THE SPIRITUAL AWAKENING

OF SCIENCE

By the same author

FREEDOM THROUGH SELF-REALISATION

YOGA FOR THE MODERN WORLD

THE SPIRITUAL AWAKENING OF SCIENCE

A. M. Halliday

SHANTI SADAN
LONDON

First published in 2010 by Shanti Sadan

Copyright © Shanti Sadan 2010
29 Chepstow Villas
London W11 3DR, UK

www.shantisadan.org

All rights reserved.
*No part of this publication may
be translated, reproduced or transmitted
in any form or by any means without the
written permission of the publisher.*

ISBN 978-0-85424-065-4

The background images of the cover design
are reproduced by kind permission of the
Space Telescope Science Institute (STScI), Baltimore, MD.

*Printed and bound by
Cromwell Press Group, Trowbridge, Wiltshire*

CONTENTS

	Preface	vii
1	The Origins of Science	1
2	Science under Islam and the Mediæval Church	22
3	Science comes of age in the Renaissance	42
4	Science faces a choice	64
5	Knowledge and Wisdom	84
6	Looking to See: The Science of Experience	106
7	Science triumphs with Newton	129
8	How the first of Newton's discoveries came to be known	152
9	How Newton came to write his most famous work	172
10	How Newton began to work out the Laws of Motion	196
11	Newton describes the Laws of Motion and the System of the World	221
12	The Publication of Newton's *Principia* and its aftermath	247
	Appendix: Foreword by Albert Einstein to Newton's *Optics*	271
13	The Vital Spark	273
14	An Example of Greatness	293
15	Herald of the Future	319
	Main Index	339
	Index of People	346

Preface

'All men by nature desire to know', observes Aristotle at the start of his *Metaphysics*. Innate in this thirst for knowledge is the desire for a full understanding which leaves no area of uncertainty or black hole ruled by ignorance.

The spiritual approach to knowledge, too, recognizes man's drive for omniscience, 'to know That, knowing which all this is known', or, in Christian terms, to know the Truth and be set free. But here the field of enquiry is the inner one. It is to heed the dictum: 'Know thyself'. To discover the spiritual principle at the core of one's own nature is to realize its identity with the ultimate Reality behind the entire realm of appearances.

In this quest, the condition of man's inner apparatus of thoughts and feelings is of supreme importance. Purity of motive, coupled with a genuine spirit of service and goodwill, renders the mind 'fruit-bearing', in the phrase of Patanjali. The spiritual knowledge dawns in a mind that is both investigative and also willing to purify itself in order to gain clear-sightedness.

In *The Spiritual Awakening of Science*, the author considers aspects of the development of science from the ancients to Clerk Maxwell, in the light of the values cherished in both the Eastern and Western spiritual traditions, and shows, by implication, that the true scientist and the seeker after spiritual truth have more in common than is generally appreciated. For example, both kinds of enquirer need to be single-minded, intelligently open-minded, and willing to detect and remove the prejudices and preferences that muddy the understanding and hinder the realization of the truth, whether scientific or spiritual.

All the chapters except the last were originally presented as public lectures at Shanti Sadan, and subsequently published in its quarterly journal *Self-Knowledge*, between 1999 and 2006. Chapter 14, 'An Example of Greatness', was also included in the author's earlier book, *Yoga for the Modern World*; its subject matter seemed particularly apposite in the present context.

Dr A M Halliday served as Warden of Shanti Sadan from 1964 until his retirement from this role in 2006, a position that was held for many years in parallel with a distinguished career in medical science. The final chapter is based on the notes prepared by him in the months prior to his passing, in March 2008.

1

THE ORIGINS OF SCIENCE

IF ONE ASKS what particularly characterizes the thought of our own age, there is little doubt that many people would answer 'the rise and predominance of science and technology'. Indeed, the advance of science, as we know it, has come to dominate our life and thought. Science is largely a phenomenon characteristic of the history of the West in the last 400 years. But the beginnings of scientific thought can be traced back to some of the early Greek philosophers and thinkers. Indeed it has been said by John Burnet[1] that:

> ....it is an adequate description of science to say that it is 'thinking about the world in the Greek way'. That is why science has never existed except among peoples who came under the influence of Greece.

The 'golden age' of science in ancient Greece began in the sixth century BC and lasted for about three hundred years. What helped to start science was the fact that the citizens of the Greek City States were, unlike the Babylonians and Egyptians who preceded them, free men in a society without a well-developed, institutionalized religious system which, in the two older civilizations, deliberately kept all knowledge secret and in the hands of

---

[1] John Burnet, *Early Greek Philosophy*, London: A & C Black, 1920.

the priestly caste. Both the Egyptians and the Babylonians had been interested in mathematics and astronomy, but progress was slow. The Egyptians, for instance, took their year as being exactly 365 days, twelve months of 30 days each, together with five extra sacred or heavenly days, but they found that, when the calendar was worked out in this way, important yearly events, like the flooding of the Nile, did not fall at the same time every year, but moved steadily back through the calendar. Early on, probably about 4,240 BC, they discovered that a better indication of the Nile flooding was the first appearance over the horizon of the star Sirius (which they called Sothius), and from then on they used this as the marker, finding, as a result, that the year actually consisted of 365 *and a quarter* days.

The Babylonians started off like everyone else counting in tens, obviously a convenient number, because the human hands have ten fingers or digits. But they discovered that it was much more convenient to use twelve rather than ten, as this can be exactly divided by 2, 3, 4 and 6 and does not involve awkward fractions like 3-*and-a-third* or 2-*and-a-half*, when one tries to divide 10 by 3 or 4. Even 12 cannot be divided by 5 but the Babylonians reduced the inconvenience of this by thinking in larger groups of 60 which can be divided by 12 or 5. This is why we still have 60 minutes in the hour and 60 seconds in the minute, and 12 months in the year, not to mention 12 signs of the zodiac.

The Greek thinkers were in a different situation to the Egyptians and Babylonians because they did not live in a society with a single authoritarian religious institution and could pursue the spirit of free enquiry into truth. As in

The Origins of Science

India, there was a free spirit of tolerance concerning different views, which allowed different schools to promulgate their own beliefs and encouraged discussion between them.

Thales & Pythagoras

The early thinkers of the sixth century BC, like Thales (c. 624-546 BC) and Pythagoras (born c. 570 BC), were particularly interested in mathematics, and both of them travelled as young men and studied with Babylonian or Egyptian priests, learning from them the method of predicting eclipses and the use of geometry to measure distances. Plutarch, writing about AD 100, speaks of Thales as one of the 'seven wise men' of Greece of his time, and as the only one 'whose wisdom stepped out in speculation beyond the limits of practical utility'.

Pythagoras, when he got back from his studies in Egypt, founded a school in Croton in Southern Italy. This was in 530 BC, the only date in his life which is known with certainty. Thales is said to have been so impressed by the younger Pythagoras's ability that he imparted to him what he himself knew. The school which Pythagoras founded was (in Sir James Jeans' words):

> a sort of brotherhood of learned men, the members of which possessed all things in common—knowledge, philosophy and goods—ordering their lives by a common moral code and forming a body rather like a modern religious order. Its members preached and practised strict self-control, temperance and purity, living simple ascetic lives and avoiding animal food because they believed that

the beasts were akin to men—one of the few instances of consideration for the animal kingdom that we meet before the modern era; indeed Pythagoras is quoted with Empedocles as the founder of this branch of morality. In brief the Pythagoreans hoped, through abstinence, discipline and religious ceremonies, to purify the soul, free it from the wheel of birth and fit it for the life after death. For they regarded the body as merely a temporary prison for the soul, Pythagoras himself advocating the doctrines of immortality and transmigration of the soul, having learned both these from his teacher, Pherecydes of Syros. Pythagoras wrote: 'When we live, our souls are dead and buried in us, but when we die, our souls revive and live.'

Pythagoras and his school believed that number ruled the universe and devoted themselves to the study of mathematics, particularly geometry. They were impressed to discover that in the notes obtained by a vibrating string, the lengths producing the perfect harmony of a note, its fifth and octave were in the ratio of 6:4:3. As the sound was so sweet to the ear, they thought that they had found the numerical basis of beauty and harmony in the world. They were also keenly interested in astronomy and carefully observed the position and movement of the stars. They suggested that the distance of the planets from the earth must follow another such simple numerical progression and that there was a corresponding music of the spheres. This Pythagorean idea was still current in sixteenth century England and finds an echo in Shakespeare's *Merchant of Venice*, when Lorenzo says to Shylock's daughter, Jessica:

The Origins of Science

> Sit, Jessica. Look how the floor of heaven
> Is thick inlaid with patens of bright gold.
> There's not the smallest orb which thou behold'st
> But in his motion like an angel sings,
> Still quiring to the young-eyed cherubins;
> Such harmony is in immortal souls!
> But whilst this muddy vesture of decay
> Doth grossly close it in, we cannot hear it.

It is clear that Shakespeare could rely on his audiences' being familiar with Pythagoras and his ideas, for we find him, in *Twelfth Night,* making fun of the belief in transmigration between the bodies of men and animals. Feste, the Clown, disguised as the curate Sir Topaz, cross-questions Malvolio, confined in the mad-house, ostensibly to assess his sanity, with the following exchange:

Feste: What is the opinion of Pythagoras concerning wild-fowl?

Malvolio: That the soul of our grandam may haply inhabit a bird.

Feste: What think'st thou of his opinion?

Malvolio: I think nobly of the soul and in no wise approve his opinion.

Feste: Fare thee well: remain thou still in darkness. Thou shalt hold th'opinion of Pythagoras ere I will allow of thy wits, and fear to kill a woodcock, lest thou dispossess the soul of thy grandam. Fare thee well.

The Spiritual Awakening of Science

One of the important mathematical discoveries of the Pythagoreans has immortalized his name in a theorem concerning right-angled triangles. (Fig 1)

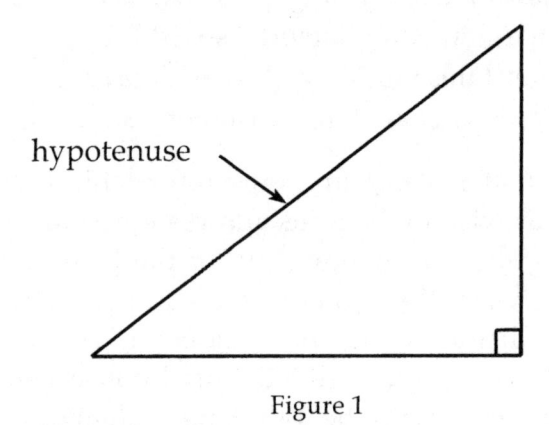

Figure 1

A right-angle triangle has one angle of 90°; the *hypotenuse* is the side opposite the right angle. They found that the sum of the squares on the two smaller sides was always equal to the square on the longer side (hypotenuse). In Fig. 2 (opposite) for instance, the two smaller sides of the triangle have lengths of 4 and 3 units respectively, the squares on which are 16 and 9. The hypotenuse has a length of 5 units, the square of which is 25, equal to 16+9. This sort of knowledge was not only interesting, but useful practically in many different ways, for example in calculating distances.

The Origins of Science

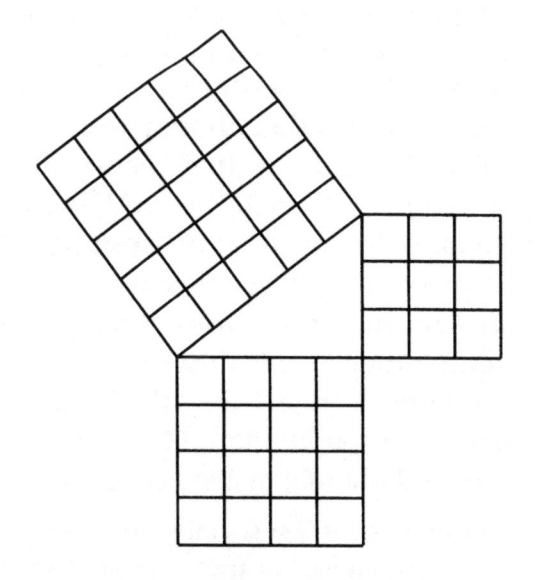

The Theorem of Pythagoras
Figure 2

Atomic Theory: Leucippus and Democritus

An atomic theory was developed by Leucippus and his pupil Democritus (460-370 BC) in the fifth century BC. Atom means literally 'uncuttable', and their idea was that matter was made of innumerable indivisible particles of different kinds which were too small to see and were in constant motion. They noticed that many (perhaps all) substances could exist in a solid, liquid and gaseous form (water, for instance, froze into ice, was normally liquid and could be turned into steam by boiling). They explained this as due to condensation and rarefaction of the constituent atoms, as they were crowded together or driven apart.

The Spiritual Awakening of Science

Scientific thought in Greece concerned itself particularly with mathematics, astronomy and physics. But the Greeks had little or no idea of testing their conclusions by experiment. As a result, although they made a number of discoveries, like the Chinese they never succeeded in developing a tradition of science. In both these cases this was largely because they over-valued abstract thought and under-valued practical tests. Neither the superior man of Chinese Confucianism nor the Greek thinker were willing to stoop to getting their hands dirty by experimenting. It was almost certainly connected with the fact that over ninety per cent of the population were slaves, and it was only slaves who did manual tasks. Xenophon wrote:

> The mechanical arts carry a social stigma, and are rightly dishonoured in our cities. For these arts damage the bodies of those who work at them... by compelling them to a sedentary life and to an indoor life, and, in some cases, to spend the whole day by the fire. This physical degeneration results also in the degeneration of the soul.[1]

The Greeks were what would now be called physical fitness fanatics. If one thinks of the way that Leonardo, Galileo, Newton and Faraday later spent their time as life-long experimenters, it is clear that the rise of science still had a long way to go! The neglect of practical experimental testing by all but a few of the scientists of the Greek world undoubtedly held back the further progress of science at that time.

---

[1] Sir James Jeans, *The Growth of Physical Science*, Cambridge University Press, 1950, p 41.

The Origins of Science

The Scientific School at Alexandria

The 'golden age' of science in ancient Greece ended about the time of the death of Aristotle in 322 BC – ten years after his former pupil Alexander the Great had invaded and conquered Greece. Alexander started building a new capital for himself at the mouth of the Nile, but died in 323 BC leaving it to one of his generals, Ptolemy. Ptolemy determined to make it the capital of the world, not only in power, but also in learning and culture, and he started a great library and what amounted to a University there, staffing it with the most eminent scholars of the time. As a result, a second centre of scientific thought arose and lasted almost a thousand years, until the Moslem invasion and the onset of the Dark Ages in AD 642.

Euclid and Archimedes

Among the greatest figures of the school at Alexandria were Euclid (c. 330-275 BC), known to every schoolboy who has ever studied geometry, and Archimedes (287-212 BC), who made major contributions to what we would now call physics. Archimedes worked out the physics of pulleys, levers and balances; and he also made a good shot at working out the value of pi (π). He is most famous for having discovered how to test the density of different substances by weighing them in water. By density is meant the weight per unit volume. He put a known weight of substance into a vessel which was already full of water, and weighed the water which overflowed the rim. A well-known story recounts how he thought out this method when he was asked by a king how to test the honesty of a

The Spiritual Awakening of Science

goldsmith to whom he had given a quantity of gold to make a crown and whom he suspected of having diluted it with cheaper metal. Archimedes suddenly realized how to do it while in his bath and rushed off exclaiming 'Eureka! Eureka!'

Aristarchus

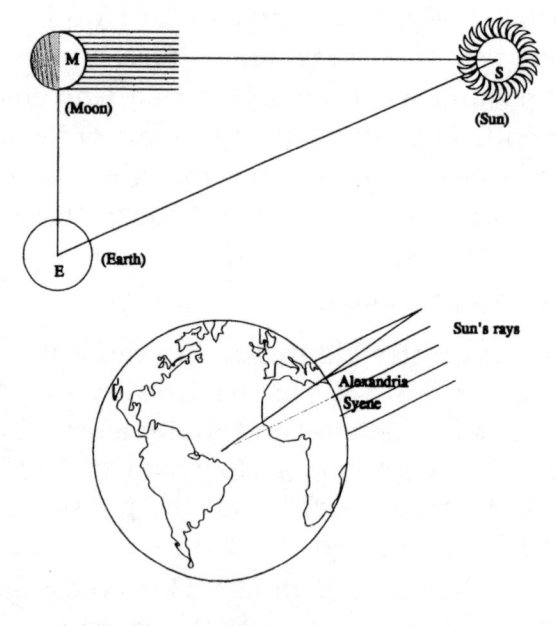

Figure 3

Aristarchus (310-230 BC) correctly suggested that the earth and other planets rotated round the sun, and that the so-called fixed stars must be vastly further away than the sun — a truth which was forgotten and had to be rediscovered by Copernicus in the sixteenth century.

The Origins of Science

He used the properties of the right-angled triangle to work out the relative distance of the moon and the sun from the earth, by observing the angle [MES] between the two at a time when the moon was exactly half visible and therefore at right angles to the sun (Fig. 3). He calculated that the sun was 19 times more distant from the earth than the moon. The true figure is 20 times greater than this, but the method was sound in principle; the difficulty was to get the exact moment when the moon was half covered, and he measured the angle as 87 degrees whereas the true value is 89 degrees 51 minutes. Unfortunately this means he calculated the other angle as 3 degrees rather than 9 minutes of arc![1] As they looked about the same size in the sky he realized that the sun, being so much further away, must be much larger.

The Destruction of the Library at Alexandria

The Christians burned a large part of the library at Alexandria in AD 390 on the orders of Archbishop Theophilus, who has been described as 'the perpetual enemy of peace and virtue, a bold bad man, whose hands were alternately polluted with gold and blood'. He had a special enthusiasm for the extirpation of all monuments of pagan culture. The job was completed by the Moslems. When Alexandria fell to the Mohammedan army in AD 642, much of the accumulated knowledge was finally lost with the destruction of the rest of the great library in Alexandria on

---

[1] Jeans, *op. cit.*, pp 86-88. We now know that the moon is on average 384,400km or 238,900 miles distant from the earth.

the instructions of the Caliph Umar—who made the infamous comment that if the knowledge contained in the books there was the same as that in the *Koran*, they were unnecessary, and if it was different they deserved to be destroyed anyway! With the sack of Alexandria the truly remarkable developments in physics, mathematics and astronomy, which had gone on steadily throughout classical times, came to an end at the onset of the Dark Ages in AD 642.

The Special Features of Greek Science

What, then, are the special features of the scientific attitude which we owe to the Greeks? Erwin Schrödinger, in his book *Nature and the Greeks*[1], suggests that there are two.

Firstly, science assumes that the world is understandable, and that its nature can be discovered by investigating it through observation, thought and experiment. The idea that Nature can be understood implies that there is an overall unity and harmony in the world, and that we can learn more about it by investigating the operation of the Laws of Nature. The universal Law is illustrated in the particular events, and we find this underlying principle by seeking the invariable in the variable. But it may be well hidden from view and require the ingenious design of special experiments to reveal it.

---

[1] Erwin Schrödinger, *Nature and the Greeks*, Cambridge University Press, 1996, Chapter VII, pp 90-98.

The Origins of Science

The second special feature of science—a less obvious one—is the value it placed on objectivity. A really important thing that the Greeks noticed early on was that, by applying measurement, particularly in geometry, one could learn new facts and establish truths which were certain and could not be gainsaid. They were, unlike most other things, no longer a matter of opinion; they were established facts and beyond mere speculation. One example (already mentioned) was the truth, discovered by Pythagoras, that in a right-angled triangle, the squares on the two shorter sides are equal in area to the square on the longer hypotenuse (Fig. 2). This is anything but obvious to the naïve observer, but is an indubitable truth, whatever anyone's opinion about it may be, and it showed therefore that it was possible to establish new truths which were beyond doubt.

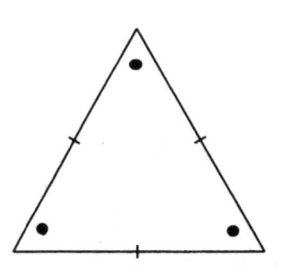

Equilateral triangle all the sides are the same length; all the angles are equal to 60°

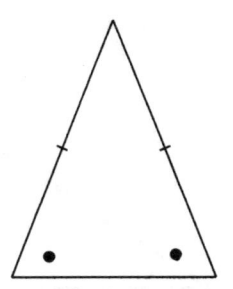

Isosceles triangle two sides and two angles are the same.

Figure 4

The Spiritual Awakening of Science

It was already known to Pythagoras's immediate predecessor and teacher, Thales, that the three angles of any triangle, when measured, always added up to a total of 180 degrees. It followed that in an equilateral triangle, where all three sides were the same length, all three angles are equal and must each measure 60 degrees, i.e. a third of 180 degrees. (Fig. 4) In an isosceles triangle with two sides of equal length, the two facing angles must be equal to each other.

But there were also other, less obvious, truths. Thales discovered that any triangle constructed on the diameter of a circle to a third point anywhere on the circumference is invariably a right-angled triangle (Fig. 5). Thales thought this so unexpected and interesting that he is said to have sacrificed an ox to the gods to celebrate its discovery by him.

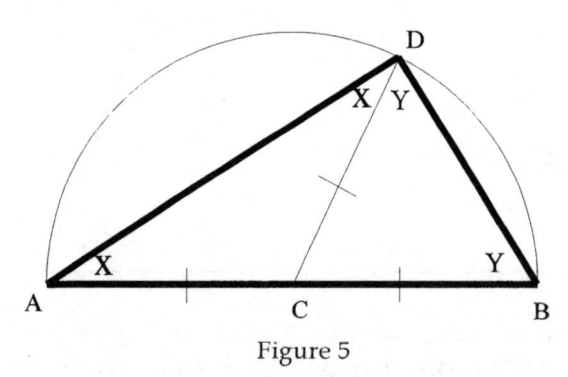

Figure 5

The reason for, or proof of, this truth is that the triangles CAD and CDB each have two sides of equal length (both being equal to the radius of the circle). They are therefore isosceles triangles with the two adjacent angles (x & x and y & y) equal to each other. It is then easy to prove that the angle at the apex of this triangle (= x+y) must be exactly equal to half of 180 degrees.

In the large triangle BAD

$$x+y+(x+y) = 180°$$

which is the same as saying

$$2x+2y = 180°$$

therefore, (dividing both sides of the equation by 2)

$$x+y = 90°$$

When we think of how satisfying it must have been to discover this sort of certain knowledge — beyond the doubts and uncertainties of mere opinion — it is easy to understand why the study of mathematics was prized so highly by those later thinkers who followed Thales, as a method of investigating the world, the stars and the moon. Astronomy was a particularly good subject to study, because the stars and planets behaved in an orderly way, day after day, year after year; and the same applied to the seasons of spring, summer, autumn and winter within the year. They could be relied on to do what one had been led to expect them to do, albeit with exceptional variations like eclipses or very cold winters, floods or droughts; and it seemed that by examining them carefully and, above all, mathematically, one could find out the laws which produced these regularities.

The presupposition of this whole scientific movement

The Spiritual Awakening of Science

was thus that, if you went about it the right way, the world was understandable, and mathematics provided the most powerful way of analyzing it. By careful observation and measurement of the facts, and thinking about them, you could work out the explanation. In this way the Greeks began the study of 'natural philosophy', or what we would now call physics.

But it must have very soon become apparent that, compared with the sun, the moon and the solar system, there were many things in the world—and perhaps, above all, people!—which were much more difficult to understand and much less predictable. Human behaviour was apparently relatively haphazard and arbitrary, dependent on the whims of the will. Human actions often seemed to proceed from sudden impulse or hidden motives, and you never knew what people were going to do next. Moreover, with regard to scientific enquiry, individuals had all sorts of strange ideas about things—including many strongly-held views and prejudices, impervious to reason—and these got in the way of finding the facts and distorted the truth, even about the world of nature. So, as well as the principle that the world was understandable when the right methods were used, science developed a strong bias in favour of objectivity, and a conviction that in investigating the world one must reject all personal preferences and put oneself in the position of an impartial observer, simply looking to see what the facts were. As far as possible, the subjective element was to be eliminated, and the scientist was to be an objective spectator in studying nature.

The Origins of Science

Schrödinger makes the point that this emphasis on objectivity came to be adopted almost unconsciously, or at least without its always being recognized and remembered. He writes of it:

> There is, however, so I believe, a second feature [of Greek science], much less clearly and openly displayed, but of equally fundamental importance. It is this, that science in its attempt to describe and understand Nature simplifies this very difficult problem. The scientist subconsciously, almost inadvertently, simplifies his problem of understanding Nature by disregarding or cutting out of the picture to be constructed, himself, his own personality, the subject of cognizance. Inadvertently the thinker steps back into the role of external observer. This facilitates the task very much. But it leaves gaps, enormous lacunae, leads to paradoxes and antinomies whenever, unaware of this initial renunciation, one tries to find oneself in the picture or to put oneself, one's own thinking and sensing mind, back into the picture.[1]

He goes on to point out that because we are unaware — or at least not fully aware — of what we are doing in adopting this scientific assumption that reality is purely objective and consists solely of the external world which exists independently of us, '...everyone willy-nilly takes himself — the subject of knowing — out of the world, and the [undoubted experience] 'I am' of [Descartes'] 'I think therefore I am' becomes 'It is' [i.e., the shared world of Nature is the only reality].'[2]

---

[1] Schrödinger, *op. cit.*, p 92.   [2] *Ibid.*, pp 92-95.

The Spiritual Awakening of Science

And he concludes:

> This is the reason why I believe it to be true that I actually do cut out my mind when I construct the real world around me. And I am not aware of this cutting out. And then I am very astonished that the scientific picture of the real world around me is very deficient. It gives a lot of factual information, puts all our experience in a magnificently consistent order, but it is ghastly silent about all and sundry that is really near to our heart, and really matters to us. It cannot tell us a word about red and blue, bitter and sweet, physical pain and physical delight; it knows nothing of beautiful and ugly, good or bad, God and eternity. Science sometimes pretends to answer questions in these domains, but the answers are often so silly that we are not inclined to take them seriously.

> So, in brief, we do not belong to this material world that science constructs for us. We are not in it, we are outside. We are only spectators. The reason why we believe that we are in it, that we belong to the picture, is that our bodies are in the picture. Our bodies belong to it. Not only my own body, but those of my friends, also of my dog and cat and horse, and of all the other people and animals. And this is my only means of communicating with them.

> Moreover, my body is implied in quite a few of the more interesting changes — movements, etc. — that go on in this material world, and is implied in such a way that I feel myself partly the author of these goings-on. But then comes the impasse, this very embarrassing discovery of science, that I am not needed as an author. Within the scientific world-picture all these happenings take care of themselves,

The Origins of Science

they are aptly accounted for by direct energetic interplay. Even the human body's movements 'are its own', as Sherrington put it. The scientific world-picture vouchsafes a very complete understanding of all that happens—it makes it just a little too understandable. It allows you to imagine the total display as that of a mechanical clockwork, which for all that science knows could go on just the same as it does, without there being consciousness, will, endeavour, pain and delight and responsibility connected with it—though they actually are. And the reason for this disconcerting situation is just this, that, for the purpose of constructing the picture of the external world, we have used the greatly simplifying device of cutting our own personality out, removing it; hence it is gone, it has evaporated, it is ostensibly not needed.

In particular, and most importantly, this is the reason why the scientific world view contains of itself no ethical values, no aesthetical values, not a word about our own ultimate scope or destination, and no God, if you please. Whence came I, whither go I?

Science cannot tell us a word why music delights us, of why and how an old song can move us to tears...

Whence come I and whither go I? That is the great unfathomable question, the same for every one of us. Science has no answer to it. Yet science represents the level best we have been able to ascertain in the way of safe and incontrovertible knowledge.[1]

---

[1] Schrödinger, *op. cit.*, pp 95-98.

The Spiritual Awakening of Science

What makes these comments especially interesting is that they are the considered view of someone who is universally recognized as one of the outstanding figures in modern science, himself personally responsible for the development of Quantum Wave Mechanics. It is clear that they are particularly germane to the answer he gives elsewhere to the question: 'What, then, is in your opinion the value of natural science?', which is:

> Its scope, aim and value is the same as that of any other branch of human knowledge. Nay, none of them alone, only the union of all of them, has any scope or value at all, and that is simply enough described: it is to obey the command of the Delphic oracle, Γνῶθι σεαυτόν, 'get to know yourself'. Or, to put it in the brief, impressive rhetoric of Plotinus (*Enneads*.VI.4.14) ἡμεῖς δέ, τίνες δὲ ἡμεῖς: 'And we, who are we anyhow?'

> He [Plotinus] continues: 'Perhaps we were *there* already before this creation came into existence, human beings of another type, or even some sort of gods, pure souls and minds united with the whole universe, parts of the intelligible world, not separated and cut off, but at one with the whole.'

> ...Our burning question as to the whence and whither — all we can ourselves observe about it is the present environment. That is why we are eager to find out about it as much as we can. That is science, learning, knowledge, that is the true source of every spiritual endeavour of man.[1]

---

[1] Schrödinger, *Science and Humanism: Physics in our Time*, Cambridge University Press, 1951, p 4.

The Origins of Science

It is also the aim of the Yoga of Self-knowledge, which maintains that it can only be done when we adopt the experimental method and turn it to the inner investigation within our own personality, abandoning pure objectivity to investigate the subject. As the *Brihadaranyaka Upanishad* puts it:

> You cannot know [as an object] the knower of knowing; you cannot understand [as an object] the understander of understanding. He is your Self, which is in all things.

2

SCIENCE UNDER ISLAM
AND THE MEDIÆVAL CHURCH

THE SACK OF Alexandria by the advancing army of Islam in AD 642 marked the beginning of a new empire which extended, at its zenith, from Southern France to the North-West region of India. It flourished for over 400 years and then declined steadily, until Ferdinand and Isabella expelled the last Arabs from Andalusia in 1493. In Europe and the Mediterranean, this left only North Africa, Turkey and the Middle East under Islamic rule, but Islam continued to spread eastward, conquering a large part of Central Asia and Northern India, and ultimately establishing a stronghold in many of the coastal countries of the Far East.

Although the Prophet Muhammed had himself been illiterate, he valued learning highly and exhorted his followers to seek it, even from China. The first small Moslem community met for the ritual prayer and the Friday service in the open courtyard adjoining the Prophet's house in Medina. When mosques came to be built elsewhere, they consisted essentially of a large open building, with no internal walls dividing it into rooms, usually sheltered from sun and rain by a roof supported on

Science under Islam and the Mediæval Church

pillars and surrounded by four arcaded walls, one of which (the *qibla* wall) faced Mecca. In the centre of this wall was a decorated prayer niche or *Mihrab*, indicating the direction of the *Ka'aba*, from which the *Imam* led the prayers, and nearby was a pulpit, the *Minbar*, reached by a short flight of steps, from which the Friday sermon was delivered. At times when no prayers or services were going on, the mosque served as a meeting place for the Moslem community, whose members could go there to study the *Koran*, the traditions of the Prophet or even wholly secular works. In effect, the mosque served as school, university, and centre for the exchange of ideas for the whole community. It was also somewhere where any matters of concern could be discussed and advice on points of law or questions of learning could be sought from experts.

Among other such activities, the mosque also provided the opportunity for those of the faithful who were able to understand and speak other languages to teach orally whoever might want to hear what they had to say. Arabic translations of scientific classics, such as Euclid, Ptolemy or Archimedes, as well as the works of Greek philosophers, like Aristotle and Plato, would be recited orally and could be taken down there and then by anyone who had the ability to write. When these manuscripts had been fair copied they would be brought back to the originator who would examine them and attest their accuracy by signing the copies, receiving an appropriate payment in return. In this way, long before printing became generally available

The Spiritual Awakening of Science

in the middle of the fifteenth century, an effective way of procuring the transmission of Greek science was produced at exactly the moment in history when it was most needed. This was providential at a time when many of the manuscripts remaining in the library of Alexandria were being used as fuel to warm the bath water of the new inhabitants of the city. Gibbon quotes one contemporary author as saying that the volumes in the library kept the 4,000 baths of the city in fuel for six months.

There was a further important factor which helped to disseminate the ancient learning and saved it from destruction. After the earlier attempt of the Christian fanatics to burn down the library in AD 390, and other incidents of the persecution of scientists, many individuals left Alexandria and settled elsewhere, taking with them any precious manuscripts which they could get hold of. There were many reminders for the scientifically-minded of the danger of remaining in the city, such as the cruel and inhuman murder of Hypatia by a band of Christians in AD 415. She was the distinguished daughter of the astronomer and mathematician Theon, and the only known woman scientist of antiquity. She had, as a pagan, acquired such an exceptional reputation on account of her profound knowledge of all the sciences that Archbishop Cyril, the nephew of Archbishop Theophilus, regarded her as a danger to Christianity. The message to other like-minded scientists was clear.

These refugees from Alexandria migrated to such places

Science under Islam and the Mediæval Church

as Athens, where Plato's Academy still existed with Proclus as its figurehead[1], or to such centres as Byzantium (Constantinople), Damascus, Baghdad or even further afield to the East. Even among the Alexandrian Christians, theological arguments were pursued fanatically with the ruthless persecution of those of contrary view. The followers of Nestorius, who refused to accept the idea that the Virgin Mary was the 'mother of God', were declared heretical in AD 431 by the council of Ephesus, and many of them were forced to flee eastwards, first to Mesopotamia and later to Persia. Once there, they were free to pursue scientific studies and, as a result, translations were made into Syriac of the works of Aristotle, Plato, Euclid, Archimedes and others. In all these ways the scientific knowledge contained in the Greek writings was preserved, so that it could be handed on to future generations.

In about AD 800 the Islamic leaders made some amends for their destruction of the library, when the eighth Caliph, Haroun-al-Raschid, ordered that the works of Aristotle and the physicians Hippocrates and Galen should be translated into Arabic; and his successor, Al-Mamun, sent missions to

---

[1] The Christians finally succeeded in closing it in AD 529, by persuading the Emperor Justinian to forbid all study of heathen learning in Athens. Proclus (AD 411-485), the last great Athenian philosopher, gave Neo-Platonism its final form and, together with the works of Plato and Aristotle, had a major influence on the mysticism of both Christianity and Islam, both of them creeds which as yet lacked a philosophy of their own.

The Spiritual Awakening of Science

Byzantium and India to bring back whatever scientific works they could find which were suitable for translation. Within a relatively few years the Caliphal library at Cordoba in Southern Spain had accumulated about 400,000 Arabic manuscripts. In this way the accumulated knowledge of the ancient world in mathematics, astronomy, physics, medicine and pharmacology was preserved and transmitted by the Arabs to the Europe of the Middle Ages and Renaissance. Among the important scientific works to be preserved in this way were Euclid's *Elements of Geometry*, Pliny's *Natural History* and Claudius Ptolemy's manual of astronomy, the *Almagest*.[1] With Euclid, work on elementary geometry was virtually complete and little further remained to be done. Pliny's work was effectually an encyclopaedia of the science of his time (AD 23-79).

In astronomy much had been accomplished, but nothing compared with what lay ahead. In the second century BC Hipparchus of Nicaea (c.190-120) had measured the exact position of the thousand stars he could see from his observatory at Rhodes, comparing them with earlier Egyptian and Babylonian records, and had found that there had been a systematic series of changes due to the movement of the earth's axis. This (as we now know) wobbles like a spinning top once every 25,800 years in what is called 'the precession of the equinoxes'. He had also

---

[1] Sir James Jeans, *The Growth of Physical Science*, Cambridge University Press, 1950, pp 93-97, 120.

Science under Islam and the Mediæval Church

studied and recorded the movements of the sun, moon and planets, and had invented trigonometry. Another later astronomer, Claudius Ptolemy (before AD 120-168) incorporated Hipparchus' discoveries in a work which was destined to become the standard work on astronomy until the sixteenth century. It was originally written in Greek, but became better known in the Arabic translation under the title of the *Almagest* (*al-Megisti* in Arabic means 'great work'). As well as describing trigonometry and giving a table of natural sines and a value of π, it recorded the positions of 1022 stars and described the well-known 'Ptolemaic' scheme explaining the movement of the sun and planets in an earth-centred world in terms of epicycles. This held sway until it was overthrown by Copernicus and Galileo in the sixteenth century.

Ptolemy also published an important five-volume work on *Optics*, in which he described the refraction or bending of light rays when they pass from air into water or glass. He noted how this makes the sun, moon and stars remain visible for some moments after they have actually passed below the horizon. One of the practical instruments which was invented either by Hipparchus or Ptolemy was the astrolabe, which enabled sea-farers to measure the altitude of the sun or stars above the horizon and was used from then onwards for navigation. Ptolemy's *Geographia* described the known world of his time and illustrated the first use of latitude and longitude. The *Almagest* circulated widely in the worlds of the Arabs and the scholastics of the Middle Ages and was first printed in Venice in 1515. The first scientific book to be printed in the West was Pliny's *Natural History* in 1469. Latin translations of Ptolemy's *Geographia* followed in 1475, and of three biological works by Aristotle in 1495. Archimedes' writings had to wait until 1544.

The advance of science under the Arabs

It would be wrong to give the impression that all progress in scientific knowledge remained on hold during the period of the Moslem ascendancy in the Mediterranean countries. This was far from the case. Significant advances were made in mathematics, optics and particularly in chemistry, which established itself as a separate science, called *alchemy*, during this period. Trigonometry was developed further, as was algebra, building on the pioneer work already started by the Greek mathematician, Diophantus, in fourth century Alexandria. The Indian mathematicians like Arya-Bhata (b.476), Brahmagupta (c.598-660) and Bhaskara (b.1114) independently developed algebra, solved quadratic equations, published tables of sines, and gave the first complete description of addition, subtraction, multiplication and division, and this knowledge, too, was transmitted to the West. The Arabs also introduced from India the new numbers (mistakenly called 'Arabic numerals' in the West), together with the new method of recording them in the decimal notation made possible by the introduction of a new symbol for zero. It enabled large numbers to be written simply and clearly by a row of figures extending to the left, standing for increasing powers of ten (units, tens, hundreds, thousands,

Science under Islam and the Mediæval Church

etc.). This was vastly superior to the clumsy Roman numerals hitherto in use. Later, this notation was to be further improved by the introduction of the decimal point, which allowed for a similar row of figures to the right of the point indicating decimal fractions (0.1s, 0.01s, 0.001s, 0.0001s, etc.), an innovation which was given its final form in 1616 by the Professor of Astronomy at Gresham's College in London, Henry Briggs (1561-1630).

There was considerable progress in chemistry (alchemy) although this later became entangled with attempts to transmute base metals into gold or to find the philosopher's stone, which encouraged secrecy and fraudulent claims. In optics much work was done on the refraction of light and Ibn-al-Haithan, known later in Europe by his Latinized name, al-Hazen (965-1038), discovered the relation between a source of light and its image formed by a lens. He was much interested in understanding how the eye saw, and was puzzled by how all that was seen managed to get through the small pupil of the eye. By experimenting he showed that when a number of lit candles were placed outside 'a small opening leading into a dark place [comparable to the pupil] with an opaque body opposite the opening, the images of these candles appear on the body or wall each distinctly'. This was what we would now call a pinhole camera or *camera obscura*. He recognized that the visual sensation passed from eye to brain via the optic nerve, but rejected the idea that the relevant image was formed on the back of the eye (where the retina actually is) on the grounds that the image there is reversed, but that we do not see the world as upside down and reversed from left to right! He therefore wrongly concluded that it must be the lens of the eye itself, and not the retina at the back of the eye, which was the sensitive element, a mistake which Leonardo da Vinci was still making in the fifteenth century.[1]

Re-awakening of learning and science in Christian Europe

During the so-called Dark Ages the true Christian tradition was kept going in the monasteries. Already in the fifth and sixth centuries Benedict of Nursia, shocked by the degenerate life of the city, had withdrawn to live in a cave. His saintliness induced others to persuade him to form a community of monks, and, after one unsuccessful try which ended in an attempt to poison him, he founded a monastery at Monte Cassino in central Italy, where he established a rule of life which became a model for all later Christian monasteries. The monks renounced all property and lived together, taking meals in common, and dividing their time between performing regular acts of turning to God in worship and remembrance nine times a day (rather as the Moslems performed the five mandatory daily acts of remembrance of Allah in the ritual prayer), combined with a period of seven or eight hours sleep and a residue of time spent in interspersed study or manual work, usually in agriculture. In addition they were expected to look after the needs and welfare of the local poor.

---

[1] An interesting account of this work may be found in an article by A.C. Crombie on 'Early Concepts of the Senses and the Mind' in *The Scientific American* for May 1964, pp 108-116.

Science under Islam and the Mediæval Church

Charlemagne, King of the Franks, who was later crowned Emperor of the Holy Roman Empire by Pope Leo III on Christmas Day 800 in St Peter's Basilica in Rome, decreed in 787 that schools should be set up in every abbey throughout his domain. This began the movement towards learning in the Christian world, which led eventually to a great awakening of Europe to classical thought in the thirteenth century under one of his successors, Frederick II (1194-1250), a reign which saw the establishment of universities in Paris (1200), Oxford (1214), Padua (1222), Naples (1224) and Cambridge (1231).

European thinkers first became acquainted with Greek thought through the Arab translations and commentaries of such writers as the Iranian philosopher Avicenna (980-1037) and the Spanish Arabian Averroes (1126-1198). Avicenna's philosophy was strongly influenced both by Aristotle and neo-Platonism; Averroes believed that truth could be found, not only in religion, but also in science and philosophy. Both of these wrote extensive commentaries on Aristotle, and exerted a major influence on Christian writers such as St Thomas Aquinas. As Copleston has written:

> The Arabian philosophy was one of the principal channels whereby the complete Aristotle was introduced to the West; but the great philosophers of mediæval Islam were more than mere transmitters or even commentators; they changed and developed the philosophy of Aristotle, more or less according to the spirit of neo-Platonism....[1]

[1] F.C. Copleston *A History of Philosophy*, London: Burns Oates & Washbourne, 1950, Vol. 2, p 186.

The Spiritual Awakening of Science

Nonetheless, copies of the original Greek texts were coming to light and being translated into Latin throughout the twelfth and thirteenth centuries.[1]

During this era students went from all over Europe to study medicine, theology, science and philosophy at the great centre of learning in Cordoba, where Arab, Jewish and Christian scholars lived in freedom and amity. This exchange with the learning of the Arab world only ceased with the final expulsion of the Moslems and Jews from Spain by Ferdinand and Isabella in 1493. They had already set up the Spanish Inquisition with papal approval in 1478, and it was used ruthlessly against Jews, Moslems and suspected Christian heretics from then on. As so often in human affairs, envy and avarice also played a significant part in this operation. The forcible expulsion of the 150,000 Jews and all the remaining Moslems from Spain was accompanied by confiscation of their property, which helped to swell the coffers of Castile and Aragon; while no small part of the many rich pickings found their way into the hands of the families of those who served on the Inquisition or played the part of accusers.

Even as the last Arab stronghold in Granada was being captured by the Christians in January 1492, Christopher Columbus was having a fateful interview with Isabella in an attempt to get permission to sail westward across the Atlantic to search for gold and an alternative route to the Spice Islands and their lucrative trade. Ferdinand was

[1] Copleston, *op. cit.*, pp 205-211.

Science under Islam and the Mediæval Church

lukewarm towards the expedition, but Isabella was an enthusiastic supporter, vowing that 'I am ready to pawn my jewels to defray the expenses of it, if the funds of the Treasury should be found inadequate.'[1] Thus opened a new chapter in the history of the West.

Science in the Middle Ages

Before this, in the thirteenth century, some of the greatest figures in the Catholic Church had shown a much more open spirit in their acceptance of the knowledge brought by the Arabs and the scientific ideas it embodied. St Albert Magnus (c.1200-1280), who held the Chair in theology in Paris from 1245, was especially interested in science and was an important influence in introducing the Greek and Arab writings into the mediæval world. He had a wide knowledge of the Arab and Jewish writers, particularly Avicenna and Averroes, and was himself a keen observer of natural phenomena. He made an intensive study of Aristotle's scientific writings, occasionally correcting them from his own observations. St Thomas Aquinas (1225-1274) was a pupil of his in Paris at the Dominican House. In 1300, another Dominican, the forty-year old Eckhart (1260-1327), came to Paris to study and stayed for two years, leaving after obtaining the title of Master in 1302.

While studying in Paris Aquinas was known among his fellow-students as the 'dumb ox', because of his heavy

---

[1] See H.V. Morton, *A Stranger in Spain*, London: Methuen, 1955, pp 182-190. Cp. pp 102-109, 217-218.

build and taciturnity, and his teacher is said to have remarked 'This ox will one day fill the world with his bellowing'! In his *Summa contra Gentiles*, written in 1259-1264, Aquinas argued that knowledge can be obtained both from the Scriptures by faith and from sense data by natural reason, and his great work, the *Summa Theologica,* was an attempt to show that the teachings of Plato and Aristotle which dealt with God's creation, were not in disagreement with the truth taught by Christ.

The newly established university at Oxford became particularly associated with an interest in mathematics and the scientific study of nature, under the influence of the first Chancellor, Robert Grosseteste (1170-1253), who was also Bishop of Lincoln, and one of his students, Roger Bacon (c.1212-c.1294), who joined the Franciscans as a simple friar, but lectured at the university. He was in constant trouble with his Franciscan superiors for his advocacy of the experimental investigation of nature and was forbidden to write for ten years, until, to his great delight, an old friend of his became Pope Clement III and in June 1266 asked him to resume his scientific investigations and send him an account of them. Within two years Bacon had despatched his *Opus Maius* to the Pope. Unfortunately for him, however, Clement died in 1269 and he was soon in trouble again with the Franciscan authorities in Paris, who had him condemned and imprisoned for most of the remaining fourteen years of his life.

Roger Bacon was a powerful advocate of science, and

Science under Islam and the Mediæval Church

believed that careful observation and experiment were the only means to acquiring knowledge of nature. He held that this alone gave certainty, while everything else was conjecture. His own main interests were in alchemy, astronomy and optics. He knew of al-Hazen's work on reflection, refraction and the properties of lenses, himself describing how they can be used to make spectacles and telescopes. He found out from the earlier Arab sources how to make gunpowder from sulphur, saltpetre and charcoal and suggested how this might be set off at a distance by means of a burning glass. He believed that mathematics should be the cornerstone of a liberal education, 'since it alone can purge the intellect and fit the student for the acquirement of all knowledge'. In the first part of his *Opus Majus* he identifies the four principal causes of human ignorance and failure to attain truth as (1) subjection to unworthy authority (something which he himself had had good reason to know about!); (2) the influence of habit; (3) popular prejudice; and (4) making a show of apparent wisdom to cover one's ignorance. He considered the last of these the worst, and gave as an example, to go on sticking to something that Aristotle is supposed to have once said when it has been clearly shown to be wrong.

It is hardly surprising that after this unpromising start, experimental science made little or no further progress during the ascendancy of the ecclesiastical authorities in the Middle Ages. Roger Bacon's fate illustrates the first of many encounters in which science, with its spirit of free enquiry, clashed with the totalitarian authority of the

Church and a strong attempt was made to suppress it. This reactionary authoritarian tendency was equally active against unorthodox spiritual views, as is shown, for example, by the trial of the aged Meister Eckhart for heresy in 1326 and the burning of Bruno at the stake in 1600. Even such revered figures as St Thomas Aquinas did not altogether escape these attempts at policing thought. A number of propositions contained in his works were condemned as heretical by the Bishop of Paris in March 1277, who threatened anyone who upheld them with excommunication.[1] The Church in Paris had earlier, in 1210, forbidden altogether the teaching of Aristotle's writings on natural philosophy, or of commentaries on them, on pain of excommunication.[2]

In all this, the attitude of the Christian Church compares unfavourably with the religious attitude of tolerance in India, which has always allowed free debate and the exposition of any variety of opinion, ranging from rank materialism to Buddhism and Jainism and the six different classical systems of Vedic philosophy including the Vedanta. The totalitarian attitude of the Church authorities towards new ideas undoubtedly stifled the progress of science in Europe at this time and, although in later times it has been less able to prevent free speech, it has proved equally slow and reluctant to come to terms with the findings of Galileo in the sixteenth century or Darwin in the nineteenth, and even in our own day it has forbidden the

---

[1] See Copleston, *op. cit.*, pp 430-432.   [2] *Ibid.*, p 209.

publication of the writings of such figures as Teilhard de Chardin or Bede Griffiths during their lifetimes. In this it has still to learn not to be afraid of truth, wherever it comes from, and also needs to realize that it does not possess a monopoly of it.

The influence of Plato and Aristotle on the history of Christianity and Science

Both Plato and Aristotle had an important influence on the Christian Church, and this gave rise to two different currents of thought in the Middle Ages. Plato's philosophy entered Christianity, which lacked a philosophy of its own, mainly through its influence on St Paul and St Augustine. Plato's other-worldly attitude, seeing the empirical world as a pale reflection of the ideal world of forms, finds its parallel in St Augustine's *City of God*, which promises to provide the ideal spiritual world so sadly missing in the empirical world of his day.

Another strand of Plato's philosophy was his emphasis on the importance of mathematics as a road to truth, crystallized in the words which he had carved over the gate of his Academy in Athens: 'Let no man enter here who is ignorant of mathematics'. It was this mathematical emphasis which made Plato in the long run a major positive influence on science, rather than a negative one.

By contrast, his great pupil, Aristotle, had a this-worldly attitude, and spent most of his life collecting and recording empirical observations on nature in its many manifestations. For him, the truth about the world could be found

The Spiritual Awakening of Science

by investigating it empirically, and in this sense he was more closely identified with the methodology of science up to his time than his great predecessor. His influence, which came to be dominant in the Middle Ages, made such figures as St Thomas Aquinas regard the world, which was God's creation, as revealing a complementary aspect of truth to the spiritual quest for beatific vision through mystical experience.

The philosopher and mathematician, Whitehead, has written well about the relevance of these two contrasting attitudes in the development of science:

> Where Aristotle said 'observe' and 'classify', the moral of Plato's teaching is the importance of the study of mathematics. Of course, neither of them was so stupid as to dissuade from observation or, on the other hand, to deny the utility of mathematics. Probably Aristotle thought that the mathematical knowledge of his day was about as much as was wanted for the purposes of physical science. Any further progress could only minister to an unpractical curiosity about subtle abstractions.
>
> An intense belief that a knowledge of mathematical relations would prove the key to unlock the mysteries of the relatedness within Nature was ever at the back of Plato's cosmological speculations.... His own speculations as to the course of nature are all founded upon the conjectural application of some mathematical construction. So far as I can remember, in every case he made a sensible shot which, in fact, went wide of the mark.
>
> Although the *Timaeus* was widely influential, yet for

Science under Islam and the Mediæval Church

about eighteen hundred years after their epoch, it seemed that Aristotle was right and Plato wrong....

Greeks, Egyptians, Arabs, Jews and Mesopotamians advanced the science of mathematics beyond the wildest dreams of Plato. Unfortunately this side of Plato's interest was notably absent among the Christian populations. I believe it to be true that no Christian made any original contribution to mathematical science before the revival of science at the time of the Renaissance. Pope Sylvester II — Gerbert, who reigned in the year AD 1000 — studied mathematics. But he added nothing. Roger Bacon proclaimed the importance of mathematics and named contemporary mathematicians. In the thirteenth and fourteenth centuries the University of Oxford cherished mathematics. But none of these mediæval Europeans advanced the subject. An exception must be made in favour of Leonardo of Pisa[1] who flourished in the beginning of the thirteenth century. He was the first Christian to make an advance in the science which in its early history illustrates the cultural union of the Hellenistic Greeks and the Near East. But, subject to this qualification, sixteenth-century mathematics was entirely based upon non-Christian sources.... We can hardly hope for a better illustration of the curious limitations of epochs and schools of civilization. It

---

[1] Not to be confused with Leonardo da Vinci. He published a book on algebra in 1202 in which he recommended the new and little known 'Arabic' system of numbers, and was also renowned for winning a tournament of mathematical problems set by Emperor Frederick II and open to all comers. Leonardo solved many of these, while no-one else solved any!

The Spiritual Awakening of Science

is especially interesting in view of the dominant influence of Plato upon Christian thought.[1]

Because of the ascendancy of Aristotle in the re-awakening of the mediæval mind to the thought of the ancient world in the first centuries of the second millennium, no one liked to question his authority. People blindly followed what he said without appreciating his devotion to the practice of looking to see what was true. Consequently they accepted his mistakes as truths. He had said that women had fewer teeth than men. So it was impious to doubt it or to suggest otherwise on the basis of looking to see what in fact was the case. This was not the only limitation of Aristotle's ascendancy. As Whitehead says:

> ...Aristotelian logic, by its neglect of mathematical notions, has done almost as much harm as good for the advancement of science. We can never get away from the questions: — How much, In what proportions, — and In what pattern of arrangement with other things. The exact laws of chemical proportions make all the difference; CO will kill you, when CO_2 will only give you a headache. Also CO_2 is a necessary element for the dilution of oxygen in the atmosphere; but too much or too little is equally harmful.... The general science of mathematics is concerned with the investigation of patterns of connectedness.... The real point is that the essential connectedness of things can never be safely omitted.[2]

---

[1] A.N. Whitehead, *Adventures of Ideas*, New York: The Free Press, 1933. 1967 edition, pp 151-153.   [2] *Ibid.*, p 153.

Science under Islam and the Mediæval Church

Galileo and particularly Newton applied mathematical measurement to the observations of natural phenomena with a view to analyzing and understanding them. So did Leonardo da Vinci before them, although he kept the results of his studies to himself. In one of his notes, he seems to have been anticipating Newton's application of mathematics to mechanics, for he says:

> Mechanics is the paradise of mathematical science, because by means of it one comes to the fruits of mathematics.[1]

But from the evidence of Leonardo's notebooks, his own use of mathematics seems to have been limited to geometry.[2]

If we think of the recent developments in modern science, such as Relativity and Quantum Theory, it is clear that Whitehead is right when he says that Plato's intense belief in mathematics as the key to unlock the mysteries of the relatedness of things within Nature has been triumphantly vindicated.

---

[1] *The Notebooks of Leonardo da Vinci*, Oxford University Press, 1952, p 9.

[2] U.Cisotti, 'The Mathematics of Leonardo' in *Leonardo da Vinci*, Vol 1, Leisure Books, Istituto Geografico De Agostini, Novara, Italy. 1964. pp 201-203.

3

SCIENCE COMES OF AGE IN THE RENAISSANCE

SCIENCE FLOURISHES where there is freedom of thought and expression, so that the search for truth can be pursued for its own sake, irrespective of the approval or disapproval of others. This was the reason for the early appearance of the scientific spirit in ancient Greece, where the City-States provided—for the first time in the West—a favourable environment, free of the stifling authoritarian regimes dominated by a priestly caste, typical of Babylonia or Egypt. Like all totalitarian regimes, up to and including Nazism and Communism in the twentieth century, such governments have attempted to control thought and maintain education in their own hands, and this implies forcibly suppressing anyone expressing dissident views. Science requires freedom to explore and experiment if it is to be successful, and ancient Greece provided such conditions for the first time in the West. When Greece fell, science was carried on in Alexandria under the Ptolemys, until it was suppressed by the rise of groups of narrow-minded and fanatical Christian monks who persecuted and attempted to stamp out all 'heathen' free-thinking.

Thanks to the attitude of the Prophet Muhammed towards learning, a much freer spirit predominated in the

Science Comes of Age in the Renaissance

Moslem world after the Arab Conquest in the seventh century, allowing science and medicine to survive and develop in such centres as Cordoba, with advances contributed, not only from the Arabs themselves, but also from the Far East, and from Jews and Christians living under Moslem rule. This was no longer the case in Europe after 1492, when the Christians were again in the ascendancy and all remaining Moslems and Jews had been expelled from Spain by Ferdinand and Isabella.

From then on persecution by the Christian authorities was a recurrent problem for those of a scientific bent of mind, just as it had been throughout the last years of the Roman Empire, and this inhibited the development of science in later mediæval times under the Church. Pioneers of science, like Roger Bacon, and later Galileo and Bruno, who did not keep their scientific interests to themselves, laid themselves open to the risk of punishment for 'wrong' thinking. It was not scientists alone, of course, who suffered in this way. Those, like Meister Eckhart, who spoke too freely of their spiritual experiences or expressed unorthodox views on the matter, fared no better. Over all unconventional thinking there hovered the threat that it would be considered heretical. In passing judgement on confirmed heretics, the Inquisition customarily pronounced the sentence that they should be 'punished with all possible clemency, and without the shedding of blood'. This may have sounded gentle and merciful, but meant, in fact, that one was to be burnt alive at the stake. Sentence was most often carried out by the Inquisition after a lengthy period of imprisonment and 'examination' or trial, often lasting

The Spiritual Awakening of Science

many years. The latter procedure effectively silenced the accused from promulgating their ideas any further, and often led to them 'recanting', or having to carry on a lengthy defence before the Inquisitors about what exactly they had said. Some, like Eckhart, were fortunate enough to die meanwhile from other causes before the sentence of heresy was finally passed.

Seen from a modern perspective, the Catholic Church was thus the main example in mediæval Europe of something we are still all too familiar with in our present-day world — a totalitarian regime which tolerates no dissidents. This effectively stifled the further development of science despite the fact that a number of eminent figures within the Church had initially taken a special interest in science and mathematics, and some had actively advocated the study of nature, particularly in the twelfth and thirteenth centuries[1].

Swami Rama Tirtha reminds us in his Notebooks that the conflict between the Christian Church and the spirit of free enquiry was a reflection of a wider and deeper problem afflicting the mind of man in every age and context, and that it represents a necessary and inevitable part of the actual development of man.

---

[1] Among them, Emperor Frederick II (1194-1250), Robert Grosseteste (1170-1253), Albert Magnus (c.1200-1280), Roger Bacon (c.1212-1294), and St Thomas Aquinas (1225-1274). There were also notable later figures, such as Nicole Oresme, Bishop of Lisieux (1323-1382) and Cardinal Nicholas of Cusa (1401-1464), who helped to loosen and break the stranglehold of the narrow-minded Church authorities and the blind following of Aristotelian authority.

Science Comes of Age in the Renaissance

The so-called conflict between Religion and Science was in reality a conflict between organized Religious Institutions and unorganized Scientific Truth. But the real essence of stubborn Conservatism [which resists and refuses to accept new truths] lies not in Religious Institutions or Theologies. The whole conflict is a struggle in the mind of man. It exists in human psychology before it is wrought out in human history. It is the struggle of realities against tradition and suggestion [or what Swami Rama calls 'hypnotism'].

If we think of the way in which totalitarian states use every means to control communication and spread their own propaganda, preventing as far as possible any contrary message reaching the minds of their subject peoples, the word 'hypnotism' seems entirely appropriate. The human mind is indeed all the time subjected to a stream of suggestions throughout its daily experience. These suggestions powerfully influence it (as every advertiser or spin-doctor knows), although it has the freedom to accept or reject them; but this freedom presupposes a spirit of independence and a habit of critical examination which can be seen to be closely allied to the scientific spirit and can only flourish in an open society.

The implication of the point that Swami Rama Tirtha is making is that truth emerges only when it is distinguished from the misconceptions and prejudices which have been implanted by wrong thinking and prejudice uncritically accepted in the past. This is a general principle with a much wider application than the religious context. As he says:

The Spiritual Awakening of Science

The progress of [the] realization [and recognition of the new truths] would still have been just such a struggle had religious theology or Churches or worship never existed. But the need for all these is part of the actual development of man. Intolerance and prejudice are not confined to religious organizations. The same spirit that burned Michael Servetus and Giordano Bruno in the name of religion for the heresies of Science, led the atheist, liberal mob of Paris to send to the scaffold the great chemist Lavoisier [in 1794] with the sneer that 'the Republic had no need of savants'.

These remarks emphasize that the rise of the scientific spirit of free enquiry represents an important part of the spiritual evolution of the mind of man towards freedom.

The origins of the Renaissance

The seeds of the coming Renaissance were already beginning to germinate in the late Middle Ages and a number of important contributory factors can be identified. The establishment of schools at the end of the eighth century AD and of universities in the thirteenth century began the great awakening of learning in Europe which radically changed the way in which people were thinking, and led to major social changes in the ordinary life of the people in the three centuries which followed. This in turn fostered a new feeling of freedom, liberating the individual to seek knowledge for himself wherever he chose, rather than being told what to think by the ecclesiastical authorities. As the historian G.M.Trevelyan has memorably put it: 'Disinterested intellectual curiosity is the life-blood

Science Comes of Age in the Renaissance

of real civilization' — a sentiment which would have been shared by all the early pioneers and lovers of science.

At this time the Church had become, not only very rich — it is estimated to have possessed somewhere between one-fifth to one-third of all the land in Europe, free of taxes — but also worldly and corrupt in many of its practices. Not surprisingly a strong element of criticism and anti-clericalism began to assert itself among the common people. Typical of this was the movement started at Oxford in the England of the fourteenth century by the religious reformer John Wycliffe. Wycliffe was a forerunner of the Reformation, not only in England, but also (through his influence on others like Jan Hus and Martin Luther) in the rest of Northern Europe. He held that all spiritual authority was conferred directly by the grace of God, and that it was forfeited where an all-too-human Christian authority was guilty of mortal sin. Both the Pope and the Church held their authority only insofar as they were not corrupt. He criticized the practices of confession and forgiveness of sins by the priests, and their sale of indulgences for money, and advocated a return to the teachings of Christ as recorded in the Bible.

This was a direct challenge to the authority of the Church. In 1377 Wycliffe was summoned before the Bishop of London to give an account of his teachings, and later that year the Pope issued several Bulls accusing him of heresy. The following year, nothing daunted, he and his helpers started preparing an English translation of the Bible. In

The Spiritual Awakening of Science

1379 he repudiated the doctrine of transubstantiation (the belief that, in the Mass, the wine and bread were literally and miraculously converted into the blood and flesh of Christ). In 1380 he began to send out his disciples as 'poor preachers' to spread his egalitarian doctrine. His followers became known pejoratively as the Lollards. In 1382 he was declared a heretic by a court convened by the Archbishop of Canterbury and subsequently expelled from Oxford. He retired to his country parish and died two years later. His English translation of the Latin Bible, made in defiance of the Church authorities, was published in 1388, four years after his death. In 1415, 31 years after his death, the Council of Constance confirmed him to be a heretic and ordered that due sentence be carried out; but it was only after another 13 years had passed that the Church had his body ceremonially exhumed and burnt in 1428. This is perhaps the only occasion on which the sentence passed on a confirmed heretic—to be 'punished with all possible clemency, and without the shedding of blood'—was actually carried out successfully to the letter.

Wycliffe believed in the direct relationship between the individual and God and held that people should go back to the Bible and strive to imitate the life of poverty and holiness of Christ and his disciples, making their spiritual life independent of the priests and prelates of the Church, many of whom had clearly become worldly and un-christian. Christ's parable concerning the blind leading the blind was all too relevant. This new spiritual freedom of the individual, introduced by Wycliffe, which was to lead

Science Comes of Age in the Renaissance

ultimately to the Reformation and the whole Protestant and non-conformist movement in institutionalized Christianity, was clearly another important seed of the Renaissance spirit.

The emphasis on self-reliance and the individual conscience was also much facilitated by the introduction of printing from movable metal type in the fifteenth century, originally at Cologne in Germany by Johann Gutenberg (1400-1468), and later brought from there, first to Bruges and then England by William Caxton (1422-1491). From then on a steady stream of printed books was produced and began to influence at least the more educated members of the general populace. Those who could read freely from a variety of sources had much more opportunity to make up their minds about things than those who could not. This spread of knowledge was also enormously widened by the appearance of books and translations in the vernacular as well as the already existing Latin and Greek texts, a change pioneered by Wycliffe's English translation of the Bible (1388), but soon also to produce secular and scientific works like Chaucer's *Canterbury Tales* (written in 1390) and Pliny's *Natural History* (1469).

The awakening of experimental science in the Renaissance

The first individual to express the fully-fledged scientific spirit and to advocate the free, unrestricted investigation of natural phenomena, not only by observation, but by actively testing and verifying any conclusions by experiment, was the universal genius, Leonardo da Vinci (1452-1519). Working at a time when the Church was still a powerful force to be reckoned with, it was probably just as well that he kept the careful records of his observations and conclusions to himself, recording them in mirror writing and writing 'backwards' from right to left (as is done, for instance, in Hebrew or Japanese). For this and other reasons they remained largely unknown to the world at large until they were deciphered and published, a task that has only been carried out in the last 150 years. His facility in mirror writing was no doubt related to the fact that he was left-handed. Fortunately for us, the confidence which this gave him meant that he could write down his own thoughts, questions, observations, experiments and results clearly and explicitly, so that they give us a marvellous account of what he thought about and of the many experiments which he did. It is an impressive record.[1]

Leonardo was the illegitimate son of a well-to-do Florentine lawyer. His father acknowledged him and, when he was old enough to leave his mother, he brought him to

[1] The translated passages from Leonardo's writings, and the contemporary accounts concerning him included in this article, have been cited from three sources, the main one being the authoritative two-volume edition by Jean Paul Richter of *The Literary Works of Leonardo da Vinci*, New York: Phaidon Publishers, 3rd edition, 1970. Also used have been the smaller collection by Irma A Richter, *Selections from the Notebooks of Leonardo da Vinci*, Oxford University Press, 1952, and L.Goldscheider's *Leonardo da Vinci: Life and Work, Paintings and Drawings*, London: Phaidon Press, 7th edition, 1964.

Science Comes of Age in the Renaissance

live in the family house in Florence. The boy soon showed his brilliant gifts as an artist, and was accordingly apprenticed to the studio of the famous Florentine painter, Andreas Verrochio. This launched the teenage Leonardo on his artistic career, which he started by helping Verrochio paint some of his pictures and doing it quite noticeably better than his master! He was admitted to the Guild of Painters at the age of 19 and soon recognized as a master painter in his own right.

Leonardo himself was never a wealthy man and earned his living by being paid for the pictures, drawings or sculpture that people commissioned from him and also from being employed as an architect, engineer or theatrical designer of pageants for rich patrons such as the Medicis in Florence, Duke Sforza in Milan or the French King. But his own main interest was in improving the techniques of his art and in his scientific studies into optics, anatomy, physiology, astronomy, the flight of birds, physics and other topics too numerous to mention. He expresses his philosophy of life—and in particular what he really values—when he writes:

> Pray hold me not in scorn! I am not poor! Poor rather is the man who desires many things. That is not riches which may be lost; virtue is our true wealth and the reward of its possessor. This cannot be lost; it does not abandon us unless life first leaves us. As for property and external riches, hold them with trembling; they often leave their possessor in contempt and ignominy for having lost them. He who possesses most is most afraid to lose.

The Spiritual Awakening of Science

He quotes with approval the saying of the ancient Roman physician, Valturius: 'Good men by nature wish to know', but he recognizes that many people will consider his scientific investigations a waste of time:

> I know that many people will call this useless work... men who desire nothing but material riches and are absolutely devoid of that wisdom which is the food and the only true riches of the mind. For so much more worthy as the soul is than the body, so much more noble are the possessions of the soul than those of the body. And often, when I see one or other of these men take this work in his hand, I wonder that he does not put it in his nose, like a monkey, or ask me if it is something good to eat.

He planned to write text-books on various subjects which he studied, and wrote some part—(or perhaps all, we do not know)—of a treatise on painting. He also certainly started on a book on human anatomy, even preparing some engravings of his anatomical drawings on copper plates for it. But (as far as we know) the only publication which actually appeared during his life was a collaborative textbook on mathematics with his friend, the Italian mathematician Pacioli. Like the scientifically-minded thinkers before him, he valued mathematics highly. He wrote on the back of one of his drawings: 'Let no man who is not a mathematician read the elements of my work.'

On his early death at the age of 67, he left all his papers to his close pupil and friend, Francesco Melzi, who was with him when he died in Cloux, near Amboise, in France.

Science Comes of Age in the Renaissance

Melzi took all the manuscripts back to Florence and treated them as precious relics during his lifetime, but, unfortunately, after his death his son starting selling them off piecemeal. As a result many of the originally consecutive leaves got separated and a number got lost. The larger collections ended up scattered all over Europe.

Scientific method: observation and experiment

One of his early notes perfectly describes — virtually for the first time in history — the now accepted methodology of Science:

> First I shall test by experiment before I proceed further, because my intention is to consult experience first and then with reasoning show why such experience is bound to operate in such a way.

> And this is the true rule by which those who analyze the effects of nature must proceed: and although nature begins with the cause and ends with the experience, we must follow the opposite course, namely (as I said before), begin with the experience, and by means of it investigate the cause.

Leonardo was well aware of the need for repeated experiments to verify the results, a feature which was to establish itself as a hall-mark of the methodology of science in the years to come, for he writes:

> ...But before you found a law on this case, test it two or three times and see whether the experiments produce the same effects.

The Spiritual Awakening of Science

And in another note, even more emphatically:

The experiment should be made many times so that no accident may occur to hinder or falsify this proof, for the experiment may be false whether it deceived the investigator or not.

His industry, and the time and patience which he expended on getting things right, was simply astonishing. He was not easily satisfied and gave up several paintings which he had started, leaving them unfinished. This was also partly because he was continually experimenting to try and improve the way of doing things, testing new ways of mixing the paints and attempting to cast in bronze a statue of Lodovico Sforza which was far larger than anything cast in that way before.

Well could he write:

Thou, O God, dost sell unto us all good things at the price of labour.

For Leonardo, experience itself (rather than theory) was the basis of a knowledge of truth.

To me it seems that all sciences are vain and full of errors which are not born of Experience, mother of all certainty, and are not tested by Experience.

All our knowledge has its origin in our perceptions.

The senses are of the earth; Reason stands apart from them in contemplation.

He had both a love for, and a reverence before, Nature:

Science Comes of Age in the Renaissance

> Nature does not break her law; nature is constrained by the logical necessity of her law which is inherent in her.

> In nature there is no effect without cause; understand the cause and you will have no need of the experiment.

He also clearly recognizes that the main difficulties in arriving at truth lie within the mind itself rather than outside.

> Experience never errs; it is only your judgement that errs in promising itself results [such] as are not caused by your experience... and are not in her power [to give]. Wrongly do men complain of Experience.

> The greatest deception men suffer is from their own opinions.

We have to approach Experience with complete honesty, putting aside (as far as humanly possible) any prejudices or pet theories of our own, and open to what Nature can teach us. This is a profoundly important characteristic about the best of science and the greatest of scientists. Newton, Faraday, Darwin and Einstein all had it. It is often the unexpected and puzzling result which is most significant scientifically and leads to the most important new insights. As such it can be at the same time difficult to accept and recognize for the very fact that it goes against our preconceived ideas. Leonardo noted something which was to astonish Charles Darwin four hundred years later: namely, the existence of the shells and fossils of sea-creatures far inland and even on the mountain tops. Having noticed this, from then on he kept an eye out for fossils. He writes, for instance, that when travelling from Milan to Rome in the Autumn of 1513, crossing the mountains between the sources of the rivers Arno and Tiber: 'I found some shells in the rocks of the high Appenines and mostly at the rock of La Vernia...' He concludes from these and other similar observations that he had made that 'The ancient bottoms of the sea have become the mountain ridges'.

His insistence on honesty is impressive and emphatic, and (it should be added) in refreshing contrast to the cynical and worldly-wise attitude of his younger Florentine near-contemporary, Niccolò Machiavelli (1469-1527).

> The lie is so vile [he writes], that even if it were speaking well of godly things it would take off something of God's grace; and truth is so excellent in itself, that, even if it dwells on humble and lowly matters, it is still infinitely above the uncertainties and lies about high and lofty matters... But you who live on dreams are better pleased by sophistical reasons and [the] frauds of wits in great and uncertain things than by those reasons which are certain and natural and not so exalted.

For Leonardo the object of studying experience is not simply to amass a knowledge about facts or to impress others; it is to *understand* nature, and to get to know how to live well.

Wisdom is the daughter of experience.

*　　*　　*

Science Comes of Age in the Renaissance

How did Leonardo appear to his contemporaries? The earliest biography that we have of him, a very short one, was written by Paolo Giovio, a doctor who had looked after Pope Leo X and was keen on painting. He was 21 years younger than Leonardo. His account was written in 1527, shortly after the sack of Rome by the combined army of the Spanish and German anti-papal forces under the Duke of Bourbon, when the author had gone to Ischia. This was only about eight years after Leonardo had died:

> Leonardo, born at Vinci, an insignificant hamlet in Tuscany, has added great lustre to the art of painting. He established that all proper practice of this art should be preceded by a training in the sciences and the liberal arts which he regarded as indispensable and subordinate to painting. He placed modelling as a means of rendering figures in relief on a flat surface before other processes done with a brush. The science of optics was to him of paramount importance and on it he founded the principles of the distribution of light and shade down to the most minute details. In order that he might be able to paint the various joints and muscles as they bend and stretch according to the laws of nature, he dissected in medical schools the corpses of criminals, indifferent to this inhuman and nauseating work. He then tabulated with extreme accuracy all the different parts down to the smallest veins and the composition of the bones, in order that this work on which he had spent so many years should be published from copper engravings for the benefit of art. But while he was thus spending his time in the close research of subordinate branches of his art he carried only a few works to completion; for owing to his

masterly facility and the fastidiousness of his nature, he discarded works he had already begun. However, the wall-painting at Milan of Christ at Supper with his Disciples is greatly admired. It is said that when King Louis saw it he coveted it so much that he enquired anxiously from those standing around him whether it could be detached from the wall and transported forthwith to France, although this would have destroyed the famous refectory. There is also the picture of the infant Christ playing with his mother, the Virgin, and his grandmother, Anne, which King Francis of France bought and placed in his chapel. Moreover, there remains the painting of the battle and victory over the Pisans in the Council Chamber at Florence which was extraordinarily magnificent but came to an untimely end owing to the defective plaster which persistently rejected the colours ground in walnut oil. It seems as if the very natural regret caused by this unexpected injury and interruption of the work was instrumental in making it famous. For Lodovico Sforza [Duke of Milan] he also made a clay model of a colossal horse to be cast in bronze, on which was to be seated the figure of the famous condottiere Francesco, Lodovico's father. The vehement life-like action of this horse as if panting is amazing, not less so the sculptor's skill and his consummate knowledge of nature. His charm of disposition, his brilliance and generosity are not less than the beauty of his appearance. His genius for invention was astounding and he was the arbiter of all questions relating to beauty and elegance, especially in pageantry. He sang beautifully to his own accompaniment on the lyre to the delight of the entire Court. He died in France at the age of 67 to the grief of his friends, which

Science Comes of Age in the Renaissance

loss was all the greater for among the crowd of young men who contributed to the success of his studio, he left no disciple of outstanding fame.

Leonardo spent the last three years of his life as the guest of the King of France, who provided him with the small château of Cloux, near the Royal Palace at Amboise. By the time he went there he was in his sixties and no longer well. The King so much enjoyed his conversation that he used to visit Leonardo practically every day while he was there.

There is an account of a visit of the Cardinal of Aragon to Leonardo in October 1517, two years before he died, written by the Cardinal's Secretary. He calls Leonardo 'a grey-beard of more than seventy[1], the most eminent painter of our time' and goes on to say that he:

> showed to his Eminence the Cardinal three pictures: one of a certain Florentine lady, painted from life at the instance of the late Lord Giuliano de' Medici [this is probably the *Mona Lisa*]; the other of the youthful St John the Baptist; and the third of the Madonna and the Child in the lap of St Anne, the most perfect of them all. One cannot expect any more good work from him, as a certain paralysis has crippled his right hand. But he has a pupil, a Milanese, who works well enough[2]: and although Messer

---

[1] This is wrong; Leonardo was only 65 at the time. Vasari in his *Lives of the Artists*, first published in 1568, also gets Leonardo's age wrong, saying he died at the age of 75, whereas on the day he died, May 2nd 1519, he was actually only 67.   [2] This was Francesco Melzi, to whom Leonardo bequeathed all his papers.

The Spiritual Awakening of Science

Leonardo can no longer paint with the sweetness which was peculiar to him, he can still design and instruct others. This gentleman has written a treatise on anatomy, showing by illustrations the members, muscles, nerves, veins, joints, intestines and whatever else is to discuss in the bodies of men and women, in a way that has never been done by anyone else. All this we have seen with our own eyes; and he said that he had dissected more than thirty bodies, both of men and of women of all ages. He has also written of the nature of water and of diverse machines, and of other matters, which he has set down in an endless number of volumes, all in the vulgar tongue, which, if they be published, will be profitable and delightful.

After leaving Amboise, the Cardinal later visited Milan, where he noted in his diary for December 1517:

In the great monastery of S. Maria delle Grazie, built at the expense of Duke Lodovico il Moro, Leonardo da Vinci, the same whom we visited two months ago outside Amboise in France, has painted a splendid picture of the Last Supper on a wall of the refectory. But unfortunately it is already damaged, I do not know whether through dampness or neglect. Among the figures represented on the painting are the real portraits of courtiers and of men in Milan of that time.

With regard to Leonardo's science, the Cardinal's account of his anatomical drawings gives us some idea of how much they impressed an intelligent layman. But their scientific standard is better attested by the impression they made much later on the great English surgeon, William

Science Comes of Age in the Renaissance

Hunter, when he was shown the drawings in the King's Library in the eighteenth century during the reign of George III:

> I expected to see little more than such designs in Anatomy as might be useful to a painter in his own profession. But I saw, and indeed with astonishment, that Leonardo had been a general and deep student. When I consider what pains he has taken upon every part of the body, the superiority of his universal genius, his particular excellence in mechanics and hydraulics, and the attention with which such a man would examine and see objects which he has to draw, I am fully persuaded that Leonardo was the best Anatomist, at that time, in the world... Leonardo was certainly the first man we know of, who introduced the practice of making anatomical drawings.

What his pioneering anatomical studies cost Leonardo himself in time, patience and perseverance in the face of great difficulties, is indicated in his own notes:

> And you, who say that it would be better to watch an anatomist at work than to see these drawings, you would be right, if it were possible to observe all the things which are demonstrated in such drawings... to obtain a true and perfect knowledge of which I have dissected more than ten human bodies,... until I came to an end and had a complete knowledge; this I repeated twice, to learn the differences.
>
> And [even] if you have a love for such things you might be prevented by loathing, and if that did not prevent you,

The Spiritual Awakening of Science

you might be deterred by living in the night hours in the company of those corpses, quartered and flayed and horrible to see[1]. And if this did not prevent you, perhaps you might not be able to draw so well as is necessary for such a demonstration; or if you had the skill, it might not be combined with knowledge of perspective; and if it were so, you might not understand the methods of geometrical demonstration and the method of the calculation of forces and of the strength of the muscles; patience may be wanting, so that you lack perseverance. As to whether all these things were found in me or not, the hundred and twenty books composed by me will give [the] verdict Yes or No. In these I have been hindered neither by avarice nor negligence, but simply by want of time.

Leonardo was anything but a cold and inhuman man, and his pursuit of knowledge, while showing admirable objectivity and freedom from prejudices and preconceptions, is always combined with a genuine love and reverence for Nature, as well as a deep feeling for the sanctity of all life:

And you, O Man, who will discern in this work of mine the wonderful works of Nature, if you think it would be a criminal thing to destroy it, reflect how much more criminal it is to take the life of man; and if this, his external form, appears to thee marvellously constructed, remember that it is nothing compared with the soul that dwells in that structure; for that, indeed, be it what it may, is a thing divine. Leave it then to dwell in its work at its good will

---

[1] Some of the bodies were those of criminals who had been executed.

Science Comes of Age in the Renaissance

and pleasure, and let not your rage or malice destroy a life—for indeed, he who does not value it, does not himself deserve it.

His attitude towards Nature as a whole is one of awe and admiration at its beauty. In this he very much resembles Albert Einstein in our own day. The range and variety of his scientific studies and his own immense creativity and genius make all the more impressive the final conclusion which he expresses about human inventiveness as compared with the creativity of Nature:

> Though human ingenuity may make various inventions which, by the help of various machines, answer the same end, it will never devise any invention more beautiful, nor more simple, nor more to the purpose than nature does; because in her invention nothing is wanting and nothing is superfluous.

4

SCIENCE FACES A CHOICE

AS WE ALL KNOW, the process of growing up inevitably brings with it new responsibilities and new problems. Science in its coming of age was no exception. The awakening of the spirit of independence in the Renaissance brought with it a new freedom of thought, allowing the individual more scope to choose for himself, but equally it made him more responsible for those choices and therefore more liable to suffer the consequences.

For Leonardo da Vinci the pursuit of science was a master-passion, inspired by the desire to understand nature and to achieve, not merely knowledge of facts about the nature of things, but wisdom — knowing how to live wisely. In his view the great obstacles to such an understanding resided in the human mind. He realized that 'the greatest deception men suffer is from their own opinions', as Roger Bacon had done before him, and that it is not experience which leads men astray, but the erroneous interpretation of experience by faulty human judgement. Complete honesty and straightforwardness is what he thought was needed in the pursuit of truth through experience, but he recognized that people in general are often better pleased by clever arguments in support of attractive dreams and the fraudulent claims of plausible confidence tricksters, who discourse on vague and uncertain matters, instead of paying attention to simple and natural things which can be observed with certainty.

Leonardo's patent honesty and directness reminds one of many of the characteristic qualities of the spiritual man enumerated in the sixteenth chapter of the *Bhagavad Gita*, among them:

> Purity of the heart and freedom from all duplicity; steadfastness in the knowledge of truth and its application in daily life; simplicity, practice of truth-speaking, truth-loving and avoidance of luxury; compassion to all beings, gentleness, non-covetousness, tolerance.[1]

Leonardo's compassion to all beings and gentleness is attested in Vasari's account of his life:

> His charming conversation won all hearts and although he possessed nothing and worked little, he kept servants and horses; of which latter he was very fond, and indeed loved all animals, and trained them with great kindness and patience. Often, in passing places where birds were sold, he would let them out of their cages and having paid the vendor the price asked, he let them fly away into the air, restoring to them their lost liberty. Wherefore Nature favoured him so greatly that in whatever his brain or mind took up he displayed unrivalled harmony, vigour, vivacity, excellence, beauty and grace.

These good qualities are contrasted in the *Gita* with the very different qualities of the deluded people:

---

[1] H.P. Shastri, *Teachings from the Bhagavad Gita*, London: Shanti Sadan, 2nd edition, 1949, p 78.

They are ignorant of what they ought to do or what they should refrain from doing, are devoid of truth in their dealings with others, and devoid of good conduct and of general purity.

Their philosophy of life is that there is no such principle as truth, that all is expediency; that there is no ethical basis of society; that there is no Supreme Being; that lust (desire) is the only basis of conduct and the cause of the birth of beings... These small-minded, petty-hearted men, without tolerance and unforgiving, indulging in violent deeds, prove the destruction of society.

The characteristics of this state of delusion are said to be:

ostentation, arrogance, vanity, anger (sometimes called indignation), insolence and ignorance of the spiritual laws.

The spiritual state produces freedom of the soul, while the state of delusion gives birth to bondage with its consequent evils and sufferings.[1]

These two prototypes represent propensities of the human mind which — by its very nature — is faced with the possibility of choosing either what the Yoga classics call *the life of the higher self* or *the life of the lower self*. Since it is a basic fact concerning the nature of the human mind, it holds true for the individual at all times and in all places. It is part of the very stuff of human experience in life.

Hence it is hardly surprising that one can readily find similar references to these two attitudes to life in what Leonardo himself has written. Firstly, he speaks of the

---

[1] Shastri, *op. cit.*, p 79.

Science Faces a Choice

rational and animal aspects of man's nature, when he writes that:

> There are four main powers or faculties of the human mind: memory and intellect, appetite and concupiscence; the first two are of the reason, the others of the senses.

He points out that:

> The senses are of the earth; reason stands apart from them in contemplation.

And that with regard to the functions of the mind:

> Every action needs to be prompted by a motive.
> To know and to will are two operations of the human mind.
> Discerning, judging, deliberating are acts of the human mind.

Like the *Gita*, he talks of the need to restrain and redirect the devilish tendencies of the mind, which are a remnant of man's animal past:

> The man who does not restrain wantonness, allies himself with the beasts.
>
> You can have no dominion greater or less than that over yourself.
>
> Blind ignorance misleads us thus and delights with the results of lascivious joys because it does not know the true light, and because it does not know what is the true light. Vain splendour takes from us the power of being...behold how owing to the glare of fire we walk where blind ignorance leads us. O wretched mortals, open your eyes!

He also notes that, in regard to the need to restrain the

lower instincts and practise self-discipline:

> It is easier to contend with evil first than at the last.

We should listen to what the wise have to say on this subject:

> Ask advice of him who governs himself well. Justice requires power, insight and will....

None of this advice could have been given by someone who did not believe in the value of self-control and training of the mind. In some of his sayings he comes even closer to the teachings of Yoga and the *Bhagavad Gita*, as when he says:

> If you governed your body by the rules of virtue, you would have no desires in this world.

If all this sounds like the pious talk of someone who is totally unworldly and has no idea of the world as it is, it is misleading. He knew all too well about those who followed the life of the lower self in the world around him, for he writes of the departing spirit looking back at the brain it had inhabited, and loudly proclaiming:

> O blessed and happy spirit, whence hast thou departed! Well have I known man and he is much against my liking! He is a receptacle of villainy; a perfect heap of the utmost ingratitude combined with every vice. But why do I fatigue myself using vain words? In him every form of sin is to be found. And if there should be found among men any that possess any good, they will not be treated any differently from myself by other men; in fact I have come to the conclusion that it is bad if they are hostile, and worse if they are friendly.

Science Faces a Choice

All this reminds us that the human mind, then and now and always, faces the same choices in life. The Chinese sage, Mencius, was saying centuries before Christ, that what differentiates one individual from another is which part of his nature he takes his stand upon as a basis for his life. And his message is not essentially different from that of the *Gita* when it contrasts those who choose to follow either the life of the higher self or the lower self. As Milton says in *Paradise Lost*:

> The mind is its own place, and in itself,
> Can make a heav'n of hell, a hell of heaven.

Niccolò Machiavelli (1469-1527), who was born 17 years after Leonardo and was also a Florentine, represented a very different view to Leonardo's. He entered government service in Florence as a clerk and rose to prominence as secretary of the ten-man council that ruled Florence when the republic was proclaimed there in 1498. He conducted missions to the French Court, the Vatican and the German Emperor on behalf of Florence in the early years of the sixteenth century and got to know many of the Italian rulers and their way of conducting diplomatic operations. When the Medici family reclaimed power in Florence in 1512, he was deprived of office and briefly imprisoned, and then — having fallen out of favour and lost his job — retired to his nearby estate and wrote a number of books, of which the most famous was *The Prince*. He also wrote several plays, the best known of which is *Mandragola* (1524) a biting satire on the corruption of contemporary Italian society.

The Prince (1532) was dedicated to the Duke of Urbino and provided advice on how a ruler should behave in order to

The Spiritual Awakening of Science

preserve and increase his power. He mentions the good qualities which such a ruler should be seen to have, but adds that it is not necessary for him actually to have them and may even not be in his interest to do so! What *is* important, according to Machiavelli, is that he should *appear* to have them. It is good to appear to be upright, religious, humane, faithful and merciful, but the ruler should not hesitate to act immorally in order to preserve his power or gain an advantage. The end justifies the means. Even in his own day Machiavelli became a by-word for cynicism and double-dealing, and his name became widely known all over Europe.

He was, in other words, an advocate of the pursuit of the interests of the lower self, by fair means or foul, along exactly the lines on which the sixteenth chapter of the *Bhagavad Gita* describes it—i.e. the ruthless pursuit of narrow self-interest at the expense of others.

Although the political philosophy of Machiavelli was not directly concerned with science, but with the governance of the State, it is clear that nothing could be further than this from the straightforward honesty in the scientific pursuit of wisdom advocated by Leonardo da Vinci. But it was not to be very long before the Machiavellian spirit found a scientifically inclined exponent in the person of Francis Bacon (1561-1626). Bacon, like Machiavelli, spent his life as a lawyer angling for position and power—in his case within the English Court of Elizabeth and James I. He pays tribute to Machiavelli in his book, *The Advancement of Learning*, where he comments:

> We are much beholden to Machiavelli and others, that write what men do, and not what they ought to do.

Science Faces a Choice

Bacon's interest in science is thoroughly pragmatic. He was not himself a scientist and made no contributions of any importance to scientific knowledge, but he recognized the possibility of using science as a means of extending man's power over nature, pointing out how the discovery of printing, gunpowder and the magnetic compass had changed the face of the world, in regard to books, warfare and navigation respectively. He recognized that this kind of knowledge came only from observation and experiment, based on inductive logic, and not from any amount of speculation. He emphasized that the successes in physics had come from careful examination of the causes — more specifically the efficient and material causes — of phenomena, whereas the enquiry into final causes — which tried to explain things in terms of aims or purposes — was sterile and got the investigator nowhere. Ruling out scientific explanations in terms of purpose, however, did not prevent him from holding that the main purpose of pursuing scientific studies is to gain power over nature.

Bacon was therefore a keen advocate of science and wrote extensively about it, and his books had a considerable influence on later thinkers. But his interest in science was entirely concerned with it as a means to an end — in what you can get out of it. In this he had the attitude typical of a politician or a captain of industry. Sadly it has to be said that Bacon's advocacy of the uses of applied science has in general appealed more powerfully to governments and accountants than the idea of pure science searching disinterestedly for new knowledge of the world. The reason why many governments support science in the modern world is that it has proved profitable. Its further pursuit promises to yield

The Spiritual Awakening of Science

further increases in man's power over nature, as it has done — often as an unforeseen incidental by-product of the disinterested search for knowledge. But the best and most important of scientific advances have invariably come from the kind of disinterested search for knowledge and wisdom advocated by Leonardo. And science without wisdom is fraught with danger.

This has become obvious in our own day when the investigation of the nature of the atom has led unexpectedly to the possibility of both atomic power and the atomic bomb, and the discovery of the genetic code has led to the equally unforeseen possibilities of changing the genetic blueprints of living things at will by laboratory techniques. It is now abundantly clear that, once knowledge is found, and the genie is out of the bottle, it is difficult to limit the spread of the know-how or to ensure that it is used wisely. As a result, the lack of consideration of the ethical questions, which had been effectively eliminated from science by the insistence on pure objectivity adopted by the Greek scientists, has become a dangerous hazard. If knowledge is power, then knowledge itself is not enough unless it also brings — or is at least accompanied by — a commensurate degree of wisdom to guide its use. This emphasizes the sanity of Leonardo's attitude to science, compared with Bacon's Machiavellian view.

Bacon himself was a true follower of Machiavelli not only in his attitude to science, but also in his life. With him the aim of science is no longer the disinterested pursuit of truth and true understanding. It has become simply an effective means of seeking increased power for the possessor. And, without being an exceptionally bad or evil man, he lived his own life on the same principles.

Science Faces a Choice

He was born into one of the most powerful families in the Elizabethan court, his uncle-in-law being none other than William Cecil, Lord Burghley, the life-long Prime Minister of Queen Elizabeth. Burghley's wife was the sister of Bacon's mother. His father was the Lord Keeper of the Seal, the head of the legal profession, but he died, leaving his two sons, Anthony and Francis, only a moderate inheritance. They not unreasonably looked to their uncle, Lord Burghley, for advancement, but he was ambitious to arrange for his own son, Robert Cecil, to succeed him as Queen Elizabeth's chief adviser, and would not help them, probably fearing that they might prove potential rivals.

Realizing that they were not to expect any help from that quarter, the two Bacons turned to the powerful Earl of Essex and, early in 1593, Anthony Bacon became Essex's private secretary, while Francis pursued an independent career as a barrister and member of Parliament. Essex, who was seven years younger than Francis Bacon, tried to get the Attorney-Generalship for him when it became vacant, and put forward his name to the Queen. But, by an ill-chance, Bacon had opposed a subsidy asked for the Crown in Parliament a few weeks before. The Queen was very angry and forbade Bacon to appear before her. The more Essex pressed his suit, the more objections the Queen raised, and finally at Easter 1594, she appointed Edward Coke, Bacon's great rival, as Attorney General. This still left the Solicitor-Generalship open, and Essex started bombarding the Queen with requests to at least give Bacon that job. Bacon meanwhile sent a rich jewel to the Queen to improve his chances, which she graciously refused and returned to him, subsequently appointing someone else to the post.

The Spiritual Awakening of Science

As soon as this happened, Essex went to Bacon and expressed his deep regret that he had been unable to help Bacon, when Bacon had served him so assiduously. To make amends, and knowing that Bacon was strapped for cash, he presented Bacon with a small property, which was worth a great deal of money at that time, and which Bacon was able to sell to pay off his debts. He also subsequently helped him to become Master of the Rolls, by writing several letters to the legal authorities concerned. All this was done at a time when Essex was particularly harassed and busy preparing for an expedition to Ireland — an expedition which was to prove his ruin, and lead to the abortive rising on his return, and his arrest and execution for treason.

By the time of the trial, Bacon had completely changed sides, offering his services to Burghley and being consulted about Essex by the Queen, while he avoided Essex's company. This could be construed as the wisdom of a man who saw that Essex was going off the rails, but it hardly excuses Bacon for then agreeing to act as the main (and most effective) prosecuting counsel at the trial of Essex which led to his execution, and also as the person who wrote the official narrative of Essex's treason afterwards. Someone who had received so many benefits and such kindness from his former patron, might have been expected (at the very least) to leave those roles to others. In this Bacon showed himself an apt pupil of Machiavelli.[1]

[1] A well-written account of the tragic rise and fall of the Earl of Essex and Francis Bacon's less than admirable role in it can be found in Lytton Strachey's *Elizabeth and Essex*, London: Chatto and Windus, 1928. The later events are detailed in A.L. Rowse's *Shakespeare's Southampton* (e.g. pp 270-272; 291), London: Macmillan, 1965, and in C.D. Bowen's *Francis Bacon*, London: Hamish Hamilton, 1963.

Science Faces a Choice

Hardly surprisingly, Bacon was never in favour while Elizabeth reigned, but his fortunes improved under James and he was eventually appointed Lord Chancellor in 1618 and raised to the Peerage as Baron Verulam. Bacon's triumphal return home after his investiture as Lord Keeper of the King's Seal is described by his biographer, C.D. Bowen, thus:

> Bacon made his way home through the streets in glory—'waited on', wrote a barrister, 'in the bravest manner I ever saw. All the lawyers and gentlemen of the Inns of Court and Chancery went before him and all the [Privy] Council, the nobility, the judges, knights and gallant gentlemen about the town rode behind him in such a deal of bravery as is almost incredible'....
>
> Lord Bacon, the world called him now. And the world paid court to Lord Bacon, begged his favour; the world doffed its hat and stood upon the York House threshold [where he lived in state], asking entrance... In ceremonies and processions the Lord Keeper had precedence over everyone except the Archbishop of Canterbury....
>
> There is no doubt that Lord Keeper Bacon enjoyed his position to the full and made the most of it; London gossips said he made too much of it. Not long after Bacon's investiture, King James went to Scotland on progress, naming the Lord Keeper as Regent of England during his absence. At the palace, Sir Francis kept almost royal state, receiving ambassadors in the banqueting hall as if he were sovereign. As summer advanced Bacon, losing caution in his new glory, made an almost fatal mistake of policy.[1]

---

[1] Bowen, *Op. cit.*, pp 120, 121 and 124-125.

The Spiritual Awakening of Science

This was to oppose, very publicly, the marriage of the youngest daughter of his old rival and adversary, Sir Edward Coke, to Sir John Villiers, the elder brother of King James's powerful favourite, the Earl of Buckingham. What Bacon did not know was that Coke had promised to provide the enormous sum of ten thousand pounds as the dowry. His opposition offended both the King and his favourite, and Bacon had a difficult time extricating himself. But he was eventually successful in restoring good relations with them, and in January 1621, he was created Viscount St Albans. But it was a short-lived success. Only a few weeks later he was arrested and charged with accepting bribes, as a judge, from the litigants appearing before him. When he saw the details of his indictment, his health collapsed and he became ill and had to be visited and examined on the charges by a group of his peers at his sick-bed. Realizing that the evidence against him was undeniable, he wrote a letter admitting his guilt and expressing his penitence. He admitted accepting bribes from those who appeared before him as Lord Chancellor, but maintained that he sold only justice, and never injustice! He seemed to have hoped that his having shown his impartiality by accepting payments with equal willingness from both sides would be considered extenuating circumstances. He was fined and banished from Parliament and the Court, and narrowly escaped losing his peerage and being confined for a long period in the Tower, but was released by King James after three days there on the grounds of his ill-health. He spent the rest of his life in retirement in his own country house and devoted his time to writing, in spite of making some unsuccessful attempts to return to the Lords, which were rebuffed.

Francis Bacon has been supposed by some to be the author of Shakespeare's plays[1], although a less probable hypothesis would be hard to find. But it is worth remembering that Shakespeare's plays were being produced during Bacon's lifetime. Shakespeare was, of course, familiar with Machiavelli's writings and reputation, although it need hardly be said that he had no opportunity to read the *Bhagavad Gita*. The *Gita* already existed in India long before his time, but the first English translation that we know of, which was by Charles Wilkins, was not published until 1785, towards the end of the eighteenth century, when it was read with interest by William Blake, among others. Notwithstanding this, there was little that Shakespeare did not know about the human heart and mind, and in one of his earliest plays, the philosophy of Machiavelli and of the life of the lower self spoken of in the *Gita*, is well personified in the character of Richard Crookback.

Let me first remind you briefly of how the *Gita* describes the thoughts of the deluded ones:

---

[1] There is indeed some evidence that Bacon attended and spoke at a notorious evening when a performance of *The Comedy of Errors* was given during the Christmas Revels on December 28th, 1594 at Gray's Inn. This was the particular Inn of Law originally attended by him as a student and to which Bacon was admitted as a Bencher in 1586. See Introduction to *The Comedy of Errors*, Cambridge, 1922, edited by Sir Arthur Quiller-Couch and John Dover Wilson, pages vii-x; xxii-xxiii.

The Spiritual Awakening of Science

Today I have gained this wealth and position; that I shall obtain in the future; this is mine now and that *will* be mine.

I have overcome this enemy today and I will slay others... There is none equal to me.

Their every thought is based on 'I'.

In *The Third Part of King Henry VI*, this is how Richard, Duke of Gloucester, dreams of achieving the crown of England, but then realizes that between him and the throne stand his brothers and their children. He then outlines his plans to pursue his own narrow self-interest by dissimulation and trickery with astounding frankness.

> Why then, I do but dream on sovereignty;
> Like one that stands upon a promontory,
> And spies a far-off shore where he would tread,
> Wishing his foot were equal with his eye,
> And chides the sea that sunders him from thence,
> Saying, he'll lade[1] it dry to have his way:
> So do I wish the crown, being so far off;
> And so I chide the means that keeps me from it;
> And so I say, I'll cut the causes off,
> Flattering me with impossibilities.
> My eye's too quick, my heart o'erweens too much,
> Unless my hand and strength could equal them...

---

[1] Lade is an old word which has fallen out of the language, meaning to draw off water with a ladle or scoop, or by means of a channel, as in a mill-race. One finds it still in old place names like Cricklade on the Thames.

Science Faces a Choice

I'll make my heaven to dream upon the crown,
And, whiles I live, t'account this world but hell,
Until my mis-shaped trunk that bears this head
Be round impaléd with a glorious crown.
And yet I know not how to get the crown,
For many lives stand between me and home:
And I—like one lost in a thorny wood,
That rends the thorns and is rent with the thorns,
Seeking a way and straying from the way,
Not knowing how to find the open air,
But toiling desperately to find it out—
Torment myself to catch the English crown:
And from that torment I will free myself,
Or hew my way out with a bloody axe.
Why, I can smile, and murder whiles I smile,
And cry 'Content' to that which grieves my heart,
And wet my cheeks with artificial tears,
And frame my face to all occasions.
I'll drown more sailors than the mermaid shall;
I'll slay more gazers than the basilisk;
I'll play the orator as well as Nestor,
Deceive more slyly than Ulysses could,
And, like a Sinon, take another Troy.
I can add colours to the chameleon,
Change shapes with Proteus for advantages,
And set the murderous Machiavel to school.
Can I do this, and cannot get a crown?
Tut, were it farther off, I'll pluck it down.

One could not get a much more accurate description of all this than the words of the *Gita*:

The Spiritual Awakening of Science

Unbalanced in mind on account of numerous imaginary and selfish projects, ambitions and desires, imprisoned in the net of infatuation (personal attachments), given to the gratification of sensual desires, they fall into the impure hells (lower states of consciousness in which discrimination ceases and ignorance of the truth increases, resulting in untold sufferings, mental and spiritual).

We can see then that when science came of age in the Renaissance, it was at once presented with this choice: either to follow the lead of Leonardo, in whom the study of nature was a way of pursuing truth and understanding the world revealed to us through experience, and the promised fruit of that pursuit was what he called wisdom; or, on the other hand, to follow Machiavelli and Bacon in the pursuit of power and narrow self-interest. The same choice still faces science today, and it has to be sadly acknowledged that governments seem far more interested in the Baconian view, than in the disinterested search for understanding which Leonardo pioneered, and which all the great scientists, like Newton, Faraday, Helmholtz, Darwin, Einstein and Schrödinger have pursued.

The idea, unconsciously adopted by the Greek scientists, that science could be pursued as a purely objective search for truth, without encountering moral and spiritual problems, was, of course, a naïve illusion from the start. And just as it was clearly recognized by scientists like Roger Bacon and Leonardo, that the biggest obstacles to the pursuit of truth were the prejudices and mistaken ideas within the mind of the scientist himself — and Francis Bacon

Science Faces a Choice

too recognizes these difficulties in his doctrine of the idols of the mind—so it is clear that the unsolved inner problems, ignored by primitive science, will finally have to be faced by the scientist if he is to achieve a full knowledge of the truth. And it is equally clear that, as the teachings of Yoga proclaim, it is only when man has turned within to achieve a more enlightened outlook through a deeper self-knowledge, that he can achieve real wisdom.

Science, having grown up, cannot avoid moral and ethical questions, because it is itself a creation of the human mind. For the Greeks, it was a search for certain knowledge about the nature of the world for its own sake, but that knowledge must be combined with understanding and wisdom if it is not to prove a Pandora's box, whose opening can release chaos and evil into the world. The use of science in the Baconian sense—simply as a means of increasing man's power over nature in the service of his narrow self-interest—is a recipe for disaster, as is becoming ever more evident in the modern world. The choice between Machiavelli and Leonardo is a spiritual choice, but it is one which affects our whole life, and the life of the whole society in which we live.

The teachings of Yoga are more than relevant to this because, in the words of our own teacher Dr Shastri:

> We have to realize that the mind is our instrument—and not our Lord and Master, nor yet a very dear and kind friend—for the mind is far from that. Its whispers are not always helpful to us, and therefore we must analyze our passions before we act on them; we must analyze our

The Spiritual Awakening of Science

thoughts also before we act on them.

We must remind ourselves every day, as often as we can, that the mind is our instrument and that we, as the thinking agents, must be able to use the mind as *we* desire, not as *it* desires to be used by us.

To attain that tranquillity of the heart which enables us to live in peace and harmony by recognizing the presence of God in, through and all around us, is the way to live well. Atman is the divine Self in man, that part of God which is covered by the mind of man.

We are reminded almost daily about our need for wisdom by the tremendous increase in the power over nature which modern developments in scientific technology have brought us. Science in the hands of worldly-wise and cynical Machiavellians is a recipe for disaster. And most governments are more interested in temporal power than truth *per se*. Worse still, the dissemination of know-how has made it possible for relatively cheap and lethal means of wreaking havoc to fall into the hands of homicidal dictators like Saddam Hussain or Milosevic, or even into the hands of small fanatical sects, like the Japanese cult which employed nerve gas on the innocent passengers of the Tokyo underground.

As well as these hazards, the widespread problem of dealing with nuclear contamination, the speed with which we are exterminating our fellow creatures, like the whales or the stocks of fish, the hazards of genetically modified crops and animal cloning, all remind us of the truth and wisdom of the words of Bertrand Russell:

Science Faces a Choice

With every increase in knowledge and skill, wisdom becomes more necessary, for every such increase augments our capacity for realizing our purposes, and therefore augments our capacity for evil if our purposes are unwise. The world needs wisdom as it has never needed it before; and if knowledge continues to increase, the world will need wisdom in the future even more than it does now.

What do we mean by wisdom and why is it something which inevitably involves a spiritual dimension? This will be the subject of the next Chapter.

5

KNOWLEDGE AND WISDOM

IF YOU LOOK UP the word 'philosophy' in the dictionary, you will find that it comes from two words, *philos* and *sophia*, meaning the love of wisdom, and that philosophy, in its original and widest sense, meant 'the love, study or pursuit of wisdom or of knowledge of things and their causes, whether theoretical or practical'. *Natural philosophy* was the name given, in particular, to the pursuit by science of knowledge of the external world, and this term gradually became identified more specifically with the study of physics.

Philosophy in general, then, concerned the pursuit of truth, whether about the world or man himself. But, as Pontius Pilate pertinently asked, 'What is truth?' Certainly it is clear that not all philosophers have had the same idea about what truth is like. So there are people who profess to offer you truth, but who are really offering very different things. In Athens in the sixth century BC, for instance, Socrates was teaching his pupils a truth representing the highest virtue and the highest beauty; the Sophists, on the other hand, also talked of truth and virtue, but gave their instructions in return for payment, and the aim of their teaching was worldly success and wealth. As a result, *sophistical* in the end became a name for specious and fallacious arguments deliberately employed to falsify and mislead the hearer.

In the Renaissance a somewhat similar choice was on offer: between Leonardo's ideal of wisdom and the cynical worldly wisdom of Machiavelli. Which of these two you chose was a question of what you considered mattered, or—to put it bluntly—whether you favoured reality or appearance. Truth is like this. Unless we choose the real truth, like Leonardo, we may choose to dissimulate, to deceive others for our own supposed advantage, like Machiavelli—but, in fact, we end up deceiving ourselves and sinking deeper into delusion. This was Leonardo's conviction and it is also that of the yogis.

Truth: real and imaginative

Russell defines truth as something which is confirmed and verified by the relevant facts, while facts, in Wittgenstein's phrase, are 'everything that is the case'. A statement is true if the state of affairs to which it corresponds is indeed a fact; and false if it is not. In other words, in saying that something is true, we are saying something about reality.

But Russell contrasts this idea of truth with what he dubs the 'engineer's idea of truth':

> Science used to be valued as a means of getting to *know* the world; now, owing to the triumph of technique, it is conceived as showing how to *change* the world. The new point of view, which is adopted in practice throughout America and Russia, and in theory by many modern

philosophers, was first proclaimed by Marx in 1845, in his *Theses on Feuerbach*. He says: 'The question whether objective truth belongs to human thinking is not a question of theory, but a practical question. The truth, i.e. the reality and power, of thought must be demonstrated in practice. The contest as to the reality or non-reality of a thought which is isolated from practice is a purely scholastic question... Philosophers have only *interpreted* the world in various ways, but the real task is to alter it.'[1]

As Russell puts it:

If love of power dominates [a man's desires], you arrive at Marx's view that what is important is not to understand the world, but to change it... And if power is all you want from science, the pragmatist theory gives you just what you want, without accretions that to you seem irrelevant. It gives you even more than you could have expected, for if you control the police it gives you the god-like power of *making truth*. You cannot make the sun cold, but you can confer pragmatic 'truth' on the proposition 'the sun is cold' if you ensure that everyone who denies it is liquidated. I doubt whether Zeus could do more.

This engineer's philosophy, as it may be called, is distinguished from common sense by its rejection of 'fact' as a fundamental concept in defining 'truth'.[2]

As Russell points out, the pragmatic theory of truth is inherently connected with the appeal to force, both as a

---

[1] From Bertrand Russell, *The Impact of Science on Society*, London: George Allen & Unwin, 1952, p 98. [2] *Ibid.*, pp 100-101.

means of suppressing the real truth and promulgating the currently preferred alternative. It is a Machiavellian concept.

Like any deliberately created appearance, this sort of 'truth' can change from time to time. In Russia, for instance, it was 'true' in 1920 that Trotsky played a great part in the Russian Revolution; but by 1930 it was 'false'. Russell comments that the results of this view of truth have been admirably worked out in George Orwell's *1984*.

This philosophy — beloved of politicians, spin-doctors and advertising executives — suggests that the truth is something open to manipulation. In Russia it led to the reports of the highly successful conclusion of each five year plan under Soviet Communism, although it turned out much later that the reality was very different — a succession of disastrous economic failures! Even scientific truth fared no better. It was announced by Lysenko under Stalin that he had succeeded in refuting the hitherto well-established Mendelian Laws of Heredity by developing crops in which acquired characteristics were inherited.[1] Ultimately the claim was proved bogus, as competent geneticists (even in Russia) had always said it was, but until after the death of Stalin in 1953 those who said so in Russia were disgraced

---

[1] This was, incidentally, long before science discovered how to carry out genetic engineering, which does actually enable one to alter the DNA and influence the 'blueprints' of genetic inheritance by modifying the coded genes in the nucleus of the cell. It was only in April 1953 that Watson and Crick discovered the chemical structure of the chromosome, and the laboratory techniques for reading and changing the coded instructions took many more years to be developed.

and lost their jobs, whereas Lysenko in 1938 became President of the Lenin All-Union Academy of Agricultural Sciences and in 1940, Director of the Institute of Genetics of the USSR Academy of Sciences.

It would be wrong to suggest that these attempted 'manipulations' of the truth are an exclusively modern development. The ecclesiastical authorities in Leonardo's time were continuously active in trying to control the truth which was promulgated, and, where possible, they bent it in their own interests. In the *Life of Leonardo* published by Vasari in his book on *The Lives of the Artists*, there are two clear examples of this. In the first edition, which appeared in 1550, 31 years after Leonardo's death, the account of his early life included the sentence:

> Leonardo was of such a heretical frame of mind, that he did not adhere to any kind of religion, believing that it was perhaps better to be a philosopher than a Christian.[1]

This sentence was expunged from all subsequent editions of Vasari's book. Somebody had decided that it should not be the truth any more.

Worse still, Vasari's account ends with a clearly spurious and mendacious account of Leonardo's death which reads:

> At length, having become old, he lay sick for many months, and seeing himself near death, he desired to

---

[1] L. Goldscheider, *Leonardo da Vinci: Life and Work, Paintings and Drawings*, London: Phaidon Press, 7th edition, 1964 p. 13, footnote 11.

Knowledge and Wisdom

occupy himself with the truths of the Catholic Faith and the holy Christian religion. Then, having confessed and shown his penitence with much lamentation, he devoutly took the Sacrament, leaving his bed, supported by his friends and servants, as he could not stand. The king arriving, for he would often pay him friendly visits, he sat up in bed from respect, and related the circumstances of his illness, showing how greatly he had offended God and man in not having worked in his art as he ought. He was then seized with a paroxysm, the harbinger of death, so that the king rose and took his head to assist him and show him favour as well as to alleviate the pain. Leonardo's divine spirit, then recognizing that he could not enjoy a greater honour, expired in the king's arms, at the age of seventy-five.[1]

Leonardo was, in fact, sixty-seven when he died on May 2nd 1519, but that is a small matter. The whole account is a complete lie. On the day Leonardo died we know with certainty that the King was far away from Amboise and Cloux with the Court, half-way across France on the other side of Paris, at St-Germain-en-Laye. There he was signing State papers on May 1st, the day before Leonardo died. Francesco Melzi, who was Leonardo's closest pupil and the heir to whom he bequeathed all his papers, was with him at Cloux when he died and wrote back to Leonardo's stepbrothers in Florence with an account of his death, but he makes no mention at all of the King being there. We can only

---

[1] Goldscheider, *op. cit.*, p.22.

The Spiritual Awakening of Science

agree with the comment of Jean Paul Richter, the great modern Leonardo scholar, when he writes:

> The incredible and demonstrably fictitious legend of Leonardo's death in the arms of Francis the First is given, with others, by Vasari and further embellished by this odious comment: '[he related the circumstances of his illness]....showing how greatly he had offended against God and man in not having worked in his art as he ought'.
>
> This last accusation is evidence of the superficial character of the information which Vasari was in a position to give about Leonardo. It seems to imply that Leonardo was disdainful of diligent labour.[1]

Richter points out that Leonardo's own writings reveal him to us:

> ...as a man whose life and conduct were unfailingly governed by lofty principles and aims. He could scarcely have recorded his stern reprobation and unmeasured contempt for men who do nothing useful and strive only for riches, if his own life and ambitions had been such as they are often misrepresented [as having been].[2]

And he refers to the tribute paid to Leonardo's exceptional qualities and character in the letter in which Melzi, the young Milanese nobleman, announces the Master's death to Leonardo's brothers:

---

[1] J.P. Richter, *The Literary Works of Leonardo da Vinci*, New York: Phaidon, 1970 Vol. II p 235.

[2] Richter, *ibid.*, and Goldscheider, *op. cit.*, p 39 (translation).

Knowledge and Wisdom

I believe the death of your brother, Maestro Leonardo, has already been certified to you. He was to me the best of fathers, and it is impossible for me to express the grief that his death has caused me. Until the day when my body is laid under the ground, I shall experience perpetual sorrow, and not without reason, for he daily showed me the most devoted and warmest affection.

His loss is a grief to everyone, for it is not in the power of nature to reproduce another such man.

It is ironic that Leonardo himself should be a victim of false propaganda, when one remembers him as writing:

> The lie is so vile, that even if it were speaking well of godly things it would take off something of God's grace; and truth is so excellent in itself, that, even if it dwells on humble and lowly matter, it rises infinitely beyond the uncertainties and lies about high and lofty matters.... But you who live on dreams are better pleased by sophistical reasons and [the] frauds of wits in great and uncertain things than by those reasons which are certain and natural and not so exalted.

The all-pervasive presence of the Catholic Church during the whole of the Renaissance period meant that one continually comes up against such examples of censorship and manipulation of the records. This thought-policing went on insidiously throughout ordinary life, in a way with which we are all too familiar in our own day from the totalitarian states under Nazism and Communism, as well as from some of the petty dictatorships in Africa and elsewhere. It also affected the progress of science.

The Spiritual Awakening of Science

In the fifteenth century, in the privacy of his own notebooks, Leonardo da Vinci (1452-1519) wrote the simple straightforward observation: 'The sun does not move', and he also noted to himself that 'The earth is a star like other stars' (nowadays we should use the word *planet*, rather than *star*, but his meaning is clear and, as such, it is correct). This is the first explicit recognition, known to us in the written records in Europe after the Dark Ages, of the truth of the discovery, originally made by Aristarchus in ancient Greece, of the fact that the sun stands still at the centre of the solar system, while the earth moves in an orbit round it like the other planets.

Some years later, the Polish mathematician and high churchman, Nicholas Copernicus (1473-1543), got to know about Aristarchus' theory while studying as a young man at the University of Bologna in Italy and became deeply interested in it. He worked for many years on devising a mathematical model which would account for the data available at that time on the movement of the heavenly bodies. When it was finished in 1530, he sent a brief summary of his conclusions, entitled *Commentariolus*, to his interested friends, but did not publish anything until 1541 and then only a short volume, entitled *De Libris Revolutionum Narratio prima*, prepared with the help of a mathematical friend, George Joachim (Rheticus), summarizing the contents of the longer book which he had already written, and which was to be called *De Revolutionibus Orbium coelestium*. In this unpublished book he had described in detail his heliocentric model of the

Knowledge and Wisdom

solar system, mentioning in it several times that Aristarchus had originally propounded it. Copernicus delayed publication of this longer book for ten years until he was on his death-bed, and then entrusted it to Rheticus to put it through the press for him. He in turn handed it on to another cleric called Ossiander, who took it on himself to remove all the references to Aristarchus and substituted an introduction of his own for the one written by Copernicus, saying that the latter's account and calculations were only 'theoretical' and 'might not be a true scheme of nature but merely a mathematical fiction which fitted the observations'. This was published in 1543, the year of Copernicus's death.

All this delay and prevarication seems to have been due to anxiety that there would be an adverse response to the idea, not only by the general readers, but by the Church authorities, either Catholic or Lutheran, with the danger of its being proscribed as heretical. One of the main objections raised by the Christians to the idea that the sun did *not* move round the earth, was that it was claimed to contradict and make nonsense of the Biblical text in the *Book of Joshua* (10.12-14), which spoke of God miraculously commanding the sun and moon to stand still until the Israelites had avenged themselves on their fleeing enemies, the Amorites. But behind this, of course, lay the even more cogent objection that it abolished the idea that the earth was the centre of the universe, and relegated it to the position of a relatively unimportant planet circling round the sun. It was therefore probably in the hope of avoiding trouble that

The Spiritual Awakening of Science

Copernicus wrote a letter to the Pope, dedicating the book to him!

Because of the watering down of what Copernicus himself had originally written before publication, little notice was taken of his book or of the heliocentric theory at the time. He had, anyway, not made a very strong case, as he was not an astronomer himself and had made no new observations. He had merely worked out an elaborate mathematical scheme to fit what past observations he could find, many of which were faulty and unreliable. Unfortunately, too, he had followed Ptolemy and the Pythagoreans in assuming that the orbits of the heavenly bodies described perfect circles, a mistake which was not to be corrected until Kepler (1571-1630) in the early seventeenth century — relying on the much fuller and more accurate observations of Tycho Brahe (1546-1601) — discovered that the planets moved, not in circles, but in ellipses. To fit the observations at all into his original earth-centred scheme, Ptolemy had needed to introduce an elaborate system of about eighty epicycles to cope with the data known in his time. In his sun-centred model, Copernicus managed to reduce this requirement to thirty-four epicycles, but this partial improvement suggested that there was still something wrong.

As a consequence of all this, it was not until 1616 (73 years after his death) that Copernicus's book was put on the Index and Catholics were from then onwards forbidden to read it. This was because by then Galileo had produced virtually incontrovertible evidence that the heliocentric

Knowledge and Wisdom

theory of the solar system was true! Galileo (1564-1642), with his newly-discovered telescope, made detailed observations on the sun, the moon and the planets, as well as the unnumbered multitude of fixed stars, and, as a result, the accumulated evidence for the truth of the heliocentric hypothesis became overwhelming. His *Letters on the Solar Spots* (1613) led to his being summoned before the Inquisition under Cardinal Bellarmine, charged with heresy. Galileo was an outstandingly good experimental scientist, and had amassed a huge body of experimental data on physics, mathematics and astronomy to support his ideas, and he was widely respected in Italy and elsewhere as a result. For this reason, he escaped the charge of heresy at this juncture, but the work was ordered to be withdrawn from circulation. Galileo himself was let off with a caution.

However, his observations had convinced him of the truth of the Copernican rather than the Ptolemaic model. He had observed, for instance, the moons circulating round Jupiter and the fact that the illumination of Venus waxed and waned like that of the moon, showing that it was illumined by the reflected light of the sun in a way that demonstrated that it must be rotating round the sun. A subsequent book on *A Dialogue on the Two Chief World-Systems, the Ptolemaic and the Copernican,* published by him in January 1632, discussed the different views in the form of a dialogue between three people, one proponent of each view and a third impartial observer. The anti-Copernican was depicted as violent and steeped in the doctrines of Aristotle — and also as desperately stupid and unable to see the simplest arguments. As a result, Galileo was

The Spiritual Awakening of Science

summoned to Rome again by the Inquisition and imprisoned, and the sale of the book was forbidden. After a trial, he was sentenced to make a recantation of all Copernican doctrines and to do penance for three years.[1]

In the long run, of course, the truth was bound to come out. Those who try and manipulate the 'truth' to maintain some idea in the interests of their own power, end up by demonstrating their own blindness. Within a few years many in the scientific world had realized that Galileo was right. But it was not until 1822, just short of two centuries later, that the Roman Catholic Church allowed the Copernican system to be taught as the truth, and it was not until 1979 that Pope John Paul II instituted an investigation by the Church into Galileo's condemnation. In October 1992, more than three-and-a-half centuries after his trial and imprisonment, the report of the papal commission finally acknowledged the Vatican's error.

One is reminded of the short poem on 'Truth' by Coventry Patmore:

> Here, in this little Bay,
> Full of tumultuous life and great repose,
> Where, twice a day,
> The purposeless, glad ocean comes and goes,
> Under high cliffs, and far from the huge town,
> I sit me down.
> For want of me the world's course will not fail;
> When all its work is done, the lie shall rot;

---

[1] See Sir James Jeans, *The Growth of Physical Science*, pp 124-134, 171-176.

Knowledge and Wisdom

The truth is great, and shall prevail,
When none care whether it prevail or not.

The need for wisdom in science, not merely knowledge

Russell has written in the introduction to his book, *The Scientific Outlook*:

Science, as its name implies, is primarily knowledge... Gradually, however, the aspect of science as knowledge is being thrust into the background by the aspect of science as the power of manipulating nature.... If, therefore, a scientific civilization is to be a good civilization it is necessary that increase in knowledge should be accompanied by increase in wisdom. I mean by wisdom a right conception of the ends of life. This is something which science itself does not provide. Increase of science by itself, therefore, is not enough to guarantee any genuine progress, though it provides one of the ingredients which progress requires.

And he goes on to say that it is important to remember that the scientific preoccupation with knowledge, combined with its neglect of the ends to which it is put, is one-sided and needs to be corrected by wisdom if a balanced view of human life is to be achieved.[1]

Differences between wisdom and knowledge

Leonardo da Vinci was arguably the most universal genius in the history of Western culture, in that he was equally great and creative in his lifelong dedication to both

---

[1] Bertrand Russell, *The Scientific Outlook*, London: George Allen & Unwin, 2nd edition, 1949, p.12.

the arts and the sciences. He was certainly totally free of that great divide between 'the two cultures' which C P Snow and others deplore in twentieth century thought, and which (it is held) has led to a disastrous lack of understanding between the adherents of the two camps. It is therefore of the greatest interest to find that Leonardo's ideal was not merely knowledge of the truth about facts. What he valued most highly was wisdom, which he called 'the daughter of experience'.

It is all the more noteworthy to find Russell, in modern times, making exactly the same distinction between knowledge and wisdom, and emphasizing the vital importance of the latter, in the pursuit of the scientific ideal. But what exactly is wisdom? Russell addresses this question in his short essay on 'Knowledge and Wisdom':

> Most people would agree (he writes) that, although our age far surpasses all previous ages in knowledge, there has been no correlative increase in wisdom. But agreement ceases as soon as we attempt to define 'wisdom' and consider means of promoting it. I want to ask first what wisdom is, and then what can be done to teach it.[1]

Russell suggests[2] that one important element in wisdom is 'a sense of proportion: the capacity to take account of all the important factors in a problem and to attach to each its due weight', but he adds that comprehensiveness should include not only intellect but also feeling.

---

[1] Bertrand Russell, *Portraits from Memory*, London: George Allen & Unwin, 1958, p 168.   [2] *Ibid.*, pp 168-172.

Knowledge and Wisdom

It is by no means uncommon to find men whose knowledge is wide, but whose feelings are narrow. Such men lack what I am calling wisdom.

He instances the philosopher Hegel, who had wide knowledge, but combined it with a feeling that his own country, Germany, was the best of all countries, the personification of the vanguard of civilization and 'the standard-bearer of progress in the world'. Comprehensive knowledge is therefore not enough in itself to constitute wisdom; for that, there must also be a certain awareness of the ends of human life. Wisdom is needed in both private and public life to influence the choice of ends to be pursued and to emancipate the individual from personal prejudice. He goes on to say:

> the essence of wisdom is emancipation, as far as possible, from the tyranny of the here and the now. We cannot help the egoism of our senses. Sight and sound and touch are bound up with our own bodies and cannot be made impersonal. Our emotions start similarly from ourselves. An infant feels hunger or discomfort, and is unaffected except by his own physical condition. Gradually, with the years, his horizon widens, and in proportion as his thoughts and feelings become less personal and less concerned with his own physical states, he achieves growing wisdom.[1]

This is very close to what the yogis say, when they speak of

---

[1] Russell, *op cit.*, p 170.

the danger of subtle egoism, distorting the clear vision of the mind of the individual, unless it is eliminated.

It is impressive to find Russell taking such a broad and sane view of wisdom and decrying the idea that knowledge and reason alone are sufficient to produce it. The need for feelings and purposes to be involved, as well as the need to escape from the narrow, blinkered outlook of the individual ego, which Russell emphasizes here, comes very much closer to the spiritual ideal of Yoga than one might have expected. The scientist, with his emphasis on objectivity and the elimination of final causes, needs to be reminded of Russell's words when he writes:

> I do not think that knowledge and morals ought to be too much separated... It is true that the kind of specialized knowledge which is required by various kinds of skill has very little to do with wisdom, but it should be supplemented in education by wider surveys calculated to put it in its place in the total of human activities. Even the best technicians should also be good citizens; and when I say 'citizens', I mean citizens of the world and not of this or that sect or nation.[1]

Writing elsewhere on *The Impact of Science on Society*, he says:

> There are certain things that our age needs, and certain things that it should avoid. It needs compassion and a wish that mankind should be happy; it needs the desire for knowledge and the determination to eschew pleasant

---
[1] Russell, *op cit.*, p.172.

myths; it needs, above all, courageous hope and the impulse to creativeness. The things that it must avoid, and that have brought it to the brink of catastrophe, are cruelty, envy, greed, competitiveness....

The root of the matter is a very simple and old-fashioned thing, a thing so simple that I am almost ashamed to mention it, for fear of the derisive smile with which wise cynics will greet my words. The thing I mean—please forgive me for mentioning it—is love, Christian love, or compassion. If you feel this, you have a motive for existence, a guide in action, a reason for courage, an imperative necessity for intellectual honesty.[1]

The conception of wisdom in Yoga

The teachings of Yoga approach the relationship of knowledge and wisdom from an entirely different perspective, but there is much in common between what they say and these comments of Western thinkers on the importance of wisdom. Swami Rama Tirtha in his Notebooks also points out the difference between knowledge and wisdom, saying that knowledge or learning is essentially backward-looking, while wisdom looks to the future; and that, as a result, the two of them are not always on speaking terms with one another![2] (Hegel is, no doubt, a good example of this.) He also, like Russell, emphasizes the close relationship of wisdom and morals.

---

[1] Bertrand Russell, *The Impact of Science on Society*, London: George Allen & Unwin, 1952, pp 113-114.

[2] Swami Rama Tirtha, *In Woods of God-Realization*, Lucknow: Rama Tirtha Pratisthan, Vols XI & XII, Notebooks, p.198 (Notebook 7).

The Spiritual Awakening of Science

The experience of others must be expressed in terms of your own before it becomes wisdom.

Wisdom is knowing what to do next. Virtue is doing it.

Wisdom which does not express itself in action is sterile and useless.

Character-building is equivalent to the formation of a 'higher heredity' — a 'second nature', formed by habit — of wisdom and virtue.

As volition passes over into action, so does science into art, knowledge into power, wisdom into virtue.[1]

All this is similar to the point that Russell was to make many years later, that wisdom also involves a consideration of *purposes* and that the will is also important, if wisdom is to express itself in acting wisely. All these observations are very much in the spirit of Leonardo, for whom wisdom was the daughter of experience; while virtue was the true expression of wisdom in action.

The early pioneers of science speak almost with one voice of the main obstacles to success in scientific enquiry originating in the habitual shortcomings of the human mind, particularly its prejudices and egotistic tendencies. When Leonardo said that the greatest deception from which men suffer arose from their own opinions, he was only echoing the views of his predecessor, Roger Bacon, who identified the four principal causes of human ignorance and the failure to attain truth as being: subjection to unworthy authority; the influence of habit; popular prejudice; and 'making a show of apparent wisdom to

---

[1] Swami Rama Tirtha, *op. cit.*, p 182.

cover one's ignorance'. His namesake, Francis Bacon, was later to echo these conclusions of his predecessors in his description of the 'idols of the mind'.[1]

By its insistence on objectivity and impartiality in the scientific enquiry, early science largely ruled out any idea of trying to improve the quality of the mind and overcome its limitations by active self-discipline. The Greeks simply tried to solve the problem by eliminating the subject as far as possible from scientific consideration, as Schrödinger has so pertinently pointed out. Wisdom had no legitimate rôle in such a view of science as purely objective, nor has the consideration of purposes or ends. It is a very short step from this view to the attitude that scientific knowledge, being itself ethically neutral and purposeless, can be legitimately applied as a means of manipulating nature at the will of whoever comes to possess it, in any way that they choose.

The view of Yoga is that the mind is a totally inadequate instrument for discovering and appreciating truth until it is brought under control and purified, and has had its innate tendency to prejudice and egoism, first mitigated, and then largely eliminated, by self-discipline and the pursuit of the inner enquiry into fuller self-knowledge. On this view, the success of the great scientists like Leonardo can be ascribed to the way in which they adopted a similar approach for themselves, an idea which is to a considerable extent verified from Leonardo's writings.

[1] See, for example, Copleston's *A History of Philosophy*, London: Burns, Oates & Washbourne, 1953, Vol. 3, pp 302-305.

The Spiritual Awakening of Science

Similar approaches can also be seen, for instance, in descriptions of the scientific working methods of such figures as Newton, Faraday, Darwin and Einstein.

For Yoga, true wisdom is indeed equivalent to full self-knowledge, which involves extending the field of scientific investigation from the outer world to the inner world of the mind and consciousness. It is in this sense that Swami Rama Tirtha can speak of Yoga as 'experimental religion'. The mastery of Yoga is said to confer on the individual who achieves it, the state of 'one established in wisdom' (*sthita-prajna*).

The methods of Yoga involve overcoming the 'mind-forged manacles', which subjugate the individual and compel him to commit sin, as if by force, against his will, and veil wisdom, like the smoke obscuring the light of a fire. This inner enemy of man in the form of desire or craving, deludes the embodied individual, having its seat in the senses and the emotional lower mind. These two correspond to the two main faculties of the lower or sensual mind spoken of by Leonardo as appetite and concupiscence, and are by him contrasted with memory and intellect, the two main faculties of the higher mind or reason, which (he says) stands apart from the lower faculties in contemplation. Like the yogis, Leonardo speaks of the need to restrain and re-direct the lower urges of the mind, which are part of man's inheritance from his animal past. As he says: 'You can have no dominion greater or less than that over yourself.' In this he echoes the teaching given in the sixth chapter of the *Bhagavad Gita*:

Knowledge and Wisdom

Let a man raise himself by himself, let him not lower himself; for he alone is the friend of himself; he alone is the enemy of himself.

To him who has conquered himself by himself, his own self is the friend of himself; but to him who has not conquered himself, his own self stands in the place of an enemy, like an external foe.

6

LOOKING TO SEE:
THE SCIENCE OF EXPERIENCE

Lead us from darkness to light,
From error to truth,
From death to immortality.

THIS WELL-KNOWN prayer from the ancient *Upanishads* may be said to sum up the purpose, philosophy and practice of the Yoga of Self-Knowledge. But the first two lines might equally well be taken as the principles which governed the life and ideals of that great figure of the Renaissance, Leonardo da Vinci. He sought light and truth, not so much from the re-awakening of the knowledge from the ancient world (although he was not unwilling to learn from it), as from examining the evidence of experience by careful observation and experiment. He believed that enquiry into truth should be pursued—*not* through speculation or theorizing and argumentation based on it, a method which had characterized much of the thought of the preceding Dark Ages—but by *looking to see* what the truth actually was. In this respect, he was the first writer in the modern world to express the spirit of science and enunciate clearly the principles on which scientific enquiry should be carried out. And he found time in his busy and productive life as

Looking to See: The Science of Experience

one of the greatest painters and sculptors the world has known, to carry out his own trail-blazing scientific investigation of the world around him.

He complained that whereas ancient writers had spent their time trying to deal with things that are beyond proof, such as what the soul and life are, they had totally ignored their own experience, with the result that (as he put it) 'those things which can at any time be clearly known and proved by experience had remained for many centuries unknown or falsely understood'.[1]

Leonardo, as the illegitimate son of a Florentine notary and a village girl, started life with the enormous advantage that he was not over-educated, although he himself knew that this was something for which people would despise him. For he wrote:

> I am fully aware that the fact of my not being a man of letters may cause certain presumptuous persons to think that they may with reason blame me, alleging that I am a man without learning... They will say that because I have no book learning, I cannot properly express what I desire to treat of — but they do not know that my subjects require for their exposition experience rather than the words of others. Experience has been the mistress of whoever has written well; and so as mistress I will cite her in all cases.

---

[1] Except where stated otherwise, the quotations from Leonardo's writings are from *The Notebooks of Leonardo da Vinci*, edited by Irma A. Richter, London: Oxford University Press, 1952.

The Spiritual Awakening of Science

He asserts his own ambition as much humbler than those of his learned critics.

> Though I have no power to quote from authors as they have, I shall rely on a far bigger and more worthy thing—on experience, the instructress of their masters.

While all around him, people were learnedly discussing what Aristotle had or had not taught, and quoting from the many past authors whose writings were now becoming widely available, Leonardo took a different path:

> I will do, like one who, because of his poverty, is the last to arrive at the fair, and not being able otherwise to provide for himself, takes all things which others have already seen and not taken, but refused as being of little value; I will load my modest pack with these despised and rejected wares, the leavings of many buyers; and will go about distributing, not indeed in great cities but in the poor hamlets, taking such reward as the thing I give may be worth.

Leonardo is not dismissive of the ancient writers where he recognized that they had something worthwhile to tell him. He was, for instance, particularly keen to read anything written by Archimedes, whom he greatly admired. Archimedes' works were not printed in Leonardo's lifetime, but he records in one of his notes that the Bishop of Padua has an Archimedes manuscript, and has a memorandum:

> Borges [the Archbishop of Bourges] will get for you the Archimedes from the Bishop of Padua, and Vitellozo the

Looking to See: The Science of Experience

one from Borgo a San Sepolcro. [1]

But although he himself had no ambition to be deeply read, he was critical of those who abbreviate works, and present 'potted knowledge' as if it were the real thing.

> The abbreviators of works do harm to knowledge and to love, for the love of anything is the offspring of knowledge, love being more fervent in proportion as knowledge is more certain. And this certainty springs from a complete knowledge of all the parts which united compose the whole of the thing which ought to be loved.
>
> Of what use, then, is he who in order to abridge the part of the things of which he professes to give complete information, leaves out the greater part of the things of which the whole is composed. True it is that impatience, the mother of folly, is she who praises brevity, as if such persons had not long life enough to acquire a complete knowledge of one single subject, such as the human body. And then they want to comprehend the mind of God which embraces the whole universe, weighing and mincing it into infinite parts as if they had dissected it. O human stupidity! Do you not perceive that you have spent your whole life with yourself, and yet are not yet aware of the thing you chiefly possess, that is, of your folly? And so with the crowd of sophists you deceive yourselves and others, despising the mathematical sciences in which is contained the true information about the subjects of which they treat. And then you would fain occupy yourself with

---

[1] See Jean Paul Richter, *The Literary Works of Leonardo da Vinci*, Vol. II, p 347; pp 354-355; 369-370, 375-376; cf .Vol I, pp 41-42.

miracles and write and give information of those things of which the human mind is incapable [of comprehending the truth], and which cannot be proved by any instance from nature.

What he says here is perennially topical and could well be taken to heart by the popularizers in our own media-dominated age, whose knowledge is usually superficial and all too often reduced to catch-phrases or sound-bites.

Leonardo's philosophy is summed up in his saying:

> To me it seems that all sciences are vain and full of errors that are not born of Experience, mother of all certainty, and that are not tested by Experience... Experience does not feed investigators on dreams, but always proceeds from accurately determined first principles, step by step in true sequence to the end; as can be seen in the elements of mathematics... Here no one argues as to whether twice three is more or less than six or whether the angles of a triangle are less than two right angles. Here all arguments are ended by eternal silence and these sciences can be enjoyed by their devotees in peace. This the deceptive, purely speculative sciences cannot achieve.

Like the eleventh century Persian philosopher, Al-Ghazali, Leonardo clearly believed that: 'The highest function of man's soul is the perception of truth.'

In his own researches, Leonardo's curiosity covered such a wealth and multiplicity of topics that it is impossible to do justice to them in a short article. But an idea of how far-seeing and innovative he was can perhaps be indicated

Looking to See: The Science of Experience

by one notable example. As both an artist and a pioneer of scientific investigation, Leonardo was especially interested in *light*, and wanted to understand its nature and behaviour, particularly as it manifested itself in what was seen by the eye of the artist. To study this he was equally concerned in gaining an understanding of the physical behaviour of light and a detailed knowledge of the structure of the eye. In the Notes which he wrote for his projected Book on Painting 'hoping [as he wrote] to arrange them later each in its place, according to the subjects of which they may treat', he deals with both these topics.

> Among all the studies of natural causes and reasons Light chiefly delights the beholder... Thus, if the Lord — who is the light of all things — vouchsafe to enlighten me, I will treat of Light...[1]

Amazingly, Leonardo had arrived at a clear idea of the wave-theory of light over two centuries before Christian Huygens (who is generally credited with this discovery). Huygens read the paper on his theory before the Paris Académie des Sciences in 1678, and published it in book form in 1690. Leonardo's fifteenth century account is worth quoting at some length, starting, as it does, from the simplest and clearest observations of something that anyone could have seen.

> I say: If you throw two small stones at the same time on a sheet of motionless water at some distance from each other, you will observe that around the two percussions

[1] Jean Paul Richter, *op. cit.*, Vol. II, p 112 & 117; pp 23-30.

numerous separate circles are formed; these will meet as they increase in size and then penetrate and intersect one another, all the while maintaining as their respective centres the spots struck by the stones. And the reason for this is that the water, although apparently moving, does not leave its original position, because the openings made by the stones close again immediately. Therefore the motion produced by the quick opening and closing of the water has caused only a shock which may be described as tremor rather than movement.

In order to understand better what I mean, watch the blades of straw that because of their lightness float on the water, and observe how they do not depart from their original positions in spite of waves underneath them caused by the occurrence of the circles. The reaction of the water being in the nature of tremor rather than movement, the circles cannot break one another on meeting, and as the water is of the same quality all through, its parts transmit the tremor to one another without change of position. Thus the water, although remaining in its position, can easily transmit the tremor to the adjacent parts, these transmitting it to other adjacent parts, while its force gradually diminishes until the end.

This is a wonderful description of the movement of transverse waves through a fluid medium, where the velocity of the wave is not produced by the movement of the fluid itself at that speed, but by the impulse travelling as a wave through the medium. This wave principle Leonardo extended to apply to sound and light, likening the light image reflected in a mirror to the sound echo

Looking to See: The Science of Experience

reflected from a wall or a mountain. He writes:

> Just as a stone flung into water becomes the centre and cause of many circles, and as sound diffuses itself in the air, so any object, placed in the luminiferous atmosphere, diffuses itself in circles, and fills the surrounding air with infinite images of itself. And is repeated, the whole everywhere, and the whole in every smallest part. This can be proved by experiment, since if you shut a window which faces west and make a hole...[1]

We will return to this example in a moment, but first we may state the conclusion which is to be experimentally demonstrated, namely that

> The air is full of an infinite number of images of the things that are distributed through it, and all of these are represented in all [of them], all [of them] in [any] one [place], and all in each.

Many of his predecessors and contemporaries held a quite contrary view, namely, that in seeing an object the mind went out to the object through the eye, took on its form and returned to the eye, bringing back the image and producing the visual sensation. Others believed that the object itself emitted the images into the surroundings. Leonardo correctly regards the creation of the images coming from the object to the eye as being a property of the luminiferous space between them, just as it was the water that gave rise to the waves produced by the stones, and within the water that they spread out in all directions.[2] He

---

[1] Jean Paul Richter, *op. cit.*, Vol. I, p 140:69. [2] *Ibid.*, Vol. I, pp 140-141:70.

argues this on the grounds that no part of the object is lost in sending out its image in all directions and to the eye, nor is anything lost from the eye in seeing the object.

> Therefore we may rather believe it to be the nature and potency of our luminous atmosphere which absorbs the images of the objects existing in it, than the nature of the objects, to send their images through the air.[1]

Nowadays it is easy for us to appreciate what he is saying when we consider how we can pick up any radio station anywhere at which the signal is strong enough, just by tuning in to its frequency. But how did Leonardo justify saying that he could prove that light images were distributed everywhere throughout the space from which the object is visible? One of his demonstrations was this:

> Accordingly if two mirrors are placed so as to exactly face each other, the first will be reflected in the second and the second in the first. Now the first being reflected in the second carries to it its own image together with all the images reflected in it, among these being the image of the second mirror; and so it continues from image to image on to infinity, in such a way that each mirror has an infinite number of mirrors within it, each smaller than the last, and one inside another. By this example it is clearly proved that each thing transmits its image to all places where it is visible, and conversely this thing is able to receive into itself all the images of the things that are facing it.

---

[1] Jean Paul Richter, *op. cit.*, Vol. I, pp 140-141:70.

Looking to See: The Science of Experience

Another demonstration, already broached, is as follows:

> I say that if the front of a building — or any open piazza or field — which is illuminated by the sun has a dwelling opposite to it, and if, in the front which does not face the sun [and is not therefore directly illuminated by it], you make a small round hole, all the illuminated objects will project their images through that hole and be visible inside the dwelling on the opposite wall which should be made white; and there, in fact, they will be upside down; and if you make similar openings in several places in the same wall you will have the same result from each. Hence the images of the illuminated objects are all everywhere on this wall and all in each minutest part of it. The reason, as we clearly know, is that this hole must admit some light to the said dwelling, and the light admitted by it is derived [by reflection] from one or many luminous bodies [the objects illuminated by the sunlight opposite the wall]. If these bodies are of various colours and shapes the rays forming the images are of various colours and shapes, and so will the representations be on the wall.[1]

The images formed in this way in what we should now call a pinhole camera or *camera obscura* had been described before Leonardo's time by al-Hazen, but Leonardo was the first to try and understand how these images were dealt with by the eye. Unfortunately he worked against great difficulties in trying to determine the detailed anatomy of the eye because of post-mortem changes in the structure, particularly in the iris and the lens. He was well aware

[1] *Ibid.*, p 141.

of these difficulties, and even tried 'fixating' the contents of the eye by boiling it in egg-white before cutting it open to study the structures in detail.[1] But he could not fully understand how we saw things the right way up, when these images were all reversed and upside down. As he notes: 'Everything that the eye sees through the small holes is seen by this eye upside down and known straight.'[2] He concluded that the eye must have some way of producing a second reversal to get the image the right way up and concluded that this must be in the lens:

> No image, even of the smallest object, enters the eye without being turned upside down; but as it penetrates into the crystalline lens it is once more reversed and thus the image is restored to the same position within the eye as that of the object outside the eye.

We know now, of course, that the retinal image *is* reversed in the eye, but that the 'second reversal' must depend on the central perceptual mechanisms of the brain, which present us with the experience 'the right way up'. In Leonardo's terms, it actually relies on the way the nervous message to the *sensus communis* is interpreted by the faculty of judgement, rather than being corrected optically, as will be explained below.

What Leonardo calls 'the triangle of vision' (or in three-dimensional terms, 'the pyramid of sight') is formed by

---

[1] D. Argentieri, 'Leonardo's Optics' in *Leonardo da Vinci*, Leisure Arts Novara, 1964. See Vol. II, pp 426-436.

[2] Jean Paul Richter, *op. cit.*, Vol. I, pp 144-145.

Looking to See: The Science of Experience

the converging light rays from the whole field of vision viewed by the eye coming to a point within the pupil. Within the whole visual field each and every object has its own pyramid, from object to eye, converging on the pupil in the same way. Leonardo points out how the correct perspective for any object can be determined by viewing it through a sheet of glass.

> Painting is based upon perspective which is nothing else than a thorough knowledge of the function of the eye. And this function simply consists in receiving in a pyramid the forms and colours of all objects placed before it... The science of painting deals with all the colours of the surfaces of bodies and with the shapes of the bodies thus enclosed; with their relative nearness and distance; with the degree of diminution required as distances gradually increase; and this science is the mother of perspective, that is, the science of the visual rays...[In practical terms] perspective is nothing else than seeing a place behind a sheet of glass, smooth and quite transparent, on the surface of which all the things may be marked that are behind the glass. The things approach the point of the eye in pyramids and these pyramids are intersected on the glass plane.

There is evidence suggesting that the contemporary German artist, Albrecht Dürer, may have especially gone to Bologna to meet Leonardo, or at least to see some of his perspective drawings, for he writes home from Venice in a letter dated 13th October, 1506: 'I shall have finished here in ten days, then I mean to go to Bologna to learn the secrets of perspective which someone there is willing to teach me.'[1]

Another puzzle for Leonardo was how the whole of our wide experience of the seen world was conveyed to us through this tiny aperture in the eye and in no other way.

> Who would believe that so small a space could contain the images of all the universe? O mighty process! What talent can avail to penetrate a nature such as these? What tongue can it be that can unfold so great a wonder? Verily none! This it is that guides the human discourse to the consideration of divine things. Here the forms, here the colours, here all the images of every part of the universe are contracted to a point. What point is so marvellous?... These are miracles...forms already lost, mingled together in so small a space it can recreate and recompose by expansion.

Leonardo rejects the idea that the mind goes out to grasp the object it is looking at and returns with the image to produce the sensation. In this he was ahead of his time, for Descartes, among others, was still maintaining in the seventeenth century that the light of vision depended on an emanation from the eye to the object, and that 'we see surrounding objects as a blind man feels them with his stick'[2], a view which can also be found in the fourteenth century Vedantic classic *Panchadashi*. Verse 30 of Chapter IV cites Sureshvara as saying the mental *vritti* actually goes out from the eye to the object, before taking on its form and coming back again. Leonardo argues against this that...

---

[1] Jean Paul Richter, *op. cit.*, Vol I, p 27.
[2] Sir James Jeans, *The Growth of Physical Science,* pp 198-202.

Looking to See: The Science of Experience

> It is impossible that the eye should project from itself, by visual rays, the visual power, since as soon as it opens, the front portion of the eye which would give rise to this emanation would have to go forth [from the eye] to the object, and it could not do this without [taking] time. And this being so, it could not travel so high as the sun in a month's time when the eye wanted to see it.

Leonardo was obviously right in principle in accepting that (like the waves on the water) it would take time for whatever it was to reach the eye (let alone travel there and back) and that what the eye actually saw must have already arrived there. He recognized that the sun was a very long way away — he speaks of 'thousands of miles' — but he can have had no real idea of the actual distance or of the speed of light, which were not determined until the late seventeenth century[1].

Leonardo speaks of the eye as 'the window of the soul' and 'the chief organ whereby the understanding can have the most complete and magnificent view of the infinite works of nature'. His analysis of the process of seeing or perception within the body in some ways quite closely parallels the Vedantic writings on the subject.

---

[1] The actual distance of the sun was first estimated with reasonable accuracy in 1672 by Cassini and Richer as about 87,000,000 miles, as compared with present-day estimates of 93,003,000 miles. The speed of light was not determined with any degree of accuracy until 1680, when Roemer noticed a 22 minute variation in the expected time of the appearance of the satellites of Jupiter, which was earlier when Jupiter was nearer the earth and later when it was further away. This led him to an estimated speed of light of 138,000 miles a second, as compared with the modern figure of 186,300 miles per second. [Jeans, *op. cit.*, pp 198-9].

In his notes for the Manual on Painting, he points out that in perception the five senses are connected by the organ of perception *(imprensiva)* to the common faculty, called the *sensus communis* or 'common sense', which receives and combines sensations from all the senses. This is the common judge of all five senses, and transmits the images sent to it by the sense-organs to the memory to be imprinted on it and retained there, more or less distinctly, according to the importance or power of the thing given. These two faculties of sensation and memory (the Vedantic *chitta*) comprise what the Vedanta calls the lower mind or *manas*.

Experience teaches us [he writes] that the eye takes cognizance of ten different qualities of objects, the first of which reveals the other nine. These are:

> Light and darkness;
> Colour and substance;
> Form and position;
> Distance and nearness;
> Movement and rest.

Leonardo writes:

> The soul apparently resides in the seat of judgement, and judgement apparently resides in the place called *sensus communis* where all the senses meet; and it is in this place and not throughout the body as many have believed; for if that were so it would not have been necessary for the instruments of the senses to meet in one particular spot; it would have sufficed for the eye to register its perception

on its surface instead of transmitting the images of the things seen to the *sensus communis* by way of the optic nerves; for the soul would have comprehended them on the surface of the eye.

And he says that this is the reason that each of the senses, vision, hearing, smell and touch, has to send its impressions by the nerves to meet in this one spot. Only when they all reach this 'common sense' are they experienced together. How the senses serve the soul in this way, rather than the reverse, is shown where one of the senses is lacking, as in the case of one who is born blind or mute. Through the 'common sense' and the memory the sensations converge and come before the faculty of judgement. The latter corresponds to what in the Vedanta is called the *buddhi* or the higher mind.

In the case of the eye

> The circle of light which is in the centre of the white of the eye is by nature adapted to apprehend objects. This same circle contains a point which seems black. This is a nerve bored through, which penetrates to the seat of the powers within where impressions are received and judgements formed by the *sensus communis*.

To sum up the matter in Leonardo's own words:

> All knowledge [of the world] has its origin in perceptions, but reasoning and contemplation stand apart in judgement. Sense experience is the starting point, but experience involves the faculty of reason and contemplation which stands above the senses and outside them.

The Spiritual Awakening of Science

The senses are earthly, but reason stands apart from them in contemplation.[1]

We are now in a position to consider what Leonardo says about art and his own methods of working in the light of his conclusions about light, vision and perception. Jean Paul Richter, after a lifetime's study of the Notebooks, summarizes Leonardo's views, saying that, although the painter renders only the surface appearance of things, he must nevertheless penetrate beneath the surface in order to realize what determines the outer appearances.[2]

> 'There is no effect in nature without a cause'. In order to understand the shapes which he sees the artist must know the form and law of their structure. But that was not enough; he must penetrate deeper and take into account the agent or agency that effected the imposition of the form. The human body was but an outward and visible expression of the soul. The body was shaped by the spirit. It was for the painter to reverse the process, so to speak, and by constructing a body give expression to a soul, a spirit.... Actions of figures must be suggestive of the motive which inspired them....Physiognomies [facial expression and features] and gestures reveal the frame of mind. The following contemporary accounts of Leonardo's methods of study are interesting in this connection.

Giovanbatista Giraldi, whose father knew Leonardo, wrote:

---

[1] Jean Paul Richter, *op. cit.*, Vol I, p 24.   [2] *Ibid.*, pp 28-30.

Looking to See: The Science of Experience

> When Leonardo wished to paint a figure he first considered what social standing and what nature it was to represent; whether noble or plebeian, gay or severe, troubled or serene, old or young, irritated or tranquil, good or wicked; and when he had made up his mind, he went to the places where he knew that people of that kind would assemble and observed their faces, their manners, their dresses and movements attentively; and whenever he found what seemed to fit in with what he wanted to do, he noted it down in a little book which he always kept in his belt. After having done this again and again, and feeling satisfied that he had collected sufficient material for the figure which he wished to paint, he would proceed to give it shape and succeeded marvellously.

G. P. Lomazzo advises students to follow Leonardo's way of studying the expressions and movements of figures.

> There is a tale told, by men of his time, his servants, that Leonardo once wished to make a picture of some laughing peasants (though he did not carry it out but only drew it). He picked out certain men whom he thought appropriate for his purpose and after getting acquainted with them, arranged a feast for them with some of his friends and sitting close to them he proceeded to tell the maddest and most ridiculous tales imaginable, making them, who were unaware of his intentions, laugh uproariously. Whereupon he observed all their gestures very attentively and those ridiculous things they were doing, and impressed them on his mind; and, after they had left, he retired to his room and there made a perfect drawing which moved those who looked at it to laughter as if they had been moved by Leonardo's stories at the feast.

Elsewhere Lomazzo refers to such studies of laughter as being in the possession of the Milanese painter Aurelio Lovino, 'where there are some who laugh so vigorously represented with such great art that nature can hardly do the same'.

Vasari in his *Life of Leonardo* also tells us something of Leonardo's manner of working:

> Leonardo then did a Last Supper for the Dominicans at Santa Maria delle Grazie in Milan, endowing the heads of the Apostles with such majesty and beauty that he left that of Christ unfinished, feeling that he could not give it that celestial divinity which it demanded. This work left in such a condition has always been held in the greatest veneration by the Milanese and also by foreigners, as Leonardo has seized the moment when the Apostles are anxious to discover who would betray their Master. All their faces are expressive of love, fear, wrath or grief at not being able to grasp the meaning of Christ, in contrast to the obstinacy, hatred and treason of Judas, while the whole work, down to the smallest details, displays incredible diligence, even the texture of the tablecloth being clearly visible so that actual cambric would not look more real.
>
> It is said that the Prior incessantly importuned Leonardo to finish the work, thinking it strange that the artist should pass half a day at a time lost in thought. He would have desired him never to lay down the brush, as if he were digging a garden. Seeing that his importunity produced no effect, he had recourse to the Duke, who felt compelled to send for Leonardo to inquire about the work, showing

tactfully that he was driven to act by the importunity of the Prior. Leonardo, aware of the acuteness and discretion of the Duke, talked with him fully about the picture, a thing which he had never done with the Prior. He spoke freely of his art, and explained how men of genius really are doing most when they work least, as they are thinking out ideas and perfecting the conceptions, which they subsequently carry out with their hands. He added that there were still two heads to be done, that of Christ, which he would not look for on earth, and felt unable to conceive the beauty of the celestial grace that must have been incarnate in the divinity. The other head wanting for him to paint, was that of Judas, which also caused him thought, as he did not think he could express the face of a man who could resolve to betray his Master, the Creator of the world, after having received so many benefits. But he was willing in this case to seek no farther, and for lack of a better he would do the head of the importunate and tactless Prior. The Duke was wonderfully amused, and laughingly declared that he was quite right. Then the poor Prior, covered with confusion, went back to his garden and left Leonardo in peace, while the artist indeed finished his Judas, making him a veritable likeness of treason and cruelty. The head of Christ was left unfinished, as I have said. The nobility of this painting, in its composition and the care with which it was finished, induced the King of France to wish to take it home with him. Accordingly he employed architects to frame it in wood and iron, so that it might be transported in safety, without any regard for the cost, so great was his desire. But the King was thwarted by its being done on the wall, and it remained with the Milanese.

The Spiritual Awakening of Science

The teenage nephew of the Prior of the Dominican Monastery of Santa Maria delle Grazie, was living in the care of his uncle while Leonardo was painting *The Last Supper* in the refectory and got to know him. Later in life he wrote a story incorporating a fascinating short account of what he saw.

> In Ludovico's time, some gentlemen living in Milan were met one day in the monks' refectory of the convent...where with hushed voices they watched Leonardo da Vinci as he was finishing his marvellous picture of *The Last Supper*. The painter was well pleased that each should tell him what they thought of his work. He would often come to the convent at early dawn; and this I have seen him do myself. Hastily mounting the scaffolding, he worked diligently until the shades of evening compelled him to cease, never thinking to take food at all, so absorbed was he in the work. At other times he would remain there three or four days without touching his picture, only coming for a few hours to remain before it, with folded arms, gazing at his figures as if to criticise them himself. At midday, too, when the glare of the sun at its zenith has made barren all the streets of Milan, I have seen him hasten from the citadel, where he was modelling his colossal horse, without seeking the shade, by the shortest way to the convent, where he would add a touch or two and immediately return.[1]

Leonardo had been in Milan working on *The Last Supper*

---

[1] L. Goldscheider, *Leonardo da Vinci*, London: Phaidon Press, 1959, pp 36-37.

Looking to See: The Science of Experience

and the clay model of the huge equestrian Sforza monument for most of the 1490s, but was back in Florence early in 1500, working on a now lost cartoon of the Holy Family and St Anne, in which Christ is shown as a one-year-old infant 'freeing himself almost out of his mother's arms and seizing a lamb and apparently about to embrace it'. A year later we find two different contemporary letters in April 1501 commenting on him, one saying that 'Leonardo's life is changeful and uncertain; it is thought that he lives only for the day. Since he has been in Florence he has worked on just one cartoon...He is entirely wrapped up in geometry and has no patience for painting'. This is borne out by a second letter, written by someone else who was trying to commission a picture from him for Isabella d'Este, which reads: 'I have this week heard, through his pupil Salai and other of his friends, of Leonardo the artist's decision, which led me to visit him on the Wednesday of Passion Week in order to assure myself that it was true. In brief, his mathematical experiments have made painting so distasteful to him that he cannot even bear to take up a brush'.[1] This shows something of the effect of his wide-ranging interests on his life.

Yet for Leonardo geometry was only a means to an end, as Richter tells us:

> In aiming at the expression of the mind and the spirit, the painter tries for something which cannot be fathomed by geometry...and mathematics alone could not achieve that

---

[1] *Ibid.*, p 37.

The Spiritual Awakening of Science

end. For geometry dealt only with quantities and not with quality, not with the beauty of the world. A science could be handed down from master to pupil, who might acquire all the master knew. But painting could not be taught to those not favoured by nature, and the actual painting was far superior to the science that preceded it. For his conception of painting being what it was, the artist in carrying out his work became a creator, like God... The soul is composed of harmony, and the harmonious proportions of a work of art are reflections of this harmony... Thus God reveals Himself in the work of man.[1]

---

[1] Jean Paul Richter, *op. cit.*, Vol. 1, p 30.

7

SCIENCE TRIUMPHS WITH NEWTON IN THE SEVENTEENTH CENTURY

IT IS STRANGE to find that two of the most decisive moments in human destiny are bound up in the popular imagination with man's encounter with an apple. The fall of Adam and Eve in the garden of Eden (we are told) was due to their succumbing to the temptation, at the suggestion of the serpent, to taste the apple of the knowledge of good and evil. In the most decisive moment in the history of science in the seventeenth century, as Newton sat in the orchard in Lincolnshire, it was not man who fell, but the apple! As Christ had told his disciples: 'There is providence in the fall of a sparrow'. In other words, even the fall of the most insignificant of things is determined and ruled by the laws governing the world, and decreed by the principles which rule the whole universe. The fall of a sparrow does not make front page news in the national press or in the media, nor does the fall of an apple in an orchard in Lincolnshire. It is no wonder that this so-called 'insignificant' event went unnoticed by the world at large, for at the time London was being, first, ravaged by the Plague, then, largely destroyed by the Great Fire. But the fact remains that the consequences of the Plague and the Great Fire of London were as nothing compared with the consequences for the whole world of the fall of the apple in Lincolnshire. What then converted this trivial occurrence into the discovery of some of the most fundamental and universal Laws of Nature? The answer is quite simply *meditation* — the application of the power of the focused mind.

Two centuries earlier Leonardo had begun to look carefully at the fall of an object under gravity. He was — among many other things — the inventor of innumerable machines and mechanical appliances to carry out practical tasks. An exhibition of these has recently[1] been seen at the Science Museum in London; they included pumps, sawmills, file cutters, rolling mills, windmills, a printing press, an instrument for measuring the velocity of the wind, spinning machines, a spring-driven clock and many other things. Many of these were powered by weights attached to pulleys which turned the driving shaft and provided the power. The control of movement by force was therefore something that Leonardo wanted to study and understand, not only as pure knowledge, but so that it could be used in practice. As he himself wrote:

Science is the captain, and practice the soldiers.[2]

Those who fall in love with practice without science are like a sailor who enters a ship without a helm or a compass, and who never can be certain whither he is going.[3]

He was therefore interested in studying the dynamics of the falling weights. According to the generally accepted doctrine propounded by Aristotle, currently being taught

---

[1] This chapter was originally given as a lecture in the year 2000.
[2] Jean Paul Richter, *op. cit.*, Vol II, p 241:1160. [3] *Ibid.*, Vol II, p 241:1161.

Science Triumphs with Newton

in the universities in Leonardo's time, heavy objects tended to fall and light objects tended to rise. That was what Aristotle had taught, so it was generally accepted that it must be true. One can imagine the Aristotelian experts of the time pointing out that the truth of Aristotle's teaching could be readily seen when you dropped a lead weight and compared it with dropping a feather; or if one saw how a cork floated in the bath while the soap dropped to the bottom! But it might have occurred to any careful and intelligent observer that the feather was responding, not so much to gravity, as to any slightest upward air currents in which the feather was being caught. In such situations there are a number of additional forces acting as well as gravity, such as air resistance and air currents, and the density and buoyancy of the air or water or any other medium in which the object is contained. So what one needed, in the first place, was to compare dropping two solid objects of different weights in air, or (better still) in a vacuum. Leonardo probably did no systematic experiments — his time was very fully occupied — but he evidently looked and made a quick note about the result:

> Every weight that descends and is free takes the direction to the centre of the earth, and that which weighs more will descend the quicker; and, the longer its descent, the greater its velocity.[1]

In this conclusion, he was both right and wrong. He was wrong in concluding that the heavier weight will descend more quickly, but where he was a good observer

---

[1] *Ibid.*, Vol II., p 219:113a.

The Spiritual Awakening of Science

was in noticing—and being among the first to notice—that the speed of its descent steadily increased during its fall. The problem in those days was the difficulty in timing or observing anything accurately; he had none of our advantages in being able to measure very short time intervals. He himself was very well aware of the importance of measurement in dynamics, for he says: 'Mechanics are the paradise of mathematical science, because here we come to the fruits of mathematics.' These words proved to be prophetic, but for the time being there were insuperable difficulties in making the necessary measurements and timing relatively fast events.

A century later, two Dutchmen in Delft, Stevinus (1548-1620) and Grotius, demonstrated, by dropping a light weight and a heavy one from the same height, that they reached the ground at almost the same time, showing that Aristotle was wrong.[1] Stevinus's other important discovery was to show how you could calculate the combined effect of two forces simultaneously acting on the same moving object, by drawing what we would now call *vectors* in a 'Parallelogram of Forces'.[2] This meant that you could calculate the effect of a wind blowing sideways on a falling object, or the effect of gravity on the course of a projectile like a cannon ball.

The Italian Galileo (1564-1642), who was born a little over a century later than Leonardo and sixteen years after Stevinus, started by confirming what Stevinus had found

---

[1] Sir James Jeans, *The Growth of Modern Science*, pp 144-145.
[2] *Ibid.*, pp 143-144.

Science Triumphs with Newton

in Delft. He tried dropping a cannon ball and a musket ball at the same time and found that, although of very different weight, they both hit the ground at almost the same moment. Galileo also confirmed what Leonardo had noticed: that the speed of falling steadily increased during the descent. But these were only qualitative observations; what he wanted to know was the law which governed this increase. In other words, what was the mathematical relationship between the speed of the fall and the distance travelled? He thought at first that the speed at each point might be proportional to the distance through which the body had fallen, but he soon realized that this couldn't be true, for, if it was, the object would never get started on its fall. So he tested whether alternatively the speed might be directly proportional to the time that had elapsed since the body had been set free.[1]

He at once ran up against the difficulty of finding any way of measuring the speed accurately with the methods available. His first solution was to try and time the fall by counting the average number of beats of his pulse during falls of different lengths, but he later improved the accuracy of measurement by collecting the amount of water escaping from a water clock during the fall, and weighing it afterwards to time the interval. As well as studying the free fall of objects under gravity he also reduced the speed of the fall, by rolling polished metal balls down a narrow, inclined groove cut in a gently sloping plank some twelve yards in length, and measuring the time which they took to

[1] Jeans, *op. cit.*, p 146.

fall through a given distance. This slowed down the descent and made measurement relatively easy and accurate. It confirmed that the balls underwent, *not uniform speed of fall*, but *uniform acceleration of the speed* throughout their descent.

Galileo did the earlier work on gravity in Pisa but never published it, but he did much fuller investigations in the twenty years which he spent in Padua where he also investigated the mathematical law governing the swinging of a pendulum. What he found was that, whatever the object was — whether a lead weight dropped from a height or a fruit dropping from the tree — the effect of gravity was the same. At the end of the second instant it had fallen four times as far as in the first instant, and at the end of the third instant nine times as far; at the end of the fourth instant sixteen times as far, and so on. *In other words the force of gravity was steadily accelerating the rate of fall so that it increased in proportion to the square of the time which it had taken.* Galileo's measurements were made in arbitrary units (see Table opposite) but we now know that the force of gravity, at the surface of the earth and near the equator, accelerates all freely-falling objects by 32 feet per second every second.

Using Stevinus's parallelogram of forces it was now possible to understand exactly how the combined force of gravity and the firing of the cannon were interacting to determine the flight path of the cannon ball. Its course followed what was known to mathematicians as a *parabola*, the resultant of the two forces: gravity pulling it down-

Science Triumphs with Newton

wards at a steadily accelerating speed and the forward force of the explosion communicated to it on firing driving it forwards. Galileo recognized that this discovery opened a gateway and a road to a large and excellent science, 'into which (he said) minds more piercing than mine shall penetrate to recesses still deeper'.

Relative Time Elapsed	Relative Distance Fallen
1 "instant"	1
2 "instants"	4
3 "instants"	9
4 "instants"	16
5 "instants"	25
6 "instants"	36
7 "instants"	49
8 "instants"	64
9 "instants"	81
10 "instants"	100

This was one of the great discoveries of science, because it showed that the effect of the force of gravity was not simply to produce motion as Aristotle had suggested, *but to produce a change in the speed (or velocity) of motion.* Force acted on a body, whether still or moving, to produce an *acceleration* in the body. It paved the way to an understanding that it was not only a body which was at rest which had no force acting on it (as Aristotle had taught), but that even a body moving steadily at a constant speed in a straight line did not need any external force to sustain that movement and would continue to move until it met some other force which could either accelerate or decelerate its motion. It is the force of friction which usually brings moving bodies to a standstill and deceives us about this. In outer space, where there is no friction to slow things down, the moving body continues to move without any change — either in speed or direction of movement — until an external force is applied to it, or (alternatively) a rocket is fired from it in a direction opposite to the movement to be induced. This again disproves the claim of the Aristotelians that all motion needed a force to maintain it and that the body on which no force acted must be standing at rest.[1]

You may ask why this experiment of Galileo's was so important, and of what interest is it to us? The answer is that, for the first time, it established the principle of a mathematically precise law ruling the world and governing events. It thus led directly to Sir Isaac Newton's extension of the same principles, which he was to show governed the movement of the planets around the sun in our own solar system, and of the moon around the earth. Far from being purely theoretical, it has formed the basis of the knowledge on which, for instance, space travel and rocket technology have been developed in the modern world.

From the Vedantic point of view it has an even more interesting implication, in that it shows how right the yogis

---

[1] Jeans, *op. cit.*, p 147.

Science Triumphs with Newton

were in calling the empirical world *'jagat'*, meaning *'the moving thing'*, because it turns out that there is no such thing as an object which is absolutely at rest. All motion is relative. It is only in relation to other nearby objects that anything can be *relatively* at rest (and never *absolutely* so). But the full implications of all this were not to be fully unfolded until the next few centuries had passed, and the two people who played the major roles in bringing this about were Isaac Newton and Albert Einstein.

Newton's early life and background

Newton was born on Christmas Day 1642, the year in which Galileo died. He was a farmer's son and the family came from a long line of yeoman farmers, who lived in a house called Woolsthorpe near a village of two or three thousand inhabitants, called Colsterworth, about seven miles from the town of Grantham in Lincolnshire. His father died three months before he was born, and he was probably premature, because his mother used to say that as a new-born baby he could have been put in a quart mug and that he was so weak to begin with that he had to wear a bolster around his neck to keep his head upon his shoulders. However, fortunately he grew up to be a healthy boy.

When he was just three, in January 1646, his mother — a strong, self-reliant woman — married again, the wealthy 63-year-old Rector of the next village, Barnabas Smith, and went to live there, but left Isaac in the care of his grandmother at Woolsthorpe. But she returned to her former home eight years later, on the death of her second husband, bringing with her the three additional children of her second marriage, two girls and a boy between the ages of 4½ and 1. Meanwhile, Newton had attended two little day schools in the village, walking there and back daily. At the age of 12 he was sent to the King's School in Grantham, which was about seven miles away. As this journey was too much to walk twice a day, he was lodged with an apothecary in the town, who seems to have been very kind to him and encouraged him to make things with his hands, which he loved to do. There are accounts of him making a model windmill and a wheeled chair for himself, as well as innumerable things like kites, lanterns and doll's furniture. He also was very fond of drawing and of collecting flowers and herbs, and used to copy out in a notebook bits which interested him from the books he was reading. Unlike some other great scientists, such as James Clerk Maxwell or Pascal, he showed no great brilliance at this stage. However there were some other traits which he showed, which were significant in the light of what he did later. He had both courage and determination, and he had an unusual capacity to get lost in thought, in other words, to meditate.

There are stories told about his absent-mindedness as a boy. In those days, when one went longer distances on horseback, it was customary to get off the horse when one reached a steep hill and lead it up to the top before remounting. Going home from Grantham, there was a particularly steep hill at one point and Newton is reported on one occasion to have got off the horse, and led it up the hill, but to have been so lost in thought that he forgot to remount and walked, leading his horse, the whole of the

Science Triumphs with Newton

rest of the way home. On another occasion, it is said that the horse, which he was leading, slipped its bridle and went home by itself while Newton walked on with the bridle in his hands without noticing anything strange. Perhaps this is an improved version of the earlier story, since when Newton became famous, the locals would no doubt make the most of it, but there is no doubt that Newton throughout his life readily got lost in thought and was an inveterate meditator, a fact attested by many different accounts. One of his modern biographers, J.W.N. Sullivan, says:

> Newton himself, when questioned, once said that if he differed from other men the difference perhaps lay in his capacity to pay attention to a problem. Like many other statements that have been attributed to Newton's modesty, this is merely an exact statement of the facts. His capacity for meditation, both in intensity and duration, has probably never been equalled. That degree of insight that other men of genius have reached only in their moments of profoundest concentration seems to have been comparatively readily reached by Newton. It was a comparatively easy matter for him to get his mind, as it were, fully under way. And he could maintain this state, an almost trance-like condition, for many hours at a time.[1]

John Maynard Keynes, who made an intensive study of Newton's papers, which ended up in the care of Trinity College, independently confirms what Sullivan says about Newton's powers of meditation:

---

[1] J.W.N. Sullivan, *Isaac Newton 1642-1727*, London: Macmillan, 1938, pp 12-13.

The Spiritual Awakening of Science

I believe that the clue to his mind is to be found in his unusual powers of continuous concentrated introspection. ... His peculiar gift was the power of holding in his mind a purely mental problem until he had seen straight through it. I fancy his pre-eminence is due to his muscles of intuition being the strongest and most enduring with which man has ever been gifted. Anyone who has ever attempted pure scientific or philosophical thought knows how one can hold a problem momentarily in one's mind and apply all one's powers of concentration to piercing through it, and how it will dissolve and escape and you find that what you are surveying is a blank. I believe that Newton could hold a problem in his mind for hours and days and weeks until it surrendered to him its secret.[1]

At the age of 17, the increasingly bookish and absent-minded Newton left school, ostensibly to take over the management of the family farm, but his mother was soon convinced by her brother, a clergyman, and Newton's old school-master, Stokes, not to try and force him to be a farmer, but instead to send him to Cambridge, where his uncle had been a student. This was probably with the idea of his becoming a country parson. So he went back to Stokes in Grantham to prepare for the University and was sent in June 1661, at the age of eighteen, to Trinity College, Cambridge. The family had little money and he went there to begin as what was then called a subsizar, a student who

---

[1] Cited in *Let Newton Be*, edited by J Fauvel *et al*, London: Oxford University Press, 1988, p 15.

Science Triumphs with Newton

paid his way through college by doing odd jobs and waiting on his tutor. He had to earn his keep by serving the Fellows and the wealthier students—cleaning boots, waiting at table, emptying chamber pots, and so forth.[1] He seems to have been rather a loner; he was deeply religious and didn't seek company, living soberly, studying and mixing little with his rather rowdy and wealthier fellow students.[2]

He was one of four hundred scholars and students in the College, who were taught mainly the philosophy of Aristotle, particularly his logic, ethics and rhetoric, together with more recent commentaries on these. But we know from his own notebooks that, from about 1664 onwards, he also read on his own account many of the contemporary books of the seventeenth century, including the English philosopher Thomas Hobbes, the Cambridge Platonist Henry More, the Frenchman René Descartes and many more. And he went on to study the scientific works of Kepler on optics, as well as those of Galileo on astronomy and motion, and of Gassendi, who wrote about current ideas concerning atoms. In all this reading he was self-taught in that he himself chose what he would read. It was later said of him as a student that 'he always informed himself beforehand of the books his tutor intended to read, and when he arrived at lectures found he knew more of them than the tutor did'.[3]

---

[1] Fauvel, *op. cit.*, pp 12-13.
[2] E.N. da C. Andrade, *Sir Isaac Newton*, London: Collins, 1954, pp 37-38.
[3] F.E. Manuel, *A Portrait of Isaac Newton*, Cambridge, Massachusetts: Harvard University Press, p 80.

The Spiritual Awakening of Science

Two years after he arrived, when he was 20, he was lucky enough to come into contact with a very gifted mathematician, Isaac Barrow, the newly-appointed Lucasian Professor of Mathematics in the University. Newton started having his first lessons from him after the Easter term of 1663. Up until this time there had been nothing brilliant or remarkable in Newton, but Barrow noticed him as being someone out of the ordinary and encouraged Newton in his mathematical studies. Later he also began to use him as his assistant. It is probably as a result of this that, in April 1664, he was elected a Scholar in the College, which meant that he no longer had to work as a sizar, but had an assured income and place at Trinity for four years. At this time he very much intensified his mathematical studies.

Newton had found his lack of mathematical background becoming an obstacle some time before this and set about remedying it with what has been described as 'ferocious application'. In midsummer 1663 he had bought a book on astrology 'out of curiosity' at the local Stourbridge Fair, but found he couldn't understand an illustration of the heavens in it 'for want of being acquainted with Trigonometry', so he bought a book on trigonometry, but found he was unable to understand the demonstrations. So he got the works of Euclid to equip himself with a basic knowledge of geometry to enable him to understand the trigonometry. This in turn led him on to study Descartes' analytical geometry, and the *Arithmetica Infinitorum* by John Wallis, the contemporary Professor of Mathematics at Oxford, as well as other current

Science Triumphs with Newton

mathematical works. Never can there have been such a compressed crash course in mathematics! But it was more than successful. Within two years Newton had become a mathematical genius. Derek Whiteside, a great scholar of Newton's mathematical papers, writes that:

> By midsummer 1665, one short crowded year after his first beginnings, the urge to learn from others was largely abated.... thereafter, though he continued to draw on the ideas of others, Newton took his real inspiration from his own fertile mind.

This led on to Newton's invention or discovery of what we now call calculus, the mathematical method which allows one to measure and study the variations in rates of change, called by Newton 'The Method of Fluxions'. Whiteside writes of his papers in the period:

> The papers...throb with energy and imagination but yet convey the claustrophobic air of a man completely wrapped up in himself, whose only real contact with the external world was through his books.[1]

He was also becoming interested in astronomy, staying up for nights on end searching for and tracking comets. He was grinding his own lenses and carrying out his first experiments with prisms.[2]

It was in his twenty-third year at this time that his genius seems to have fully awakened and he worked excessively — so much so that he became ill. It was at this

---

[1] Manuel, *op. cit.*, pp 80-81.   [2] *Ibid.*, p 78.

The Spiritual Awakening of Science

time that he noted: 'I found the method of infinite series'. He took his B.A. in January 1665, but this was scarcely more than a formality, occurring automatically after he had been in Cambridge for three years. It is now chiefly memorable in that Barrow, who examined him, found him 'deficient in Euclid'!

And then fate took a hand. In August that summer he was suddenly and unexpectedly forced to leave Cambridge when the University was closed down and the students sent home because of the danger of plague. This dreaded disease had started in London the year before and had become very severe so that in the three month period from July to September 1665 one in ten Londoners died from the disease.[1] It was a terrible scourge, spreading fear throughout the population, but it was (quite incidentally) to bring about the most momentous two years in the history of science, by providing Newton with the ideal conditions for undisturbed meditation.

He went back to live at the family home at Woolsthorpe, where his mother was living. The house had been repaired and partly rebuilt, having been in rather a poor condition during his childhood. He lived there in relative isolation for the next two years until the University reopened in the spring of 1667, that is between the ages of 22 and 24. During that time he had made virtually all the greatest discoveries on which his fame rests, the recording

---

[1] Andrade, *op. cit.*, p.39.

and eventual publication of which was to occupy him for the rest of his long life.

The three most important of these were:

In **mathematics**, the discovery of how to measure variations in the rate of change of things, the technique now known as calculus;

In **optics**, the demonstration that white light was made up of a mixture of lights from all the colours of the spectrum. Each of these colours consisted of light rays of a distinct and invariable kind (or *wavelength* as we would now say) which was characterized by the degree to which it was deflected in passing through a glass lens or a prism;

In **physics**, the laws of motion and the characteristics of the force of gravity, combined with the demonstration that gravity ruled, not only the way in which the apple fell from the tree in the orchard, but also the movements of the moon around the earth and the planets round the sun. In other words he had established some of the most important universal laws governing the whole of nature and the universe.

Over fifty years later Newton gave his own more detailed account of his discoveries during those two momentous years at Woolsthorpe:

> In the year 1665, I found the method of approximating [infinite] series, and the rule for reducing any dignity [i.e. any power] of any binomial to such a series. The same year in May I found the method of tangents of Gregory

and Slusius, and in November had the direct method of fluxions [the differential calculus], and next year in January had the theory of colours and in May following, I had entrance into the inverse method of fluxions [the integral calculus] and in the same year [1666] I began to think of gravity extending to the orb of the moon and... from Kepler's Rule of the periodic times of the planets, I deduced that the forces which keep the planets in their orbits must be reciprocally as the squares of their distances from the centres about which they revolve; and thereby compared the force requisite to keep the moon in her orbit with the force of gravity at the surface of the earth, and found them answer pretty nearly. All this was in the two plague years of 1665 and 1666, for in those days I was in the prime of my age for invention and minded mathematics and philosophy more than at any time since.[1]

By 'philosophy' here Newton means 'natural philosophy' or physical science — what we would now call physics.

One of Newton's modern biographers, Professor Andrade, a Professor of Physics at Imperial College and an acknowledged Newton expert, draws attention to how isolated Newton must have been there at Woolsthorpe. He was always greatly attached to his mother, who would have been living with him during this period, and he was probably well cared for by her, but she would have been no use to him in discussing what he was thinking about. He was intellectually quite alone, without anyone to talk to about his ideas and without meeting or exchanging

---

[1] Jeans, *op. cit.*, p 184.

Science Triumphs with Newton

correspondence with any learned men. He himself, when asked how he made his discoveries, answered quite simply: 'By thinking about them all the time'; and he repeated this on another occasion when he explained: 'I keep the subject constantly before me and wait till the first dawnings open little by little into full light.' Professor Andrade comments:

> Even for great men of science it is hard to keep the mind concentrated on a problem, to the exclusion of everything else, for more than an hour or two: I believe that Newton, however, could sit for hours with the whole power of his mind fixed on whatever difficulty he was concerned with. I imagine him, then, as sitting there at Woolsthorpe, perhaps in the orchard on a summer afternoon or in the kitchen on a winter's evening, completely ignorant of what was going on around him, pondering on the motions of the heavenly bodies, or new mathematical methods, or the nature and behaviour of light.[1]

and he goes on to say:

> Isaac Newton was a devoutly religious man, and in many ways a mystic, but he did not believe that religion or mystery had anything to do with the mathematical laws of planetary motions, although they had to do with the First Cause. Late in his life, he wrote, when discussing the Creator at the end of his book on *Opticks*, 'Such a wonderful Uniformity in the Planetary System must be allowed [to be] the Effect of Choice,' that is, it must be admitted to come about by design and not by chance. That was his belief throughout his life.

[1] Andrade, *op. cit.*, pp 42-43.

The Spiritual Awakening of Science

In his old age, on April 15th 1726, when Newton had left London to escape the atmosphere of the city and retired into the heart of the country to a little village called Kensington, he was visited by his friend, the physician, Dr William Stukeley, who wrote later:

> After dinner, the weather being warm, we went into the garden and drank thea [sic], under the shade of some apple trees, only he and myself. Amidst other discourse, he told me, he was just in the same situation, as when formerly, the notion of gravitation came into his mind. It was occasion'd by the fall of an apple, as he sat in a contemplative mood. Why should that apple always descend perpendicularly to the ground, thought he to himself. Why should it not go sideways or upwards, but constantly to the earth's centre? Assuredly, the reason is, that the earth draws it. There must be a drawing power in matter: and the sum of the drawing power in the matter of the earth must be in the earth's centre, not in any side of the earth. Therefore does this apple fall perpendicularly, or towards the centre. If matter thus draws matter, it must be in proportion of its quantity. Therefore the apple draws the earth, as the earth draws the apple. That there is a power, like that we here call gravity, which extends itself through the universe.
>
> And thus by degrees he began to apply this property of gravitation to the motion of the earth and of the heavenly bodies....[1]

---

[1] Cited in Rosamond Harding, *An Anatomy of Inspiration*, Cambridge: Heffer, 1942, pp 100-101.

Science Triumphs with Newton

Another account by Newton, obtained by Henry Pemberton at about the same period, adds some further details:

> As he sat alone in the garden, he fell into a speculation on the power of gravity: that as this power is not found sensibly diminished at the remotest distance from the center of the earth, to which we can rise, neither at the tops of the loftiest buildings, nor even on the summits of the highest mountains; it appeared to him reasonable to conclude, that this power must extend much further than was usually thought; why not as high as the moon, said he to himself? and if so, her motion must be influenced by it; perhaps she is retained in her orbit thereby. However, though the power of gravity is not sensibly weakened in the little change of distance, at which we can place ourselves from the center of the earth; yet it is very possible, that so high as the moon this power may differ much in strength from what it is here. To make an estimate, what might be the degree of this diminution, he considered with himself, that if the moon be retained in her orbit by the force of gravity, no doubt the primary planets are carried round the sun by the like power. And by comparing the periods of the several planets with their distances from the sun, he found, that if any power like gravity held them in their courses, its strength must decrease in the duplicate proportion of the increase of distance.[1]

---

[1] Cited in Manuel, *op. cit.*, pp 82-83.

The Spiritual Awakening of Science

In other words, the force of gravity exerted by two bodies on each other must diminish with the square of the distance between them.

This was a tremendous new insight. Newton realized that, like a weight whirled in the air at the end of a string, the moon is prevented from flying off in a straight line as the weight does if the string is released, and that it is the pull of the string which keeps it in its circular motion. The attractive force of gravity plays the same role in keeping the moon circling round the earth as it does in the fall of the apple and the orbiting of the planets round the sun. But the force of gravity exerted by the earth, which pulls the moon towards its centre, is much weaker at the moon's distance than at the earth's surface. Newton deduced from Kepler's third Law, relating the square of the duration of the planetary year to the cube of its distance from the sun, that the pull of the sun on the planets was in proportion to the inverse square of the distance of one from the other. He compared the distance of the centre of the earth to the apple, about 4,000 miles, with that of the centre of the earth to the moon, about 240,000 miles, he squared them and compared them inversely, giving the pull on a given mass at the moon's distance as about 1/3,600 of that of the same mass at the surface of the earth. It worked out as about right for the pull required to keep the moon in her orbit. As Newton himself said[1]: 'I thereby compared the force requisite to keep the moon in her orb with the force of

---

[1] Andrade, *op. cit.*, pp 45-46.

Science Triumphs with Newton

gravity at the surface of the earth, and found them answer pretty nearly.'

But he put the problem aside and did not publish anything about it for many years, because he was not completely satisfied with what he had done. For one thing he had not proved that it was legitimate to regard the whole of the mass of a body like the earth or the moon acting at a single point in its centre, and it was only later that he was able to prove this theorem mathematically. How Newton's discoveries in 1665-1666 eventually became known to the world at large and how the world was changed by what it learnt is in itself a fascinating story.

8

HOW THE FIRST OF NEWTON'S DISCOVERIES CAME TO BE KNOWN

WE HAVE already seen[1] how the many, wide-ranging scientific discoveries of Leonardo da Vinci were unknown to the world at large because they remained recorded only in the immense collection of notes, handwritten by him in mirror-writing, which he bequeathed to the care of his most trusted student, Francesco Melzi. After Melzi's death these were broken up and sold piecemeal by his son and became lost or dispersed in libraries throughout Europe, where they lay virtually unknown until the late nineteenth century, when they were collected, copied, deciphered and published.

Galileo's published scientific writings on astronomy were declared heretical and banned by the Inquisition, because of his promulgation of the heliocentric Copernican view of the solar system, first in 1613, when his *Letters on the Solar Spots* was ordered to be withdrawn for 'corrections', and again in June 1633 when his *Dialogue on the Two Chief World-Systems, the Ptolemaic and the Copernican* was prohibited by public edict, and remained forbidden reading matter for Catholics until 1822. Fortunately, however — human nature being what it is — this did not

---

[1] See above, p 52, and also Chapter 6.

How the first of Newton's discoveries came to be known

prevent knowledge of his work spreading rapidly throughout the Catholic and non-Catholic worlds. In Italy in 1633, the price of remaining copies of the banned book rose all through the summer following the ban—from the original half *scudi* to 4 and then 6 *scudi*—as interested people rushed to buy any now illegal copies while they were still available. Within two months of the ban a copy had found its way across the border to Strasbourg, where a Latin translation was prepared, which became available throughout Europe in 1635. An English translation followed in 1661.

Galileo's last work, *Dialogues concerning Two New Sciences including Centres of Gravity and Force of Percussion*—in which he recorded his lifetime of studies on the physics of motion—could not be published in Italy, being the work of a declared heretic, but was smuggled out of the country in instalments and published in Holland in 1638, four years before his death in January 1642. This was the same year in which Isaac Newton was born. Although, from the time of his first appearance before the Inquisition in 1613 onwards, Galileo was forbidden to receive visitors, both Thomas Hobbes and John Milton were among those who visited him in old age, a fact that is mentioned by Milton in his *Areopagitica*.

In this way knowledge of Galileo's important scientific

---

[1] See *Galileo's Daughter* by Dava Sobell, London: Fourth Estate, 1999, pp 365-366. This book gives a fascinating and detailed account of the human events and difficulties of Galileo's life, so different from Newton's.

The Spiritual Awakening of Science

discoveries in astronomy and dynamics spread rapidly and was assimilated by other scientifically-minded thinkers. It was at about this time that groups of such men began to join together in societies, the members of which met regularly to discuss the latest important results and advances in science and also to correspond and interchange ideas with similar groups in other parts of Europe. Such a society had already been started in Rome (1603), and others soon sprang up in Florence (1651) and Naples (1660). In England, a society began meeting in 1645 in Gresham's College, London, but moved to Oxford in 1648 because of the Civil War. It returned to London in 1662 after the Restoration of the Monarchy in 1660 and was granted a Royal Charter by King Charles II in 1662 as 'The Royal Society of London for Promoting Natural Knowledge'. A similar Society was formed in France in 1666. The Royal Society of London adopted as its motto *Nullius in verba*, which (Professor Andrade suggests) can be freely translated as 'We don't take anybody's word for it!', meaning that any claim had to be verifiable by experiment — by 'looking to see'.

Examination of Newton's contemporary notebook and the Buttery Books in Trinity College for the two plague years, shows that Newton actually left Cambridge because of the decision to close the University in June 1665, but that he came back briefly at the end of March 1666, when it was believed the epidemic was subsiding. This proved to be over-optimistic, and he was back in Lincolnshire by June 1666, remaining there for almost a year, until April 1667.

How the first of Newton's discoveries came to be known

When he got back to Cambridge early in 1667, he had already made the three major discoveries, whose development and publication would occupy many years of his subsequent life. But he was not someone who was ever looking to 'make a name for himself', nor did he think of himself as exceptional. He was happy to settle down again at Trinity as an assistant to Isaac Barrow, who asked him to help in preparing Barrow's lectures on optics for publication. Newton gave Barrow an account of some of the new mathematical methods which he had developed while at Woolsthorpe—initially, probably his method of infinite series and his calculations on the area of the hyperbola. He may have also mentioned the method of fluxions. Within six months of his return Newton was elected a Minor Fellow of Trinity and he became a Major Fellow in the following year, when a vacancy became available on the death of an incumbent.

Newton had by this time given Barrow a full, written account of some of his new mathematical ideas, entitled *On Analysis by equations with an infinite number of terms (De Analysi)*. Barrow described it as a work of unparalleled genius. As he anyway wanted to return to his theological studies, he decided to resign his Chair and recommended the now 26-year-old Newton as his successor, praising him as 'a man of quite exceptional ability and singular skill'. He showed the paper on infinite series to a number of colleagues in Cambridge at this time, and it evoked considerable interest, and eventually became known quite widely there and among the more mathematically-minded members of the Royal Society and elsewhere. Newton was duly appointed Lucasian Professor of Mathematics on October 29th 1669 at the age of 26. This appointment gave Newton ample time for his meditations and experiments and an assured income of £100 a year, with very light duties in lecturing and teaching. He gave his first series of lectures in 1669 on his own work on light, as well as considering the current views on the subject. The lectures themselves seem to have been poorly attended, both then and later, judging by the comments of his assistant and amanuensis throughout the 1680s, who wrote:

> I never knew him to take any recreation or pastime either in riding out to take the air, walking, bowling, or any other exercise whatever, thinking all hours lost that was not spent in his studies, to which he kept so close that he seldom left his chamber except at term time, when he read in the schools as being Lucasianus Professor, where so few went to hear him, and fewer that understood him, that ofttimes he did in a manner, for want of hearers, read to the walls.

He was required to provide a handwritten copy of all his Lectures to be deposited with Trinity College, but the Optical Lectures were to remain there, more or less neglected, until they were eventually published in 1728, the year following his death.

The Nature of Light

Newton had first become interested in optics, probably under Barrow's influence, from 1663 on, and this interest continued. We now know, from a study of his manuscripts

How the first of Newton's discoveries came to be known

and notebooks, that he was reading about current theories on colour and also performing carefully planned experiments between 1664 to 1672 and again in about 1687.

This was a topic which had also interested Leonardo da Vinci two centuries before. He had recorded in his notes the beautiful colours seen in the wings of butterflies or mother-of-pearl, and in the feathers of peacocks or the necks of pigeons. He also made notes about the colours exhibited by the rainbow. And he was also interested in the colours produced directly by the sun's rays passing through water or glass. He writes:

> If you place a glass full of water on the window-sill so that the sun's rays will strike it from the other side, you will see the aforesaid colours formed in the impression made by the sun's rays that have penetrated through that glass and fallen on the pavement in the dark at the foot of a window, and since the eye is not used here, we may with full certainty say that these colours are not in any way due to the eye.

Whether or not Leonardo succeeded in determining the laws of refraction between air and water, he certainly recognized the need for it to be done, for he describes a simple but ingenious arrangement for doing it:

> Have two trays made, parallel to each other, and let one be 4/5 smaller than the other, and of equal height. Then enclose one in the other ... and paint the outside, and leave uncovered a spot the size of a lentil, and have a ray of sunlight pass there coming from another opening or window. Then see whether or not the ray passing in the

water enclosed between the two trays keeps the straightness it had outside. And form your rule from that.

By Newton's time the popularly-accepted explanation of colours, derived from Aristotle, was that they were an admixture of light with darkness, the latter being held to be a property of matter. Red was due to a smaller amount of darkness added to light than blue. To this it was reasonably objected by some that darkness did not seem to be anything other than the absence of light.

René Descartes had a more sophisticated theory that explained light in terms of the pressure exerted by the motion of small spherical particles moving through space. When reflected they were set spinning by the friction of the contact with the reflecting surface. When entering the eye, their rotary movement was seen as colours and the moving particles themselves as light. Differences in colour were due to the different speeds of rotation of the particles, the most rapid being red, while particles with progressively slower speeds of rotation produced successively sensations of yellow, green and blue in that order. There were endless and inconclusive arguments about the different theories concerning the nature of light. Newton's approach was entirely different and practical, and very much more on the lines that Leonardo had been suggesting.

The experiments on colour

Like Leonardo, Newton was an inveterate and skilful experimenter, able to turn his hand to anything from

How the first of Newton's discoveries came to be known

grinding lenses, creating new metallic alloys to make good mirrors and himself polishing them—he was the first person to use pitchblende to do so—or building a brick furnace for chemical experiments without the help of a bricklayer. Asked in later life where he had obtained the necessary tools, he replied that he had made them himself, and added: 'If I had staid for other people to make my tools and other things for me, I had never made anything of it.'

As he wrote in a letter to Oldenburg, the Secretary of the Royal Society, dated February 6th 1672, Newton, two centuries after Leonardo, also carried out his own light experiments:

> ...In the beginning of the year 1666 I procured me a Triangular glass-Prisme, to try therewith the celebrated Phaenomena of Colours. And in order thereto having darkened my chamber, and made a small hole in my window-shuts, to let in a convenient quantity of the Suns light, I placed my Prisme at its entrance, that it might be thereby refracted to the opposite wall. It was at first a very pleasing divertisement, to view the vivid and intense colours produced thereby...

The sunbeam was bent in passing through the prism, and the emerging light spread out into a strip of colours—red, orange, yellow, green, blue, indigo and violet—in an invariable series which we now know as *the spectrum*. He was impressed by the fact that the length of the spectrum was about five times as great as its breadth, and was not at all like the circular image predicted by the known law of refraction.

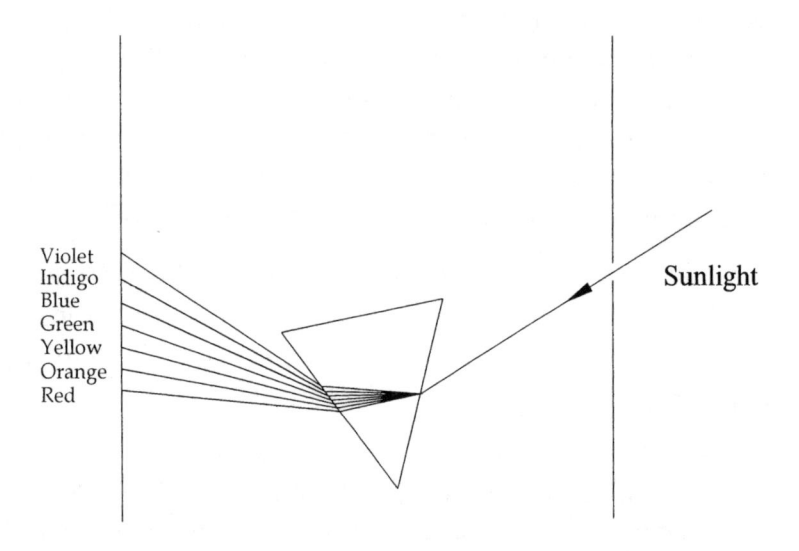

```
              Violet
              Indigo
              Blue                              Sunlight
              Green
              Yellow
              Orange
              Red
```

Newton realized that this was because the different colours were bent to a different extent by their passage through the glass, the violet being the most, and the red the least, deflected. He found that, if they were all recombined by passing them all through a second, reversed prism, white light was again produced, but, when any one of the colours was isolated by passing it alone through a narrow slit in a board, the light retained that colour, no matter what one did with it, although its brightness could be diminished or extinguished. Each isolated colour could be shown to undergo the same characteristic deflection by

How the first of Newton's discoveries came to be known

exactly the same amount on being passed through a second prism, and this could be repeated many times. The degree of bending was constant, but different for each colour, with red invariably the least deflected and violet the most.

Newton had thus demonstrated conclusively by experiment that *white light was made up of a combination of all the colours, and that the coloured lights, when isolated, each had an unalterable identity associated with the degree to which it was deflected in passing from air through a glass prism*. There was nothing to argue about. The results were crystal clear.

In all this Newton did not discuss what colour is or how it is produced, as Aristotle and Descartes had done. He knew that he didn't know this, and recognized that arguments about which theory was right (if any!) were futile. What mattered was to look to see, to examine the facts. Only then would it be worth trying to explain them.

Newton also noticed in his experiments that similar colour fringes, produced in the same way, could be seen around the images produced by a convex glass lens, a defect that we now call 'chromatic aberration'. He investigated this further by preparing an oblong strip of card with one half painted red and the other half blue, and winding some very fine black silk thread round it. When lit by a candle (all he had!) an image of the black lines can be focused by a lens onto a sheet of white paper, but he found that when the lines on the red paper were sharp, those on the blue paper were out of focus, and *vice versa*. The paper had to be nearer the lens to get the blue lines into focus and further away for the red lines. This again showed the effect of the greater bending of the blue rays than the red.

The telescopes available at that time, used, for instance, by Galileo, Kepler and Huygens, were all made using glass lenses and suffered from this defect. But Newton realized that you could avoid this by using a concave *mirror* rather than a *lens* to form the image, as the light does not then pass from air into glass and all the colours are reflected at the same angle. He therefore made a reflecting telescope employing a one-inch concave mirror made of a special alloy, which he himself prepared from copper, tin and arsenic, and which could be polished to produce a good reflection. It was the first of its kind, with a tube six inches long and magnifying the image forty times.

When he subsequently showed the telescope to some of his colleagues in Cambridge, it aroused great interest and news of it eventually spread by word of mouth to London and the members of the Royal Society, who expressed an urgent wish to see it. By this time, over five years had elapsed since he had first made it and he had lost the original telescope, and already made a second improved one, which again seems to have gone missing, although its subsequent history is obscure. So Newton made yet a third telescope, again with improvements, which was exhibited to the Royal Society sometime in the year 1671. This telescope had a two-inch mirror and a tube nine inches long. It attracted a great deal of attention, and was examined by various dignitaries, including the King. As a

How the first of Newton's discoveries came to be known

result the Bishop of Salisbury proposed Newton for membership of the Royal Society, and he was elected a member on January 11th 1672.

All this seems to have surprised Newton, who didn't pay particular attention to his achievements and certainly wasn't looking for fame. He wrote in a letter to the Secretary of the Royal Society, Oldenburg, dated January 6th 1672:

Sir,

At the reading of your letter I was surprised to see so much care taken about securing an invention to me, of which I have hitherto had so little value. Therefore since the Royal Society is pleased to think it worth the patronising, I must acknowledge it deserves much more of them for that than of me, who, had not the communication of it been desired, might have let it remain in private as it hath already done some years.... I am very sensible of the honour done me by the Bishop of Sarum in proposing me candidate, which I hope will be further conferred upon me by my election into the Society. And if so, I shall endeavour to testify my gratitude by communicating what my poor and solitary endeavours can effect towards the promoting of your philosophical designs.

He was duly elected and wrote immediately afterwards asking for the time of the weekly meetings of the Society, saying that he proposed to submit to them a discovery which had induced him to make the telescope, and which, he believes, will prove much more interesting than the

The Spiritual Awakening of Science

instrument itself, 'being in my judgement the oddest, if not the most considerable detection, which hath hitherto been made in the operations of nature'. The promised paper was sent to the Society the following month. This gave a full and detailed account of his experiments with a prism, already described, and explained why he had devised the reflecting telescope to avoid the chromatic aberration occurring with use of glass lenses. This was the first scientific paper published by Newton and it appeared in the *Philosophical Transactions of the Royal Society* in February 1672, described as his *New Theory about Light and Colours*. A Committee of members of the Royal Society was formed to discuss the paper.

Newton, who was now 29, had led rather a sheltered existence hitherto, limited almost entirely to the life in Trinity College Cambridge, with interludes in which he returned home to the farm in Lincolnshire. But now he was to experience, virtually for the first time, the human mind in some of its less admirable aspects. Two centuries later, when Michael Faraday, another very religious and abstemious man of humble origins, told Humphry Davy that he wanted to give up trade, which he found vicious and selfish, to work in science, which he thought must make its pursuers amiable, liberal and idealistic, Davy was amused and said he would leave it to a few years' experience to set him right about the moral feelings of scientists. Newton too was now to undergo a somewhat similar experience.

How the first of Newton's discoveries came to be known

The report on the paper was written by a member, Robert Hooke, an able scientist but a vain man who always wanted to appear better than those he regarded as competitors, and was not too scrupulous about how he achieved it.[1] Already, when Newton had sent his telescope to the Society at their request, Hooke was recorded as putting it about that:

> He had made a little tube of about an inch long to put on his fob, which performed more than any telescope of fifty inches long made after the common manner. But that, because of the plague and the fire intervening, he had neglected to prosecute the same, as he was unwilling to let the glass grinders know anything of the secret of how to make it.

In the Report on the prism experiments he criticised Newton's interpretation of the results from the point of view of the theory which Hooke himself had put forward in his recently published book, *Micrographia*. Newton on this occasion took his criticisms well and answered them carefully. Huygens also criticised Newton's work, which was perhaps understandable, as he had himself made great use of a telescope using glass lenses, this type of instrument having been originally invented in Holland.

What these critics did not understand was that Newton was not in any way arguing about the nature of colour or

---

[1] It is not surprising to find that he was an out-and-out disciple of the pragmatic view of Francis Bacon in his attitude to science, whereas Newton was inspired by the same idealistic spirit as Leonardo. Manuel, *A Portrait of Isaac Newton*, Cambridge, Mass: Harvard, 1968, pp 134-137.

how it was produced, but simply describing experiments to show how white light and colours behaved and how they exhibited constant and measurable properties. He patiently wrote back:

> ...the theory, which I propounded, was evinced by me not by inferring 'tis thus because not otherwise, that is, not by deducing it only from a confutation of contrary suppositions, but by deriving it from experiments concluding positively and directly.

Another critic was a French priest, Father Pardies, who put his criticism courteously, and was answered patiently in kind by Newton, who again said:

> For the best and safest method of philosophising [doing scientific work, we should say] seems to be, first to enquire diligently into the properties of things, and of establishing these properties by experiment, and then to proceed more slowly to hypotheses [theories] for the explanation of them.

The Frenchman in the end apologised to Newton for having misunderstood him.

Not all critics were so courteous or understanding. A Professor Linus from Liège sent 'some absurd and not very polite criticisms of the work', suggesting that Newton's experiments were just incorrect, and accusing him of gross carelessness and of misrepresenting the facts. These adverse comments were duly printed in the *Transactions* of the Royal Society in October 1674. Newton at first refused to answer them, but when the Secretary wrote urging him to reply, he wrote back:

How the first of Newton's discoveries came to be known

I am sorry you put yourself to the trouble of transcribing Fr Linus's conjecture, since (besides that it needs no answer) I have long since determined to concern myself no further about the promotion of philosophy. And for the same reason I must desire to be excused from engaging to exhibit yearly philosophic discourses.... If you think fit, you may, to prevent Fr Linus's slurring himself further in print with his wide conjecture, direct him to the scheme in my second answer to P. Pardies, and signify (but not from me) that the experiment, as it is represented, was tried in clear days, and the prism placed close to the hole in the window, so that the light had no room to diverge, and the coloured image made not parallel, (as in his conjecture), but transverse to the axis of the prism.

Your humble servant,

Isaac Newton

After four years of responding to all these objections to his first 1672 paper, during which ten of these from half a dozen authors had been published in the pages of the Royal Society's *Transactions*, together with eleven replies by Newton, he sent a further paper in 1675 on *An hypothesis explaining the properties of light, discoursed in my several papers* which he wished to be read out at one of their meetings, but not to be published. In it he proposed a hypothesis as an 'illustration' for the convenience of those who did not understand his work when he talked 'abstractedly' about light and colours. This was in line with his belief that it was only sensible to begin to speculate about the explanation of things when one had first obtained and established the experimental facts. But he clearly did not want it to be a permanent record of his own firm conclusions. Rather it was an attempt to arrive at a reasonable working hypothesis as a basis for further investigation. He no doubt hoped it would bring the long-drawn-out controversy to an end.

But Linus persisted with his objections, and the matter was still dragging on two years later. All this had a very unfortunate effect on Newton, who hated dispute of this kind and clearly regarded it as a complete waste of precious time. He expressed his exasperation when he wrote in a letter to Oldenburg on November 18th 1676:

> I see I have made myself a slave to philosophy, but if I get free of Mr Linus' business I will resolutely bid adieu to it eternally, excepting what I do for my private satisfaction, or leave to come out after me; for I see a man must either resolve to put out nothing new, or become a slave to defend it.

Sullivan also writes about Hooke's jealous attitude to Newton's experimental work and its effect on Newton:

> ...although he confirmed the veracity of Newton's experiments, [he] shows an uneasy, apprehensive vanity, varying from the patronising to accusations that Newton had got his ideas from him. Newton's reaction to Hooke's claims and criticisms was at first quite mild, if a trifle contemptuous. He was content to say: 'For I am still of the same judgement, and doubt not but that upon severer examinations, it will be found as certain a truth as I have asserted it.' But finally Newton was provoked into writing

How the first of Newton's discoveries came to be known

a detailed analysis of Hooke's attitude and claims. The result was crushing and unanswerable, and its effect on Hooke, which was greatly to exacerbate his bitterness, was not lessened by its tone. After discussing Hooke's hypotheses, he concludes: 'If I would proceed to examine these his explications, I think it would be no difficult matter to show that they are not only insufficient, but in some respects to me at least, unintelligible.'

Hooke's claims and criticisms were one of the main reasons that Newton decided he did not want to submit any more communications to the Royal Society.

This first experience of publication by Newton had a profound effect on him, because he hated controversy and valued, above all, peace of mind so that he could get on with what he really wanted to do. From then onwards he changed in his attitude towards publication and declaring his discoveries. Even before his first paper on light, he had written, in replying to a request for permission for a mathematical result of his to be published, agreeing to it, but only provided it was done anonymously: 'For I see not what there is desirable in public esteem, were I able to acquire and maintain it. It would perhaps increase my acquain-tance, the thing which I chiefly study to decline.' Newton was very modest about his own powers; he ascribed any success he had achieved to 'nothing but industry and patient thought'. But he was 'passionately fond of his quiet', as the Frenchman Bernard de Fontenelle later testified.

Sullivan writes of this attitude:

The Spiritual Awakening of Science

His aloofness was, in part at least, an acquired characteristic. We have already referred to the difference in style between Newton's earlier and later writings. This difference in style is significant. In his first paper Newton frankly appeals to his reader's interest, and frankly reveals his delight in his work. He narrates the genesis and history of his ideas, and describes at length the difficulties he had to overcome. There is a spontaneity and frankness about the paper which has been called youthful and even naive. Newton writes as if he imagined that his paper would be welcomed by other scientific men in a spirit of joyous approbation and collaboration. The numerous criticisms it met with undoubtedly surprised him, the more so as most of them seemed to him remarkably unintelligent. And it is this reception which is probably the reason that no other paper of Newton's exhibits any of the 'human' qualities that characterised his first paper. The formal, abstract, and, as it were, armour-plated style of his later writing was less due to his natural frigidity than to what he felt was an appropriate attitude.

So, at least for the time being, the world at large learned nothing of the other great discoveries he had made.

This did not mean that Newton lost interest in his investigation of the nature and behaviour of light. He continued his experiments sporadically for some time but kept them to himself. The results were not to be published until his great work, the *Opticks: or a Treatise on the Reflexions, Refractions, Inflexions and Colours of Light* appeared in 1704, a year after the death of Robert Hooke. By this time Newton himself was 61 years old. The

How the first of Newton's discoveries came to be known mathematical paper on infinite series, *De Analysi, On Analysis by equations with an infinite number of terms,* which had so much impressed Isaac Barrow as 'a work of unparalleled genius' in 1669, was not published until seven years later, in 1711.

Newton writes in the Preface to the *Opticks*: 'To avoid being engaged in disputes about these Matters, I have hitherto delayed the printing, and should still have delayed it, had not the Importunity of Friends prevailed upon me.' And he goes on to explain once again that he is not trying to suggest hypotheses to explain the properties of light, but to propose and prove them by reason and experiment. The work, written in English, first deals with the prism experiments and their results, and then goes on to give a precise account of how he polished the mirror of the reflecting telescope. He then discusses how the colours which we see around us are made up by a combination of the colours provided by the incident light and the innate colour in objects which absorb or reflect back each of the different spectral colours of the incident light to a different extent. Mixing paints (which absorb different colours from the incident light and reflect what remains—the so-called 'subtraction colours') gives quite different colours to mixing lights reflected from a white surface ('addition colours', which lose nothing of the incident light). Newton also explains how the rainbow is produced by the refraction of the sun's rays in the droplets of moisture in the sky. He goes on to deal with the colours seen in such things as soap bubbles, flakes of mica or a thin film of air

The Spiritual Awakening of Science

trapped between a thin slightly curved lens face pressed onto plate glass, a phenomenon known as 'Newton's rings'.

It appears that all the experimental work on colour was done while Newton was in Cambridge, the first part in the period up to 1675, when it was written up for the Royal Society for oral communication but not published, and the second in a period twelve years later, just after Newton had finished his great book, the *Principia*. The *Opticks* ends with a number of 'Queries' in which he allows himself to become more speculative about possible explanations of the experimental results he has reported. He enlarged this section in a second edition which was published in 1717. Among these additional Queries are two on polarized light and another suggesting that the forces which hold atoms together may be electrical—an amazing anticipation of findings only to be verified still far in the future.

There were two mathematical appendices published with Newton's *Opticks* in 1704: one dealt with his Method of Fluxions and the other described ninety-two species of cubic curves. Like the *Opticks* itself, the Appendix on Fluxions was only published by Newton because of the strong pressure put on him by a friend—in this case, John Wallis, the Professor of Mathematics at Oxford—who was concerned that Leibniz had by then published his own version of the calculus and was claiming priority as its inventor, although Newton's unpublished method had preceded his by ten years. This led to a prolonged controversy between the English and continental mathematicians as to who had been first, and whether

How the first of Newton's discoveries came to be known

either had plagiarised the discovery of the other. Newton's habit of keeping things to himself to avoid controversy over their publication, tended to lead to this sort of trouble instead.

Newton was not ever surprised to learn that others had independently made the same discoveries as he had. He himself always acknowledges what he had learnt from others. He writes in the course of a letter to Hooke about his colour experiments on February 5th 1676:

> There is nothing which I desire to avoid in matters of philosophy more than contention, nor any kind of contention more than one in print; and, therefore, I most gladly embrace your proposal of a private correspondence. What's done before many witnesses is seldom without some further concerns than that for truth.... If I have seen farther, it is by standing on the shoulders of giants. But I make no question, you have diverse very considerable experiments besides those you have published, and some, it's very probable, the same with some of those in my late papers.

This well illustrates Newton's genuine desire for reconciliation with someone who had consistently criticized his work.

But he resented deeply the false accusation that he had stolen the discoveries of others and presented them as his own. When such false accusations were made against him, as they were later by Robert Hooke regarding the inverse square law and Leibniz over the invention of the calculus,

The Spiritual Awakening of Science

Newton defended his honour vigorously. As he wrote to Bernoulli after Leibniz's death:

> I have never grasped at fame among foreign nations, but I am very desirous to preserve my character for honesty, which the author of that epistle[1], as if by the authority of a certain great judge, had endeavoured to wrest from me. Now that I am old I have little pleasure in mathematical studies, and I have never tried to propagate my opinions over the world, but have rather taken care not to involve myself in disputes on account of them.

---

[1] Newton refers here to an anonymous letter published by Leibniz in which Newton was accused of plagiarism on the evidence of 'a certain eminent mathematician'.

9

HOW NEWTON CAME TO WRITE HIS MOST FAMOUS WORK

HENRY OLDENBURG, the first Secretary of the Royal Society, with whom much of Newton's early correspondence with the Royal Society was carried on, had been born and brought up in Bremen, North Germany, the son of a Professor at the University of Dorbat. After a period in his early manhood when he acted as a diplomat in negotiations with Cromwell, he came and settled permanently in England and soon became a good English speaker. He was particularly interested in current scientific developments, which led to his friendship with Robert Boyle, and this, in turn, to his becoming a founder member of the Royal Society and later, in 1663, its first Secretary. He was an indefatigable correspondent with a wide circle of English and continental contacts which even included Spinoza, someone whom he encouraged to publish his philosophical ideas. For the Royal Society itself, it has been said that

> ...not only was [he] a central clearing house for scientific papers, but constantly urged publication upon scientists who might otherwise have tended to shut themselves off from their fellows. There were those who charged that he fired jealousies among them in the course of his activities as an intermediary; but his tireless attention to foreign and domestic letters helped to make the Royal Society of

London the most prestigious scientific body in the world, and towards Newton at least this heavy activist from Bremen showed a measure of sensitivity.

Like Newton, Oldenburg did not escape Robert Hooke's jealous and troublesome personality. His last days were embittered by a complaint from Hooke, currently the Curator of the Society, that he had not done justice in the Society's *Philosophical Transactions* to Hooke's invention of the hair-spring for pocket watches, an accusation that Hooke repeated in a book which he published. The resulting quarrel lasted for two years. It was finally settled by the Council of the Society, which investigated the complaint and declared that Oldenburg had conducted himself faithfully and honestly in the management of the intelligence of the Royal Society and had given no just cause for the reflections which Hooke had tried to cast on him. Sadly, Oldenburg died suddenly in his fifties in September 1677, shortly after the prolonged published correspondence on Newton's first paper had come to an end. The Society subsequently appointed Dr Grew and Robert Hooke as joint Secretaries in his place.

These events were hardly likely to have encouraged Newton to send any further contributions to the *Transactions*. He had no taste at all for science as a gladiatorial show, in which rival theories were hotly debated by their proponents in public. He detested public controversy, believing that 'truth is the off-spring of silence and unbroken meditation', as he was to tell John Conduitt in his old age. He was therefore determined to avoid any further entanglement with public controversy of the kind

How Newton came to write his most famous work

that had followed the communication of his experiments with the prism on the dissociation of white light into its constituent colours. Having, at Oldenburg's urging, answered a mass of criticisms and objections in the pages of the *Philosophical Transactions* and tried to meet the misunderstanding of his critics on the various current ideas about the nature of light in his conciliatory paper of 1675 (which he expressly asked should *not* be published, but only read to the Society at one of their meetings), he was well content with the proposal made by Robert Hooke in his letter of January 1676 that they should in future agree to exchange their ideas and discuss their differences by private correspondence only, rather than in the meetings and publications of the Royal Society.

This did not mean that he was in any way deciding to give up his own scientific investigations. John Conduitt, who married Newton's niece, Catherine Barton, said that he had never known Newton to be idle, and wrote to Fontenelle:

> At the University he spent the greatest part of his time in his closet and when he was tired of his severer studies of [Natural] Philosophy [i.e., physics] his only relief and amusement was going to some other study [such] as History, Chronology, Divinity and Chymistry, all of which he examined and searched thoroughly as appears by many papers that he has left on those subjects.

In Trinity his duties as Lucasian Professor were not onerous. Between January 1670 and October 1683 he lectured every year, as required, but the number of lectures varied from only three to ten a year. He apparently had

The Spiritual Awakening of Science

very few listeners and hardly any students to tutor. The majority of his time was therefore given to his own reading and research. His old Professor and benefactor, Isaac Barrow, came back to Trinity in 1673, when King Charles appointed him Master of the College, to the great delight of both Newton and the other fellows, for he was very popular. Although only twelve years older than Newton, he had shown himself an unusually kind and intelligent colleague, recognizing and encouraging his exceptional qualities as a student and getting his abilities known by showing the paper on infinite series to other eminent mathematicians like John Collins, and, above all, by resigning his Chair in favour of Newton. It was he who had proudly taken the reflecting telescope of his former pupil and assistant up to London to be demonstrated to the Royal Society and the King. He also provided Newton with the freedom of his own rich private library of science, theology and history, which was particularly valuable to him at a time before Trinity College Library existed. Sadly, Barrow died of a chest complaint in 1677 at the early age of 47, having unwisely tried to treat himself with opium.

Even more tragically for Newton, his mother died in May or June 1679. Newton's half-brother, Benjamin Smith, had fallen ill with a malignant fever at Stamford, and Newton's mother went there to nurse him through his illness. But he died and she herself caught the same infection from him. Newton is recorded as having left Cambridge on 15th May 1679, when he went home in order to look after her. He himself nursed her during her illness, personally attending to her immediate needs, dressing her sores, and staying up through the nights to watch over her.

How Newton came to write his most famous work

In spite of his ministrations, however, the disease proved fatal in her case too; although, mercifully, Newton himself seems to have escaped with his health unimpaired. It is evident that he was always very greatly attached to his mother, and Isaac was her favourite among her children. But he was sensitive and secretive about his relationship with her and took great care to destroy all her letters and whatever other evidence there may have been of the relationship between them. Of their letters, only a few charred fragments have survived among his mass of papers.

After his mother's death (probably within nine days of his arrival in Lincolnshire — the exact date is uncertain) he seems to have returned briefly to Cambridge on 24th May, but must have been back in Lincolnshire by 4th June, the day when it is recorded that his mother was buried 'in woollen' at Colsterworth Parish Church.[1] As the sole executor of his mother's will he was present when probate was granted on 11th June 1679 and, except for a brief further return to Cambridge for nine days in July, he stayed in Lincolnshire until the end of November 1679, no doubt involved in making the necessary arrangements as sole executor concerning the family and the estate. As the elder brother he became virtually the head of the whole extended

---

[1] In an attempt to bolster the failing wool trade, Parliament had recently passed two Acts in 1666 and 1678 ordering that all bodies should be buried in a shroud made of wool, and with the coffin lined with wool. The penalty for non-compliance was a fine. But, although it was not repealed until the nineteenth century, it soon fell into neglect. The expression 'died (dyed) in the wool' eventually came to imply extreme die-hard conservatism.

family of the children and grandchildren of his deceased step-father, the Reverend Barnabas Smith, and he was now the one to whom they turned for support in time of need. At his death in 1727, when he had left no will, eight of these children from his mother's second marriage became his legal heirs.

After this half-year in Lincolnshire, Newton returned to Trinity College on 27th November 1679 to find a letter from Hooke, dated 24th November, waiting for him. In the course of it Hooke, writing now as one of the new Secretaries of the Royal Society, says:

> ...I hope therefore that you will please to continue your former favours to the Society by communicating what shall occur to you that is philosophical, and for return I shall be sure to acquaint you with what we shall receive considerable from other parts or find out new here. And you may be assured that whatever shall be so communicated shall be no otherwise further imparted or disposed of than you yourself shall prescribe...

And he goes on to acquaint Newton with some of the latest scientific news. Newton's reply, written four days later, but only the day after he had himself returned to Cambridge, reads:

> Sir, I cannot but acknowledge myself every way, by the kindness of your letter, tempted to concur with your desires in a philosophical correspondence. And heartily sorry I am that I am at present unfurnished with matter answerable to your expectations—for I have been this last half year in Lincolnshire cumbered with concerns among

my relations till yesterday when I returned hither; so that I have had no time to entertain philosophical meditations, or so much as to study or mind anything else but country affairs. And before that, I had for some years past been endeavouring to bend myself from philosophy to other studies in so much that I have long grutched (*sic*) the time spent in that study unless it be perhaps at idle hours sometimes for a diversion; which makes me almost wholly unacquainted with what philosophers at London or abroad have of late been employed about... And having thus shook hands with philosophy and being also at present taken off with other business, I hope it will not be interpreted out of any unkindness to you or to the R. Society if I am backward in engaging my self in these matters... However I cannot but return my hearty thanks for your thinking me worthy of so noble a commerce and in order thereto frankly imparting to me several things in your letter...

Newton then goes on to express polite interest in the scientific ideas of which Hooke has sent him news. He then incautiously adds something more, which he calls 'a fancy of my own about discovering the earth's diurnal motion'. He was later to tell Halley that this was something which he only included in order 'to sweeten his answer'. In it he draws attention to the fact that any point on the earth's surface, as it rotates in an easterly direction once in every 24 hours, does so with a speed of rotation which depends on where it is situated on the earth's surface, being at its fastest for the points at the equator and correspondingly slower for those nearer the poles, where the circumference of the earth is much smaller and it has less far to go in the same time. This suggests that a stone dropped from a height should fall to the east of the spot originally vertically underneath it, since it starts off with a greater velocity than this spot of ground because of its greater distance from the earth's centre and it therefore moves forward faster in relation to it as it falls. He also predicts that in its journey down towards the centre of the earth such a body would pursue a spiral path, since (as well as its forward velocity) it will also be pulled sideways towards the earth's centre.

Having enlarged on this, Newton ends his letter by returning to his main point with the words:

> But yet my affection to philosophy being worn out, so that I am almost as little concerned about it as one tradesman uses to be about another man's trade or a countryman about learning, I must acknowledge myself averse from spending that time in writing about it which I think I can spend otherwise more to my own content and the good of others: and I hope neither you nor anybody else will blame me for this averseness. To let you see that it is not out of any shyness, reservedness, or distrust that I have of late and still do decline philosophical commerce but only out of applying myself to other things, I have communicated to you the notion above set down (such as it is) concerning the descent of heavy bodies for proving the motion of the earth; and shall be as ready to communicate in oral discourse anything I know, if it should ever be my happiness to have familiar converse frequently with you. And possibly if anything useful to mankind occurs to me I may sometimes impart it to you by letter.

How Newton came to write his most famous work

So wishing you all happiness and success in your endeavour, I rest,

Sir, Your humble servant to command,

Isaac Newton.

In spite of the promise made by Hooke in his letter to Newton three years before that he would not communicate anything he told him without his express permission, Hooke read Newton's letter to the Royal Society at the next meeting where it aroused considerable enthusiasm. To make matters worse, Hooke thought about the problem himself and — again in direct contradiction to his agreement to discuss any differences in their opinions privately by letter — took the opportunity at the next meeting of the Society to read a rebuttal of Newton's hypothesis, in which he showed that the path followed by such a stone would not be a spiral, but either an excentrical elliptoid or an excentric ellipti-spiral, according to whether there was resistance or not in the medium through which it was falling. When Newton received details of these communications by Hooke, he wrote immediately to him, acknowledging that Hooke was correct in saying that the path would not be simply a spiral, but he did not agree that it would be as Hooke had described it, and went into a lengthy discussion of why this was so. Hooke read this second letter to the Royal Society and carried out several experiments on the lines suggested by Newton. He then wrote to Newton telling him of the successful results. But Newton had barely been able to write to him the first time, and returned no answer. He seems to have been annoyed at Hooke's failure to abide by their agreement, as well as irked by his own careless error in regard to the exact path of the falling body.

It is hardly surprising that, having just arrived back in Cambridge the day before, after many months in Lincolnshire with the worries of settling all the affairs of the family on his mind, let alone the upset of his mother's death, that his 'fancy' should not have been fully thought out; but to find it—very much against his wishes—communicated without his fore-knowledge to the assembled Royal Society and publicly repudiated in the same way, demonstrated clearly once again that Hooke could not resist trying to establish his superiority over Newton if he were given the slightest chance.

The one good outcome of this exchange was that it stimulated Newton into considering more carefully the mathematical problems involved in calculating orbiting bodies. As a result he proved mathematically that the orbit of a planet influenced by an attractive force varying inversely as the square of the distance from its centre would be an ellipse. He wrote down the proof of this major discovery and thought no more of it, subsequently losing the paper on which it was written. Then he seems to have dismissed the whole subject from his mind for the next five years. In this regard, it has to be remembered that physics (or 'philosophy' as he called it) was only one—and not the most important—of his interests. He worked on it only sporadically (albeit intensively when he did) and spent much more of his time on experiments in chemistry and

How Newton came to write his most famous work

biblical studies, as well as mathematics, than he did on physics. As his biographer, J.W.N. Sullivan, has said: 'The paradox of Newton's scientific career was due to the fact, probably unique in the history of scientific men, that he was a genius of the first order at something that he did not consider of the first importance.'

His interest was eventually aroused again as a result of a meeting of three other members of the Royal Society in January 1684, where they discussed their suspicion that the elliptical orbits of the planets (observed and described to be the case by Kepler) could be due to an attractive force from the sun varying inversely as the square of the distance. The circumstances are described by Edmund Halley:

> I met with Sir Christopher Wren and Mr Hooke, and, falling in discourse about it, Mr Hooke affirmed, that upon that principle all the laws of celestial motions were to be demonstrated, and that he himself had done it. I declared the ill success of my own attempts; and Sir Christopher, to encourage the enquiry, said, that he would give Mr Hooke or me, two months time, to bring him a convincing demonstration thereof; and beside the honour, he of us that did it, should have from him a present of a book of 40 shillings. Mr Hooke then said, that he had it, but he would conceal it for some time, that others trying and failing might know how to value it, when he should make it public. However I remember that Sir Christopher was little satisfied that he could do it; and though Mr Hooke then promised to show it to him, I do not find, that in that particular he has been so good as his word.

The Spiritual Awakening of Science

As no solution was forthcoming by August, over five months later, Halley went to Cambridge to see if Newton could suggest a solution. He asked Newton: 'What would be the curve described by the planets on the supposition that gravity diminished as the square of the distance?' and Newton immediately replied: 'An ellipse!' Struck with joy and amazement, Halley asked him how he knew it, and Newton replied: 'Why, I have calculated it!' But when asked for a copy of the proof he couldn't find the paper on which he had written it five years before. In the event, he had to re-do it and produced not one, but two, equally valid alternative proofs, which he sent to Halley in November 1684.

Halley's visit was the stimulus which rekindled Newton's interest in the problem of gravity and the laws of motion, to such an extent that he prepared and gave a series of nine lectures *On the motion of bodies in an orbit (De Motu Corporum in gyrum)* in Cambridge in the Michaelmas Term 1684. Meanwhile Halley was so excited by the two proofs when he received them in November that he went back to Cambridge in December to persuade Newton to publish them. While he was there, Newton showed him the manuscript of the whole course of lectures and Halley at once realized its immense importance. He got Newton to promise that he would send it to the Society to be registered so that Newton's priority would be safeguarded and, as soon as he returned to London, he started making arrangements for it to be published by the Royal Society. Unfortunately, the Royal Society had just depleted its funds

How Newton came to write his most famous work

by producing a very handsome and expensive book on the *History of Fishes* which sold badly. So Halley also agreed to finance Newton's book out of his own pocket. In this way, to quote Professor Andrade, 'The stage was now set for the appearance of what is held by most men of science to be the greatest scientific book ever written, Newton's *Principia*.'

Newton while writing the *Principia*

By February 1685 Newton was writing to his old friend Aston, who had now become Secretary of the Society, saying:

> I thank you for entering in your *Register* my notions about motion. I designed them for you before now, but the examining several things has taken a greater part of my time than I expected, and a great deal of it to no purpose. And I am now to go into Lincolnshire for a month or six weeks. Afterwards I intend to finish it as soon as I can conveniently.

As it turned out, it was going to take him the next seventeen months to complete what he had begun. But, as Sullivan tells us:

> By now Newton was fully immersed in the subject. He was, we may say, completely in the grip of his mathematical genius. He now enters on a period when his personal will, his own preferences and distastes, hardly seem to be concerned. He behaves like a man dominated by an irresistible force. And it did not relax its grip until it had pushed him on to the accomplishment of the greatest intellectual feat of his life, the greatest intellectual feat in the history of science.

The Spiritual Awakening of Science

It seems probable that it was sometime during the year 1683, the winter of which was memorable for its very cold frost, that Newton recruited his namesake, Humphrey Newton, as an amanuensis. Humphrey was no relation, but came from Stamford. He was to be with Newton as his personal assistant until 1688, helping him by copying out the text of the *Principia* for the press, and in his chemical experiments, as well as acting as his sizar. Newton took immense pains in writing the *Principia*, and was obviously in a state of total absorption in it over the 17-months period during which he was completing the manuscript for publication. Humphrey Newton has left a revealing account of him during this period in two letters which he wrote to John Conduitt more than forty years later, after Newton's death:

> ...His carriage was then very meek, sedate and humble, never seemingly angry, of profound thought, his countenance mild, pleasant and comely. I cannot say I ever saw him laugh but once... He always kept close to his studies, very rarely went a visiting, and had as few visitors, excepting two or three persons, Mr Ellis, Mr Laughton of Trinity, and Mr Vigani, a chemist, in whose company he took much delight and pleasure at an evening when he came to wait upon him... Foreigners he received with a great deal of freedom, candour and respect. When invited to a treat, which was very seldom, he used to return it very handsomely, and with much satisfaction to himself. So intent, so serious upon his studies, that he ate very sparingly, nay, ofttimes he has forgot to eat at all, so that, going into his chamber, I have found his mess [meal]

How Newton came to write his most famous work

untouched, of which, when I have reminded him, he would reply—'Have I?' and then making to the table, would eat a bit or two standing, for I cannot say I ever saw him sit at table by himself. At some seldom entertainments, the Masters of Colleges were chiefly his guests. He very rarely went to bed till two or three of the clock, sometimes not until five or six, lying about four or five hours... I cannot say I ever saw him drink either wine, ale or beer, excepting at meals, and then but very sparingly. He very rarely went to dine in the hall[1], except on some public days, and then if he had not been minded, would go very carelessly, with shoes down at heels, stockings untied, surplice on, and his head scarcely combed... He was very curious in his garden, which was never out of order, in which he would at some seldom time take a short walk or two, not enduring to see a weed in it... He very seldom went to the chapel, that being chiefly the time he took his repose; and, as for the afternoon, his earnest and indefatigable studies retained him, so that he scarcely knew the house of prayer. Very frequently, on Sundays, he went to St Mary's church[2], especially in the forenoon... He was only once disordered with pains in the stomach, which confined him for some days to his bed, which he bore with a great deal of patience and magnanimity, seeming indifferent either to live or die. He seeing me concerned at his illness, bid me not to trouble myself;

---

[1] The Colleges were built on the model of the mediæval monasteries and the hall was the refectory where the members customarily went to share meals together. They also met at services in the College chapel held twice a day. [2] St Mary's is a large church in the centre of Cambridge, unconnected to any College.

The Spiritual Awakening of Science

'For if', said he, 'I die, I shall leave you an estate,' which he then mentioned...

In a second letter to Conduitt a month later, Humphrey Newton adds some further interesting reminiscences of Newton's behaviour during the time he was writing the *Principia*. Speaking of Newton in his garden, he says:

> When he has sometimes taken a turn or two, [he] has made a sudden stand, turn'd himself about, run up the stairs like another Archimedes, [and] with an *eureka* fall to write on his desk standing without giving himself the leisure to draw a chair to sit down on. At some seldom times when he designed to dine in the hall, [he] would turn to the left and go out into the street [i.e. in the opposite direction to what he had intended], when making a stop when he found his mistake, [he] would hastily turn back, and then sometimes instead of going into the hall, would return to his chamber again... He would with great acuteness answer a question, but would very seldom start one... His brick furnaces, *pro re nata* [i.e., wherever necessary], he made and altered himself without troubling a bricklayer. He very seldom sat by the fire in his chamber excepting that long frosty winter, which made him creep to it against his will. I can't say I ever saw him wearing a night gown, but his wearing clothes that he put off at night, at night do I say, yea, rather towards the morning, he put on again at his rising. He never slept in the daytime that I ever perceived; I believe he grudged the short time he spent in eating and sleeping... In a morning he seemed to be as much refreshed with his few hours sleep as

How Newton came to write his most famous work

though he had taken a whole night's rest. He kept neither dog nor cat in his chamber, which made it well for the old woman his bedmaker, she faring much the better for it, for in a morning she has sometimes found both dinner and supper scarcely tasted of, which the old woman has very pleasantly and mumpingly gone away with. As for his private prayers, I can say nothing of them; I am apt to believe his intense studies deprived him of the better part. His behaviour was mild and meek, without anger, peevishness, or passion, so free from that, that you might take him for a stoic... When he was about thirty years of age his grey hair was very comely, and his smiling countenance made him so much the more graceful. He was very charitable, few went empty handed from him...

The one occasion when Humphrey Newton heard Newton laugh (mentioned near the beginning of the first letter) was after he had lent a friend a copy of Euclid's Geometry to look at, who, when he returned the book, asked Newton what use and benefit in life the study of Euclid might be. The question was said to have made Newton very merry indeed! But others found Newton's sense of humour much more in evidence, at least in later life. William Stukeley, who knew him in old age, said that he had often seen him merry and 'that upon moderate occasions' and that, although he was of a 'very serious and compos'd frame of mind... He had in his disposition a natural pleasantness of temper, and much good nature... attended neither with gayety nor levity. He us'd a good many sayings bordering on joke and wit. In company he behaved very agreeably; courteous, affable, he was easily made to smile, if not to laugh.'

It is recorded that Newton took neither snuff nor tobacco, declaring to his amanuensis 'that he would make no necessities to himself'.

Frank Manuel comments that 'the few accounts of Newton's behaviour during the Cambridge period when his genius was most productive, speak of an indifference to bodily needs and a divorcement from the world which, though hardly equal to the asceticism of the mystics in the desert, had something of their denial of the flesh in the holy service'.

The *Principia*

According to Newton himself, he began the *Principia* at the end of December 1684 and finished it in May 1686 when the last part was sent to the Royal Society. It contains 192 propositions in three books. Except for two of these propositions, which he had already solved in December 1679, and twelve more that were composed in June and July of 1685, all were created in this seventeen-month period. As Sullivan says:

> It is this rapidity of execution, besides the importance of the work, that makes Newton's achievement incomparable. If the problems enunciated and solved in the *Principia* were the result of a life-time's meditation, Newton's position in the history of science would still be unique. But that these problems should have been both originated and solved within seventeen months is so

How Newton came to write his most famous work

incomprehensible that it can only be accepted as a historical fact. It just happens to be so.

A recently published modern English translation of the book runs to 604 large pages, not including a profusely annotated introductory guide of 370 pages containing notes and commentary on the main text.

Sullivan has justifiably said that the work is written 'in a style of glacial remoteness which makes no concession to the reader'. This was to some extent deliberate. Newton explains all the mathematics in the *Principia* in terms of classical Euclidean geometry, which was difficult for people then and with which only a few mathematicians are really familiar even today. This was partly because he greatly admired the mathematical methods of the ancients; but this was not the only reason. He told a friend, the Rev. Dr Derham, that 'to avoid being baited by little smatterers in mathematics he designedly made his *Principia* abstruse; but yet so as to be understood by able mathematicians'. We see again his horror of being pestered by people who could not understand him, and his desire to avoid all those tiresome and unnecessary distractions which disturbed his peace of mind, which he valued above all things and which was so essential to creative meditation! If duller men queried anything in his work, he considered that they were wasting his valuable time and energy. Besides, as Sullivan says:

> That the style which Newton has adopted was suitable to the dignity and importance of the subject Newton was doubtless fully aware. He was consciously engaged in

The Spiritual Awakening of Science

giving permanent expression to what he felt were permanent truths. And this was done in the abstract, as it were, an address to the human intelligence, for there is no indication that he was ever anything but completely indifferent to the contemporary reception of his work. Provided that nothing disturbed his tranquillity, he could be his benign, placid and unresponsive self. His lack of desire for fame was perfectly genuine...his sense of personal responsibility, and therefore of merit, would not have been involved.

Professor Andrade sums up Newton's personality at the end of his excellent *Brief Life of Newton* in the words:

> Well, there is this extraordinary man, of the world yet not of the world; supreme in the exact sciences but a mystic at heart... A man who mixed freely with other men of different birth, of different temperaments and pursuits, but always a man withdrawn, guarding, in the ultimate, his own secrets as to what he believed and what he was above all seeking: a man revealing great mysteries of nature's machinery but reticent about much which he had profoundly pondered...

After drawing attention to the modesty of Newton's final assessment of his own achievements in his saying, frequently quoted, about feeling like a boy, playing on the seashore, and diverting himself by now and then finding a smoother pebble or a prettier shell than ordinary, while the great ocean of truth lay all undiscovered before him, Andrade comments:

> We can explain this, perhaps, by supposing that Newton's

How Newton came to write his most famous work

aim was to understand the whole scheme and mystery of the world, in which he believed that the truths of exact science were only a part of a greater truth. His religious and mystic interests would fit in with this suggestion.

10

HOW NEWTON BEGAN TO WORK OUT THE LAWS OF MOTION

AS SOON AS Newton had made up his mind to undertake something, he could show quite extraordinary determination and persistence in carrying it through to a successful conclusion. Of what he was able to do during his life, only a fraction became known to his contemporaries, and both the number of his interests, and amount of handwritten notes he has left of his thoughts and researches on them, is truly phenomenal. It is only in modern times that people have seriously begun to study them in detail.[1] This enormous output was largely because he wasted no time and, once he had decided to do something, he would not allow any irrelevant distractions to deflect him from quietly getting on with its pursuit.

This characteristic, which played a large part in enabling him to achieve success, not only in science and the

---

[1] As, for instance, in the 8-volume edition of the *Mathematical Papers of Isaac Newton*, edited by D.T. Whiteside, Cambridge University Press, 1967-1981; J. Herival, *The Background to Newton's 'Principia': A Study of Newton's Dynamical Researches in the Years 1664-1684*, Oxford: Clarendon Press, 1965; B.J. Dobbs, *The Foundations of Newton's Alchemy*, Cambridge University Press, 1975; *Unpublished Scientific Papers of Isaac Newton*, edited by A.R. Hall & M.B. Hall, Cambridge University Press, 1962.

How Newton began to work out the Laws of Motion

other fields which interested him—chemistry, theology, world history and many more—was in large part due to this habit of disciplining himself and using his time and energy efficiently and economically in pursuit of his goals. This was a life-long feature of his character, and, like his exceptional powers of focused concentration and meditation, it showed itself early in his life in an incident from his days in the grammar school at Grantham.

He had gone from the village school to Grantham at the age of twelve and was placed in the lowest form and near the bottom of the class.[1] On the way to school one morning, one of the other boys gave him a hard and painful kick in the stomach. According to the account given by Conduitt, who must have had it from Newton himself in old age:

> As soon as the school was over he challenged the boy to fight, and they went out together into the church yard; the schoolmaster's son came to them whilst they were fighting and clapped one on the back and winked at the other to encourage them both. Though Sir Isaac was not so lusty as his antagonist he had so much more spirit and resolution that he beat him till he declared that he would fight no more, upon which the schoolmaster's son bade him use him like a coward, and rub his nose against the wall; and accordingly Sir Isaac pulled him along by the ears and thrust his face against the side of the church.

With anyone else, this might have been the end of the

---

[1] R.S. Westfall, *Never at Rest: A Biography of Isaac Newton*, Cambridge University Press, 1980, pp 59-60.

matter, honour having been satisfied. But Newton there and then seems to have decided that beating the boy in fight was not enough, and he determined to beat him at school as well. Once he had started out in this way, he rose steadily in his school-work, eventually becoming the first in the school.

The same strength of mind and singleness of purpose was to characterize much of what Newton did for the rest of his life. It was particularly evident in the period during which he completed his greatest work, the *Principia*. Halley, who had been shown the manuscript of the nine lectures *On the motion of bodies in an orbit* (*De Motu Corporum in gyrum*) in November 1684, was eager to go ahead with publication, but he was going to have to wait for seventeen months, while Newton expanded the original few pages into a large volume containing three books. This was because Newton had begun to realize the full implications of what he had discovered, namely that three Laws of Motion governed the movement of each and every object throughout the universe, and that mathematics enabled one to calculate and predict the results of their interaction with precision. But to show the fuller implications of this and reveal clearly what he called 'The System of the World', the original lectures needed expanding. To do this Newton virtually gave up everything else (including his chemical investigations, of which he was particularly fond), from August 1684 to the Spring of 1686.

It was not as if there were not other distractions occurring around him, but he took no notice of them. Early

How Newton began to work out the Laws of Motion

in February in 1685,. King Charles II died after a short illness, and the crown passed on to his brother and heir, James II, who was a convinced and publicly proclaimed Catholic and was determined to return his kingdom to the Catholic faith. Moreover, his wife had recently presented him with a son and heir. There were very difficult times ahead, as the kingdom became increasingly divided into warring parties of Protestants, Catholics and Dissenters. But Newton remained largely untouched by these events, wholly absorbed in what he was doing, until he had finished writing his masterpiece. By good fortune it was only in 1687 that the threat actively involved Cambridge University, when James commanded them by Royal Decree to set aside the law which prevented Catholics being appointed to University posts and to appoint a Jesuit, Alban Francis, as an M.A. It was part of a general plan to return the seats of learning to Catholicism, and James had at the same time dissolved Parliament which was then the only effective body able to challenge what he was doing. But all this lay some way ahead.

Isaac Newton's *Philosophiae Naturalis Principia Mathematica* — *Mathematical Principles of Natural Philosophy* — commonly known as 'the *Principia*' — which appeared in 1687, was the culmination of a radical change in the understanding of motion, which had been building up in his mind since the 1660s. When he began as a student, the classical view of motion, derived from Aristotle, was still being widely taught. Matter in itself was motionless; motion was something imposed on it by an outer force; when the outer force ceased to act on it, matter reverted to its motionless state. Originally, said Aristotle, motion was imposed on the world by the First Unmoved Mover, God.

But Galileo (1564-1642) had by then applied mathematics to the study of the motions of projectiles and falling weights and had shown that the force of gravity produced a constant and mathematically predictable acceleration of the speed of falling; he had also used the telescope to study planetary motion, and this had confirmed the heliocentric theory of the solar system, originally suggested by Aristarchus and promulgated by Copernicus. Tycho Brahe's careful observations too had been shown by Johannes Kepler to reinforce the truth of this new view, and, as a result, many of the classical ideas in dynamics and cosmology were crumbling fast.

Plutarch had pointed out nearly a millennium-and-a-half earlier that the moon is prevented from falling into the earth by her motion and by the swing of her revolution — just as objects put in slings are prevented from falling by their circular whirl. Borelli, the Professor of Mathematics in Galileo's old University in Pisa, took up this model to explain the solar system, arguing that (although there was no obvious 'sling' in this situation) there must be some force drawing the planet towards the sun, the pull of which was just equal to the opposing force of the whirling motion pulling it away; between the two the planet revolved continually round the sun at a definite distance from it. Robert Hooke in England was expressing the same idea at almost the same time in his book *Attempt to Prove the Motion*

How Newton began to work out the Laws of Motion

of the Earth (1674), later reprinted in his *Lectiones Cutlerianae* (1679).

All this was intelligent speculation, but, without any measurements or a detailed examination of the forces involved, little progress could be made in proving or disproving what had been suggested. This was the importance of the contributions made by Galileo to the more exact measurement of the speed of objects falling under gravity, and of the examination by Kepler of the laws governing the movement of the planets.

A currently popular alternative to the Aristotelian view of motion was that of René Descartes (1596-1650), the mathematician and philosopher who had introduced modern algebraic methods into geometry and mathematical analysis. He explained motion speculatively as due to a system of vortices made up of small and invisible particles which filled all space and swept up larger material objects as if they were fragments of debris in a system of whirlpools, impelling them in this direction or that. The planets (he said) were carried round the sun in one such great vortex. In his view space had no independent existence; it was simply the name for the place where matter was and matter completely filled it. He therefore maintained that there was no such thing as space and that no place could exist without matter in it. Everywhere the world was entirely filled with the vortices of small particles — matter made up largely of particles so small that they could not be sensed. He also held that all the motions undergone by matter were in some way circular. Descartes was no scientist and did no experiments, but this did not prevent him from condemning Galileo's experiments as without foundation, because (he said) he ought first to have determined the nature of weight!

As Sir James Jeans has written:

> The [Cartesian] vortices were whirlpools in a sea of particles; ordinary material objects were like floating corks which revealed how the currents were flowing in the whirlpools.... The planets were corks caught in the whirlpool of the sun and whirled round its centre, while a falling leaf was a smaller cork being drawn towards the centre of the earth's whirlpool. In a later elaboration, there was supposed to be so much agitation at the centre of a large whirlpool that objects became luminous; this explained why the sun and the stars shone.
>
> The system attained to a vogue out of all proportion to its scientific merits. It largely held the field until it was superseded by Newton's incomparably better theory of universal gravitation.

What Newton learnt from Kepler

Johannes Kepler (1571-1630), who was born in Stuttgart, suffered an attack of smallpox in childhood, that left him permanently disabled in both hands and with poor eyesight. But he was an intelligent man who became interested in the heliocentric Copernican hypothesis and managed to obtain a post as lecturer in astronomy at Graz. He was also much interested in Pythagorean ideas. A book which he wrote in his early twenties impressed the Danish

How Newton began to work out the Laws of Motion

astronomer, 53-year-old Tycho Brahe (1546-1601), who invited Kepler to come as a guest to his observatory in Prague and later appointed him as his assistant.

Tycho had just moved to Prague in 1599, in what turned out to be the last two years of his life, after spending many years making accurate and reliable observations on the movement of the stars and planets in the well-equipped observatory, Uraniborg, provided for him by King Frederick II of Denmark. The King died in 1588, leaving Tycho without his main source of support, and in 1599, he accepted an invitation from the German Emperor Rudolph II to go to Prague, where he was provided with a castle as an observatory and granted a pension. Unfortunately, Tycho died shortly afterwards in October 1601, after contracting a sudden illness. But the data he had collected in Denmark on the stars and planets were published in a star catalogue in 1602, which he left for Kepler to study.

Tycho did not himself believe in the Copernican hypothesis, but he had set Kepler the task of using the vast number of planetary observations which he had accumulated to settle the question of whether Copernicus had been right or not. Kepler found he could not make the data fit the Copernican model with its perfectly circular orbits, even with all the complicated superimposed epicycles which had been posited to explain the anomalies. But he solved the problem—and made a major advance in astronomy—by reviving an idea originally suggested by the Spanish astronomer, Arzachel, who had lived in Toledo in about AD 1080 under the Caliphate of the Arabs at

The Spiritual Awakening of Science

Cordoba. Arzachel had maintained that the planets moved round the sun, not in perfect circles, as Pythagoras and the *Almagest* maintained, but in ellipses. Kepler found that, viewed in this way, all the difficulties in explaining the planetary orbits in terms of the actual observations were immediately solved.

A circle has a single point as its centre, and every point on its circumference is equally distant from the centre point; but an ellipse (which can be thought of as a stretched circle with a symmetrical oval outline) differs from a perfect circle in having two centres rather than one (these being called mathematically *foci*). An ellipse has the property that *the sum of the distances from each of the two foci is the same for any point on the circumference.*

Kepler discovered three 'Laws' concerning the planetary orbits, the first two of which were described in his book *Astronomia Nova*, published in 1609. These were that

[1] The planet (Mars) moves in an ellipse which has the sun as one of its foci.

In its generalized form Kepler's first Law says that the planets move in orbits which are elliptical, not circular, and that one of the two foci of the planetary ellipse is invariably the sun. The other focus Kepler named 'the empty focus'.

[2] the line joining the sun to the planet sweeps out equal areas in equal times. (*Figs 1 and 2*)

Kepler's second Law expressed mathematically the fact that a planet moves faster as it gets nearer to the solar focus, in

How Newton began to work out the Laws of Motion

such a way that the line joining the planet to the sun sweeps out the same area in unit time throughout the year. This means that it goes faster and further in unit time when the planet is nearer the sun than when it is further away.

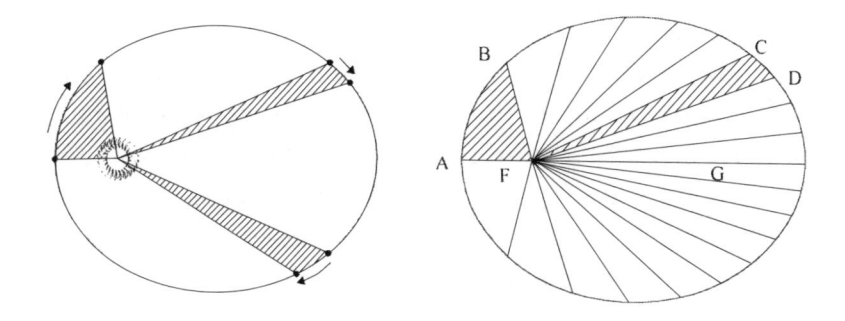

Figs 1 & 2. Kepler's second Law states that the line joining a planet to the sun sweeps out equal areas in equal times — this means that the planets move faster when they are nearer to the sun, and slower at the far extremities of their orbits. In Figure 2 the two foci of the ellipse, solar (F) and empty (G), are shown; the adjacent lines joining the solar focus to the orbit enclose equal areas throughout.

Ten years after publishing this book, Kepler added a third Law, stated in his book *Harmonices mundi*, published in 1619. This Law says that

> [3] the planetary 'year', (i.e., the time taken to complete one whole orbit) is determined by the size of the orbit (measured as the mean radius i.e. the average distance from the solar focus), such that the square of the planetary 'year' (orbiting time T^2) is proportional to the cube of the mean radius ($\bar{r}^3$): $T^2 \propto \bar{r}^3$.

The Spiritual Awakening of Science

Kepler's insight, based on the analysis of actual observations, was a major advance in the understanding of the movement of the heavenly bodies. It at last provided an explanation which fitted the astronomical data and dispensed, once and for all, with all the implausible attempts to make them fit circular orbits by superimposing complicated systems of epicycles on their supposedly circular path. It also explained the variation in the speed of rotation of the planet at different parts of the orbit and what determined the length of the planetary year. It was the beginning of a mathematically convincing explanation for the motion of the planets through space.

Newton read Kepler's works while still a student at Cambridge, and his mathematical insight led him, by simple deduction from Kepler's third Law, to the conclusion that the force holding a planet in its solar orbit must fall off inversely with the square of the distance from the sun. This discovery he made in 1666, during the plague years spent in isolation at Woolsthorpe, when he saw the apple fall and began to think about the forces concerned in mathematical terms.[1]

---

[1] Still under the influence of Descartes' ideas on vortices he had discovered how to 'estimate the force with which a globe revolving within a sphere presses on the [inner] surface of the sphere' and had found that the strength of the centrifugal endeavour (*conatus*) in uniform circular motion, which is balanced by the centripetal endeavour (force) in uniform circular motion at speed v in a circle of radius r, is proportional to v^2/r. This had been independently discovered by the Dutch scientist, Huygens, at about the same time.

How Newton began to work out the Laws of Motion

What Newton was thinking about in the 1660s

In the two years before this, from 1664 to 1666, Newton had been honing his mathematical skills and was deeply immersed in the modern methods of analysis introduced and described by Descartes in his *Geometry*, which Newton read in the annotated edition by Schooten. He obtained his background knowledge of algebra from the many works of Viète [1510-1603], the French lawyer who had largely invented the algebraic notation. He also studied infinitesimals in the writings of John Wallis. But it is clear from the careful modern examination of all his notes from that time that he was himself developing the methods further, as he studied them with astonishing rapidity and creativity. Whiston, his room-mate at Trinity, much later remarked that in mathematics Newton 'could sometimes see almost by intuition, even without demonstration....' Newton's biographer Westfall, who gives a detailed account of this

---

[1] (continued from p 206) Combining this with Kepler's 3rd Law, relating the radius to the period of rotation, $r^3 \propto T^2$, it can be shown that centripetal endeavour keeping the planets in their orbits must be proportional to $1/r^2$.

E [the centripetal endeavour] $\propto v^2/r = 1/r \times (2\pi \, r/ \, T)^2 = 4\pi^2 r^2/ \, rT^2 \propto r^2 /rT^2$

Since Kepler's third Law says that $T^2 \propto r^3$

$E \propto r^2/rT^2 \propto r^2/r^4 = 1/r^2$.

For a fuller discussion, see Westfall, *op. cit.* pp 151-155; and Section 3.6 of the Guide to the recent English translation of the *Principia* by Cohen (particularly pp 14 & 67) in Isaac Newton, *The Principia: A New Translation* by I.B. Cohen & Anne Whitman, Univ. of California Press, 1999.

The Spiritual Awakening of Science

period, comments on the paper that emerged at the end of it:

> Taken all in all, the tract of October 1666[1] was a virtuoso performance that would have left the mathematicians of Europe breathless in admiration, envy and awe. As it happened, only one other mathematician in Europe, Isaac Barrow, even knew that Newton existed, and it is unlikely that in 1666 Barrow had any inkling of his accomplishment. The fact that he was unknown does not alter the other fact that the young man not yet 24, without all benefit of formal instruction, had become the leading mathematician of Europe.

This is not just over-enthusiastic exaggeration, but reasoned judgement. Leibniz was much later to speak in similar terms of Newton, when, in 1701, he was asked his opinion of Newton by the Queen of Prussia during a dinner at the Royal Palace. His reply was recorded by someone present:

> Taking mathematics from the beginning of the world to the time of Sir Isaac, what he had done was much the better half! He added that he had consulted all the learned in Europe upon some difficult point without having any satisfaction and that when he wrote to Sir Isaac, he sent him an answer by the first post to do so and so and then he would find it out.

---

[1] The last of three papers which Newton had written that year detailing mathematical methods for analyzing the motion of moving bodies. (Westfall, *op. cit.*, p 137.)

How Newton began to work out the Laws of Motion

In 1666 Newton had turned from pure mathematics to the mechanics of motion. As Westfall says: 'Newton was not a man of half-hearted pursuits. When he thought on something, he thought on it continually.' He had begun a notebook in 1664 based on his reading of the current literature on the mechanics of motion and was well aware of what Galileo and Descartes had written on the subject. He was at this time greatly influenced by the ideas of Descartes, accepting the idea that a force inherent within bodies keeps them in motion—a drive which Descartes called a *conatus* (endeavour). Descartes had said that 'Every thing naturally perseveres in the state in which it is unless it has been interrupted by some external cause.... A body once moved will always maintain the same speed, quantity and determination of its movement.'

This was all very well as an idea but how did one examine it mathematically? Newton recognized that a definite amount of force was required to stop or move another body. He concluded that there must be a rigorous mathematical relationship between the external cause which changes the movement and the change which it produces. Rather than thinking of a body as an active vehicle of force impinging on others, it was more reasonable to think of the body as the passive recipient of external forces impressed upon it. What one could measure were the changes in motion associated with the exchanges of force between bodies. From this he went on to conclude that in all such exchange the total amount of force remained unchanged, although it could be redistributed.

The Spiritual Awakening of Science

He now thought about the problem of bodies colliding with each other and the way forces were exchanged between them on impact, and also about circular motion, which was more difficult to deal with mathematically. In the analogy of the stone in the sling, the role of the sling was easy to understand as a resisting force holding the stone tied to the centre, but the source of the centrifugal force driving the stone to fly off into outer space was more difficult to understand or to measure accurately. Descartes maintained that all forces were intrinsic and that an interaction of motion could only occur through a direct contact. This was the essential point of the vortex theory.

Newton first considered the idea that the orbiting body met some kind of resistance in striving to fly outwards and was deflected back by an opposing force into its orbit round the ellipse. He considered what Descartes had to say on impact, but rejected it in favour of what seemed much more in line with actual experience and common sense: that the amount of force with which one body struck another determined what happened; that equal forces effected an equal change in similar (equal) bodies; that an exchange of force takes place from one body to the other on impact; and that the bodies themselves are passive sufferers of this exchange of force. He also recognized that any two bodies isolated from external influences constitute a single system whose common centre of gravity moves inertially whether or not they impinge on each other.

On the topic of circular motion, Newton was again dissatisfied with what Descartes had to say, but it led him to his measurements of the strength of the force holding the

How Newton began to work out the Laws of Motion

moon in its orbit round the earth, by using Kepler's third Law, as already mentioned. He seems at this time to have been thinking that, irrespectively of how they were produced, the two forces holding the moon or the planets in orbit must be equal in order to maintain the *status quo*, and by comparing their strength at the moon and the earth's surface, and also for the sun and the planets, he found that the strength varied roughly in proportion to the inverse square of the distance. It looks as if he did not yet have any clear idea of a universal force of gravitation at this time. For one thing, he did not yet accept the idea of *action-at-a-distance*, which Descartes ruled out as impossible.

However, already in 1668, in an essay on gravity (*De gravitatione*), he was beginning to turn against the Cartesian picture of motion. He called Descartes' idea of space being entirely filled with matter 'absurd,... confused and unreasonable'. He himself now maintained, on the contrary, that force is the cause of both motion and rest and that space and time are absolute. Force may be either external—generating or destroying or otherwise changing the motion in some body to which it is applied—or it may be an internal principle by which any existing motion or rest is conserved in a body, and by which it endeavours to continue in its present state and opposes change by resisting it.

His most serious charge was that Descartes, by separating body and mind, denied the dependence of the material world on God. 'The ultimate cause of atheism', Newton asserted, 'is this notion of bodies having, as it were, absolute and independent reality in themselves....' He drew a parallel between God, with His capacity to move matter, and the human soul, with its capacity to move its body. Even created mind (he wrote) 'is of a far more noble a nature than body, so that perhaps it may eminently contain it in itself'. Whereas Descartes' distinction separated mind and body, his view allowed them to combine.

Newton believed that God is everywhere; as he says explicitly in the final Scholium which he added to the second edition of the *Principia*. He notes elsewhere: ''Tis not the place but the state which makes heaven and happiness. For God is alike in all places. He is substantially omnipresent and as much present in the lowest hell as in the highest heaven....'

From 1669 onwards Newton's interests in motion gave way to his work on colour and his duties as Lucasian Professor of Mathematics. The construction of the reflecting telescope and the first paper to the Royal Society on his prism experiments and its aftermath, already described in an earlier chapter, must also have occupied part of his time until about 1678. But he was already pursuing his other main interests in alchemical experiments and reading in theology and Church history. Each year he was also required to give a course of lectures on algebra, and the College laid down that the manuscript of these lectures should be deposited in the College afterwards.

How Newton began to work out the Laws of Motion

Newton turns to the physics of motion again in 1679

When Newton turned to mathematics and motion again in 1679 as a result of the correspondence with Hooke, his attitude underwent a major re-orientation. Among the new publications from France that year was a book by Fermat dealing with the geometry of Apollonius (260-200 BC) who had studied conic sections in great detail in ancient times, being the first to introduce this subject. He lived about 100 years after Euclid. Conic sections was the branch of geometry which dealt with ellipses rather than circles. Newton was encountering classical geometry for the first time and he became an enthusiastic and serious student of it. His largely self-taught mathematical training as a student had ignored this subject in favour of algebra and Descartes' modern analysis, a fact which incidentally explains why he had been censured as 'deficient in Euclid' at his examination by Barrow for a scholarship at Trinity in April 1664.[1] Now the tables were turned and he developed a high regard for the ancient geometers. As Henry Pemberton later said:

> Of their taste, and form of demonstration Sir Isaac always professed himself a great admirer. I had heard him even censure himself for not following them yet more closely than he did; and speak with regret of his mistake at the beginning of his mathematical studies, in applying himself to the works of Descartes and other algebraic writings, before he had considered the elements of Euclid with that attention which so excellent a writer deserves.

---

[1] The accounts of this differ. See Westfall, pp 98-99, 102; Manuel, p 96.

The Spiritual Awakening of Science

He considered that to many problems the solutions of the classical mathematicians in purely geometric terms were more elegant.

> Men of recent times, [he wrote] eager to add to the discoveries of the ancients, have united the arithmetic of variables with geometry. Benefiting from that, progress has been broad and far-reaching if your eye is on the profuseness of output, but the advance is less of a blessing if you look at the complexity of its conclusions. For these complications.... often express in an intolerably round about way quantities which in geometry are designated by a single line.

He called Cartesian algebraic geometry: 'The analysis of the Bunglers in mathematics.' It was as a result of this new attitude towards geometry that Newton used geometrical proofs throughout the *Principia*.

By this time Newton's concept of the forces at work in orbiting bodies (such as the planets, the moon and the satellites of Jupiter and Saturn) had undergone a major change. He had abandoned Descartes' view that force could only be exerted by direct contact between particles, and had accepted action-at-a-distance. This was an idea rejected out-of-hand by Cartesian thinkers like Huygens. After Hooke's letters in 1679 he showed, using Kepler's second Law of equal areas in equal times, that, for an elliptical path, the central force of attraction varies inversely as the square of the distance as for a circular one, a much more difficult mathematical task than deducing it from Kepler's third Law assuming a simple circular orbit. He had also

How Newton began to work out the Laws of Motion

accepted the idea of the force of inertia. The two essential opposing forces holding the body in orbit were now the centripetal attraction and the inherent, inertial force of the tangential momentum, continually attempting to drive the body in a straight line into space and being diverted round the orbit by the force of attraction from the centre. (*Fig*.3)

Fig. 3. The two elements responsible for circular motion, the innate tangential drive of the orbiting body to continue in a straight line *PQ* (due to its momentum), and the centripetal attraction pulling it into the circular orbit *QR*. Note that the orbiting shown in Figs 3 & 4 is anti-clockwise, rather than clockwise as in Figs 1 & 2 (p 205).

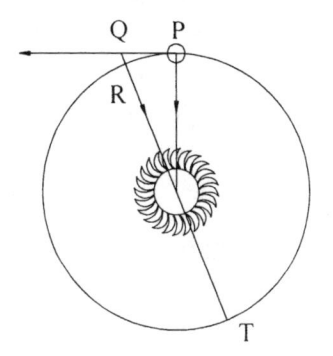

Newton seems to have come to regard Descartes' rejection of action-at-a-distance as another example of his atheistical views. After all, God was omnipresent and could move things as He chose. Newton saw that there were innumerable examples of action-at-a-distance throughout nature. As well as the movements of bodies in the cosmos, there were innumerable unobservable examples among the particles of which bodies are composed. He said of them:

> If any one shall have the good fortune to discover all these [forces of attraction drawing particles together], I might almost say that he will have laid bare the whole nature of bodies so far as the mechanical causes of things are concerned. I have least of all undertaken the improvement of this part of philosophy. I may say briefly, however, that

nature is exceedingly simple and conformable to herself. Whatever reasoning holds for greater motions, should hold for lesser ones as well. The former depend on the greater attractive forces of larger bodies, and I suspect that the latter depend upon the lesser forces, as yet unobserved, of insensible particles. For, from the forces of gravity, of magnetism and of electricity, it is manifest that there are various kinds of natural forces, and that there may be still more kinds is not to be rashly denied. It is very well known that greater bodies act mutually upon each another by those forces, and I do not clearly see why lesser ones should not act on one another by similar forces.

Newton's main evidence for this view came from his chemical experiments, particularly reactions which generated heat or revealed affinities. It found expression in Query 31 of the *Optics*.

Hooke's exchange of letters with Newton in 1679 was a crucial stimulus awakening the latter's interest in dynamics again after a long pause. It was associated with a major change in his approach, in that he abandoned the belief in some centrifugal force balancing out the pull of gravity to maintain the circulation of orbiting bodies. Instead he clearly realized that it was the inherent inertial force of the circulating body itself trying to continue tangentially in a straight line which was competing with gravity and being continually deflected around the circle by the centripetal force. It is not clear whether Newton got this idea from Hooke or whether he had already come to the same conclusion himself, but it is clear that Hooke was mathematically incapable of incorporating the idea into a

How Newton began to work out the Laws of Motion

test of the dynamics of the bodies circulating in elliptical orbits.

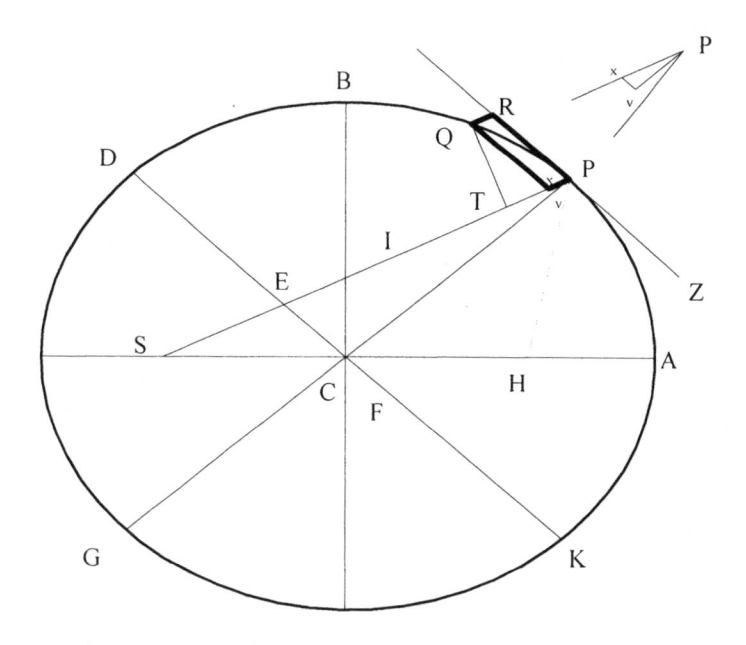

Fig. 4. The illustration for Newton's two alternative proofs of the inverse square law for an elliptical orbit from the *Principia* (Book I; Proposition 11; Problem 6). For the proofs themselves — (too long to include here) — see Cohen and Whitman (1999) *op. cit.*, pp 462-463. The parallelogram of forces *QxPR* allows the centripetal force towards the solar focus (S) to be calculated for each part of the orbit.

Newton's proof involved the use of the parallelogram of forces to calculate the resultant of the interaction of the tangential and centripetal vectors for an elliptical orbit. He accepted Kepler's second Law that the satellite orbited equal areas in equal times, and then showed that the forces vary inversely as the square of the distance for every point on the ellipse. The problem of circular motion was solved. It was explained as the interaction between gravity—a centripetal attractive force—and the inherent force of inertia in the moving body. Newton, having solved it, characteristically lost all interest, told no one and mislaid the paper on which he had written the proof.

Newton's new discovery concerning the path of comets

In November 1681 his interest was aroused again in astronomy when a comet appeared. He had first made observations on a comet as a student in December 1664, sitting up all night to do so and finding himself (as he later told Conduitt) 'much disordered by lack of sleep and learning from it to go to bed betimes.' The comet was first sighted before sunrise early in the month. He had a telescope mounted at the top of the stairs down to the garden from which he could make his sightings and made observations throughout November until the comet vanished into the morning sun at the end of the month. Two weeks later, in mid-December, what was widely regarded as a second comet appeared moving away from the sun. By the end of the month it was immense with a tail four times as broad as the moon and more than 70 degrees long. 'I believe scarce a larger has ever been seen', was the comment of Flamsteed, the Astronomer Royal. During the whole period Newton kept meticulous records of its course and he also wrote to Flamsteed and to some of his friends for descriptions of their sightings. He even started making a new reflecting telescope four feet long and designed to magnify 150 times with a silvered glass mirror. What he

How Newton began to work out the Laws of Motion

was really interested in was finding out if comets behaved at all like planets in their paths, although they were generally regarded as quite distinct in their behaviour. Flamsteed, for instance, did not believe that they went round the sun. He rightly thought that the supposedly two comets seen in November and December were one and the same comet going to and from the sun, but his own theory was that the comet was magnetic and had been attracted to the sun magnetically, but became reversed on close approach and was then repelled in the opposite direction.

Newton later met Halley, probably in 1682, and questioned him about his observation of the comet on 8th December 1681, the earliest sighting on its second appearance coming back from the sun. In 1682 a further comet appeared (the one which we now call 'Halley's comet'), and Newton again carefully recorded observations of its changing position. He systematically collected information on all recorded comets and classified them in various ways according to features of their appearance and behaviour. At this time neither Hooke, Halley nor Flamsteed believed that comets were subject to the attraction between cosmic bodies. It was generally accepted that they moved in a straight line with uniform velocity. Newton worked out from all the scattered data he had collected, by meticulous successive approximation and correction, that the comets had an elliptical path obeying the same inverse square law as the planets. This must have been a major step in his growing belief in universal gravitation. It was in the autumn and winter of the year 1684-85 that it came to full fruition.

The Spiritual Awakening of Science

In the late 1670s and early 1680s the problem of how to derive Kepler's Laws from the principles of dynamics was beginning to intrigue many people and to feature as a topic of general discussion among interested persons. Newton and Wren had had a conversation in 1677 on 'Determining the Hevenly motions upon philosophical principles'. Wren had already arrived at the inverse square law at this time, but neither Wren, Hooke nor Halley had been able to demonstrate its truth for elliptical orbits mathematically from dynamic principles. Newton, of course, had arrived at the inverse square law for circular orbits from Kepler's third Law over ten years before in 1666; and he had demonstrated its association with elliptical orbits following the correspondence with Hooke in 1679, but kept it to himself and lost the paper on which the proof was written. It was not until after the discussion of the problem by Wren, Hooke and Halley in 1684, and Wren's offer of a prize for the successful solution, that Halley visited Newton in Cambridge and triggered in him the renewed interest which led him to plan and give the course of lectures on the motion of orbiting bodies in Trinity College that autumn and culminated, two and a half years later, in the publication of the *Principia*.

11

NEWTON DESCRIBES THE LAWS OF MOTION AND THE SYSTEM OF THE WORLD

NEWTON'S *PRINCIPIA* — or, to give it its full name in English, *Mathematical Principles of Natural Philosophy* [meaning Physics or Science] — is entirely devoted to the study of movement and the forces governing movement. This might seem at first sight a rather specialized and circumscribed topic, but a little further thought should quickly serve to dispel this judgement. It is not without reason that the Vedanta philosophy called the external world *'Jagat'* — 'the moving thing', regarding motion as its prime characteristic. Modern science, too, which has recognized even solid matter to be merely another manifestation of electromagnetic energy in a different state, emphasizes the fundamental character of the world as a manifestation of the energy of Nature. The Vedanta philosophy is in close agreement with this view, regarding not only the external world of matter, but also the internal world of mind, as a product of the power or energy of Nature (called by the Vedantins *Prakriti Shakti*).

Newton himself presumably had virtually no access at all to the wisdom of ancient India, but he was very much of the opinion that the things he was discovering had been already known in some form by the Ancients. This belief of

The Spiritual Awakening of Science

his is now well recognized and beyond dispute, mainly as the result of the careful and intensive study of Newton's surviving notes and papers during the last half century. A much clearer idea of his thought in the various wide-ranging fields of his interests has emerged, as can be seen, for instance, in the large variety of topics covered in the twelve chapters of the multi-authored anthology *Let Newton Be*, published by Oxford University Press in 1988. One of these chapters was entirely devoted to *Newton and the Wisdom of the Ancients*. It points out how unexpected it is to find someone, honoured largely for the major new advances in knowledge which he had made, expressing the modest view that much of what he had done was effectively only a rediscovery of what had already been known (at least in some form) by previous thinkers; and, in particular, showing a deep respect for the Greek mathematicians. As the author writes:

> It is all the more surprising, then, to find that in his secret thoughts Newton held a vision of history, which would have very much astonished the *philosophes* [of the eighteenth century], had they been acquainted with it. It reduced all he had discovered to a rediscovery of scientific truths well known to some of the great thinkers of the ancient world... These were not random observations based on a cursory reading in ancient sources. Newton worked on the problem with the same assiduity and concentration that marks his scientific work. Gregory[1]

---

[1] David Gregory, the young Scottish mathematician who cultivated Newton's friendship. For details of his meeting with Newton, see Westfall, *Never at Rest*, Cambridge University Press, 1980, pp 499-501.

Newton describes the Laws of Motion & the System of the World

came into possession of a set of fifteen folio sheets in which Newton assembled a formidable array of classical authorities to support key propositions of the *Principia*.[1]

And the chapter goes on to list a number of these, including the universal force of gravity exercised by the bodies in the solar system on each other and extending in all directions, but decreasing with distance and proportional to the amount of matter in each body. Several notable examples have already been mentioned, such as the recognition by Aristarchus that the planets circled round the sun rather than the earth and Plutarch's analogy of the stone in the sling to characterize the force of the earth's attraction holding the moon in orbit.[2]

Another interesting example of the influence of ancient thinkers on Newton's ideas concerns his prism experiments on colours, as it explains his division of the spectrum into seven colours[3]. Newton, while resolutely refusing to commit himself in print on the causal explanation of the different colours of light in the spectrum, does speculate in his paper read to the Royal Society in 1675. In it he goes so far as to suggest that the different degrees of deflection

---

[1] Piyo Rattansi, 'Newton and the Wisdom of the Ancients' in *Let Newton Be*, Oxford University Press, 1988, pp 185-201. See also Westfall, pp 434-5; 510-514.

[2] See Dampier, *A Shorter History of Science,* Cambridge University Press, 1944, pp 28 & 50; Sir James Jeans, *The Growth of Physical Science,* Cambridge University Press, 1947, pp 86-89 & 181.

[3] See Chapter 8, p 159f.

(refrangibility) of various colours in passing through the prism might 'best be interpreted by supposing that bodies could be excited so as to cause vibrations in the ether of various depths and bignesses, and that the largest of these beget a sensation of red colour, the least or shortest of a deep violet, and intermediate sizes sensations of intermediate colours, just as waves in air according to their bignesses make several tones in sound'.[1] The apparently arbitrary division of the continuous spectrum into seven colours reflects Newton's interest in Pythagorean ideas on the production of sound vibrations in air, where the seven notes of the scale obviously provided a model of what he had in mind.[2] This was in the course of discussing Hooke's suggestion that light was composed of transverse waves in the ether. He himself tended to favour the view that light consisted of small particles emitted from the surface of shining bodies, but he thought that the differing prismatic deflections of these too might be due to variation in the size of the particles of different colours.[3] He describes his own investigations of this topic in the last Section of the first Book of the *Principia*. But he could never finally decide definitely whether light was made up of waves or particles — another example, perhaps, of his prescience!

[1] See Sir James Jeans, *The Growth of Physical Science*, p 207.

[2] This is discussed further in the chapter on 'The Harmonic Roots of Newtonian Science' in *Let Newton Be*, pp 100-126. See especially pp 118-120.

[3] Casper Hakfoort, 'Newton's optics: the changing spectrum of science' in *Let Newton Be*, pp 80-99.

Newton describes the Laws of Motion & the System of the World

What the *Principia* is about

The *motion* that Newton was mainly considering in the *Principia* was the movement through space of solid bodies like the earth and the planets and their satellites, as well as the path of comets. This movement was due either to their inherent momentum or to externally applied forces. Innate movement was invariably in a straight line, but a change in speed or direction of movement was more complex and implied the action of an external force deflecting a body from its own original undisturbed course.

In his Preface Newton writes that:

> The ancients studied this part of mechanics in terms of the five powers which relate to the manual arts and paid hardly any attention to gravity (since it is not a manual power) except in the moving of weights by these powers. But since we are concerned with natural philosophy rather than manual arts, and are writing about natural rather than manual powers, we concentrate on gravity, levity, elastic forces, resistance of fluids, and forces of this sort, whether attractive or impulsive. And therefore our present work sets forth mathematical principles of natural philosophy. For the basic problem of philosophy seems to be to discover the forces of nature from the phenomena of motions [i.e. experimental observations or 'looking to see'] and then to demonstrate the other phenomena from these forces. It is to these ends that the general propositions in Books 1 and 2 are directed, while in Book 3 our explanation of the system of the world illustrates these propositions. For in Book 3, by means of propositions

demonstrated mathematically in Books 1 and 2, we derive from celestial phenomena the gravitational forces by which bodies tend towards the sun and towards the individual planets. Then the motions of the planets, the comets, the moon, and the sea are deduced from those forces by propositions that are also mathematical. If only we could derive the other phenomena of nature from mechanical principles by the same line of reasoning! For many things lead me to have a suspicion that all phenomena may depend on certain forces by which the particles of bodies, by causes not yet known, either are impelled towards one another and cohere in regular figures, or are repelled from one another and recede. Since these forces are unknown, philosophers have hitherto made trial of nature in vain. But I hope that the principles set down here will shed some light on either this mode of philosophising or some truer one.

Newton's mathematical approach to the analysis of circular motion.

The study of gravity involves the problem of orbiting bodies, a more complex problem than movement in a straight line or a simple change of direction. In his approach to discovering the forces governing the movement of objects in a circular orbit, Newton developed three completely different approaches in the course of the short, but intensive, periods during which he concentrated on it. There are traces of all these three mathematical approaches to circular movement in the *Principia* itself.

Newton describes the Laws of Motion & the System of the World

His first approach was noted down in an entry made in the mid-1660s in what is known as 'the Waste Book', the large commonplace book, inherited from his step-father, in which he used any available blank spaces to note down his mathematical discoveries. It was begun when he was still under the influence of Descartes' ideas, which emphasized the supposed principle that it was *only by direct physical contact between bodies* that force could be exerted — as would be the case for a body swept along in a rotating vortex of invisible matter. The force acting on the orbiting body he modelled in terms of the impacts of a perfectly elastic ball against the sides of some impenetrable resisting walls enclosing it. In its simplest form, this could be represented by the reflection of a ball bouncing round the four walls of a square box, without losing any energy at each impact (Fig.1). This simple model could then be replaced by a many-sided polygon of n sides (Fig. 2). Simply increasing the number of sides to infinity, led in the limit to a perfect circle (Fig. 3).

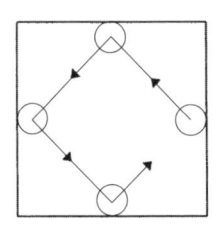

Figure 1 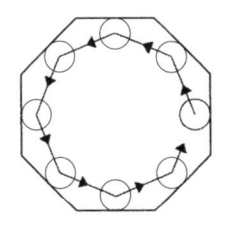   Figure 2 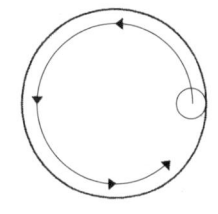   Figure 3

The Spiritual Awakening of Science

Clearly this model was an appropriate way of conceiving circular motion in Cartesian terms, which only recognized the effect of any material particle on its neighbours through direct contact, and denied the existence of action-at-a-distance.[1]

Newton, however, soon became disillusioned with this Cartesian picture, and developed another based on his knowledge of Galileo's experiments on the parabolic path of projectiles under the influence of gravity, and the constant acceleration due to gravity which he had observed in falling objects. This involved a continuous, rather than an intermittent, change in the straight path of the object, whether projectile or planet. Newton was able to measure acceleration due to gravity with much greater accuracy by developing Galileo's use of a pendulum. The distance that the weight on a pendulum fell in each swing could be measured, and the mean time of the fall could be determined more accurately by dividing the total time taken for a large number of swings. He considered the two components of motion acting at a point on the orbit: one uniform and linear along the tangent, and the other producing a constant acceleration directed centrally. For any one point, this is equivalent to the course of a projectile

---

[1] Cohen, *op. cit.*, pp 70-84 (see below, p 230, note 2); Westfall, *op. cit.* pp 148-149. The original model of the circulating body undergoing successive impacts on the sides of a polygonal container appeared in the *Principia* in propositions 1 & 2 of Book 1 (Cohen, pp 444-448), where the centripetal force is treated as a regularly repeated centripetal impulse driving the tangentially directed body towards the centre.

describing a parabolic path under the influence of gravity, as in Galileo's experiments.[1]

In 1679, Hooke's letter stimulated him to look again at the problem of circular motion, but now in relation to the more complicated problem of the planets circulating in elliptical orbits. He had, in fact, already solved the problem of finding the forces concerned fifteen years before this, as we know from another note in the Waste Book:

> If the body is moved in an Ellipsis then its force in each point (if its motion at that point bee given) may bee found by a tangent circle of equal crookednesse to that point on the ellipsis.

Newton's manuscript shows that he knew the main steps in finding the curvature of an ellipse as early as December 1664, but there is no evidence that he applied it in practice until two weeks after the exchange of letters with Hooke in 1679, when he used it to work out — not what type of orbit would be followed by a body attracted by an inverse square force — but the strength which a central force located at one focus of an ellipse exerted on a body circling round it in an elliptical orbit. He found it to be an attraction varying in proportion to the inverse square of the distance from the focus. He showed this first for the points at the two ends of the ellipse (the two apsides) and then demonstrated that the same relation holds for every other point on the ellipse. This showed for the first time that

---

[1] The parabolic model is exemplified in the *Principia* in Book 1 Propositions 4, 6, 10 and 11, where the model posits a continuously active force.

Kepler's Laws applied equally to elliptical orbits, as they did to circular orbits.[1] As Westfall says, this demonstration was one of the two foundation stones on which the concept of universal gravitation rested. The other was the acceptance by Newton of the existence of action-at-a-distance, a major change in his outlook which he implicitly accepts without demur in his demonstration that an elliptical orbit round a central point implied a central force falling off in proportion to the reciprocal of the distance squared.[2]

Some Fundamental Concepts

Newton starts his book by defining certain fundamental concepts, such as the '*quantity of matter*', which is a product of its volume and density and is called by him '*body*' or '*mass*'. It is invariably proportional to the weight. And this may be accurately determined by making measurements with a pendulum.

The '*quantity of motion*' is a measure of motion arising from the *velocity* and the *quantity of matter* of the body.

---

[1] Westfall, *op. cit.*, pp 387-388.

[2] Newton's third mathematical approach to the analysis of circular movement, using the variation in the curvature of the circle indicated by the tangent, does not appear clearly in the first edition of the *Principia*, except in proposition 28 of Book 3 (see Cohen, *The Principia: A New Translation*, University of California Press, 1999, pp 844-846). But Newton planned to add alternative proofs in the second edition of the work employing this technique (Cohen, pp 73-76), and there is evidence to suggest that he himself used it much more extensively than these few examples would suggest.

Newton describes the Laws of Motion & the System of the World

Newton next defines the *'inherent force of matter'* [*inertia*], which he characterizes as 'the power of resisting by which every body, so far as it is able, perseveres in its state either of resting or of moving uniformly straight forward'. This inertial element had already been recognized by Leonardo before him when he noted that 'a body has weight in the direction in which it is moving'. It is sometimes called *'the force of inertia'* [*vis inertiae*] by Newton, but it is not an active force so much as *a resistance to change*, since it is only exerted and apparent when a body is subjected to an externally impressed force. Newton notes that it is commonly regarded as *resistance* in relation to resting bodies and as *impetus* [*or momentum*] in relation to moving bodies. But he points out that motion and rest, in the popular sense of the terms, are distinguished from each other only by one's point of view, and bodies commonly regarded as being at rest are not always truly so.

The fourth definition concerns an *externally impressed force*, which 'is the action exerted on a body to change its state either of resting or of moving uniformly straight forward'. It may be due to the impact of a collision, or pressure or to a centripetal force like gravity.

The remaining four definitions concern *centripetal force* which is 'the force by which bodies are drawn from all sides or are impelled towards some point as to a centre'. Newton cites the force of gravity towards the centre of the earth and the force which holds the planets in their circular orbits round the sun, and also the magnetic force by which iron is drawn to a lodestone.

In the final scholium to these definitions he adds that *time, space, place,* and *motion* are familiar to everyone and are properly conceived solely with reference to the objects of sense perception, but he points out that it is useful to distinguish these quantities into *absolute* and *relative, true* and *apparent, mathematical* and *common* conceptions to eliminate misunderstanding. And he considers this problem in some detail.[1]

The Three Laws of Motion

After defining the fundamental concepts, the *Principia* begins with a statement of Newton's three laws of motion, acknowledging what he owes to Galileo in putting them forward.

1. **The first law says that a body will remain in its present state, either at rest or in uniform motion in a straight line, unless acted on by an external force.**

   This law is sometimes known as **the law of inertia.**

   This is, of course, a direct denial of Aristotle's idea that matter is by nature motionless and only moves as a result of an external force and only for as long as that force is acting on it. We are misled about this by the customary slowing-down of moving objects by air resistance or friction. In empty space, where no other forces are acting, the planets and comets continue indefinitely in their courses. The law asserts, on the contrary, that there is what

[1] Cohen, *op. cit.,* pp 408-415.

Newton describes the Laws of Motion & the System of the World

Newton characterizes as 'an inherent force of inertia' within a material body by reason of which it endeavours to resist change and persevere in its present state, whether of motion or rest. In everyday life we are very familiar with it when the driver of the bus puts his foot on the brake and we continue to move forward until we can catch hold of something to save ourselves from falling flat. A similar feeling can be experienced in a vertical direction in a fast lift which suddenly comes to an abrupt halt at its destination!

2. **The second law says that the effect of an external force acting on a body is to cause a change in either the rate or direction of movement, and its strength is measured in terms of the rate of that change.**

In other words the force either speeds things up or slows them down or changes their direction of movement. A motionless body will continue at rest unless it is accelerated into movement by some force. But equally a body already moving at uniform speed in a straight line will also continue indefinitely at the same speed in the same direction until a force either speeds it up or slows it down or changes its direction of movement.

3. **The third law of motion is that when a force acts on a body, action and reaction are equal and opposite.**

This law is well illustrated, for instance, by the firing of a cannon, where the force of the explosion propels the cannon ball out towards the target, but equally drives the (much heavier) cannon itself in the opposite direction, producing the recoil. We are all much more familiar with this principle nowadays, because of the use of rockets to accelerate space vehicles in a particular direction, which is done by the rocket directing an explosive force backwards in the opposite direction to that in which the rocket itself is to go. Note that this manoeuvre is effective even in empty space, requiring no other extrinsic element against which the forces have to be exerted.

In arriving at his laws of motion, Newton conceived any motion as due to the interaction of two elements, what he called the *inherent force* in the body (the force of inertia, *vis inertiae*) and the *impressed force*, acting on the body from outside. Gradually, however, he realized that the inherent force was not really a force at all but a resistance to change due to the mass of the body. As he writes:

> The inherent force of matter is the power of resisting by which every body, as much as in it lies, perseveres in its state of resting or of moving uniformly straight forward. This force is always proportional to its body and does not differ at all from the inactivity of the mass except in our mode of conceiving it. In fact a body exerts this force only in a change of its state effected by another force impressed upon it, and its exercise is *resistance* and *impetus* [i.e. momentum] which are distinct only in relation to each other.

Of the principle embodied in the third law, he writes:

> As much as any [one] body acts on another, so much does it experience in reaction.... In fact this law follows from...

Newton describes the Laws of Motion & the System of the World

[the inherent force of a body to persevere in its state of resting or moving uniformly] and...[the force brought to bear and impressed on a body to change its state] in so far as the force of the body exerted to conserve its state is the same as the force impressed on the other body to change its state, and the change of state of the first body is proportional to the first force and of the second body to the second force.

In other words the externally applied force and the innate inertia of each of the bodies determine the exchange of forces between them, [i.e., action and reaction are equal and opposite] but the *total force* only undergoes redistribution and is not increased or reduced in the exchange.

A Vedantic Parallel to the Laws of Motion

To anyone familiar with the Vedanta philosophy, Newton's three laws of motion will be at once recognizable as closely related to the three qualities or modes (*gunas*) which make up the energy of nature (*Prakriti Shakti*) in the classical doctrine. These are inertia (*tamas*), activity (*rajas*) and the balanced equilibrium between the two (*sattva*), which is also the quality of light, balance or harmony. Although, in Vedantic literature, the *gunas* are not in any sense limited to physical movement, but also characterize the mental qualities, *tamas* and *rajas* conceptually correspond closely to the aspects of motion described in the first and second of the Newtonian laws (i.e., inertia and active force for change), and the parallel is even more striking when the aspect of *sattva* as the balanced equilibrium or harmony between *rajas* and *tamas* is taken into account.

The Spiritual Awakening of Science

As has already been said, there seems little chance of Newton having had any channels through which information from the ancient Indian writings could have reached him. But it is worth remembering that the doctrine of the qualities or modes (*gunas*) is very old. It goes back to the *Bhagavad Gita*, a work in which it is extensively written about, which modern Western scholarship dates at somewhere around 200 BC. It is even briefly mentioned in the classical *Upanishads*. According to Deussen, it was taken over from the *Sankhya*, one of the oldest branches of Vedanta philosophy.[1]

Book 1 of the *Principia*

Having established the three laws of motion, Newton goes on to show how you can measure these forces quantitatively from the movements that they produce, and also calculate the way they interact. It is only possible here to briefly outline the large range of topics which the rest of the work covers.

In the first Book, for instance, he deals mathematically with the motion of a body, such as a planet, acted on by a centripetal force, such as the gravitational pull of the sun, and shows that such a force, obeying the inverse square law (i.e., falling off in proportion to the inverse square of the distance), will result in orbital movements exactly obeying the three Laws that Kepler had found to be true in his observations of the planets.

---

[1] P. Deussen, *The Philosophy of the Upanishads,* New York: Dover Publications, 1966, pp 250-253.

Newton describes the Laws of Motion & the System of the World

He demonstrates that (as Kepler had suggested) the imaginary line joining an orbiting body to a fixed point (for instance, the planet joined to the sun) sweeps out an area proportional to the time if the force acting on that body is directed towards that point. He goes on to show that the converse is also true: that if a line between a fixed point and a moving body always describes areas proportional to the times, then the force acting on the moving body is directed towards that point. This is **Kepler's second Law** of 1609, that the line joining a planet to the sun does indeed sweep out equal areas in equal times. By calculating this for each planet it can be shown that the forces acting on each of them to keep them in orbit, point towards the sun. He goes on to show that for a body revolving in an ellipse, the centripetal force towards the focus of the ellipse obeys an inverse square law. This allows him to generalize the view that the forces acting on each and every planet must obey such a law.

He then goes on to show that Kepler's third Law (see page 205) relating the period (T) of the planetary 'year' to the mean distance ($\bar{r}$) from the sun by the formula $T^2 \propto \bar{r}^3$, can also be deduced from the same principles. In this way, Newton shows that one and the same set of simple mathematical laws governs the movements of all the solar planets, and he goes on to show the same for the force which holds the moon rotating round the earth. Finally, he shows that exactly the same force is active in the fall of the apple, in spite of the fact that it is at the surface of the earth. Newton then argues that the economy of nature requires us to make gravity responsible for the orbital force acting on each of the planets and on all the bodies in the universe. As John Roche says, writing of the *Principia*:

> Today we take the notion of universal gravitation so much for granted that we find it hard to imagine a period when gravity was thought of as confined to the earth's surface only. This is the measure of Newton's success.[1]

In Section 11 he abandons the mathematical treatment of the sun or the earth as an abstract point (or centre of force) from which the force of gravity acts, on the grounds that such a situation 'hardly exists in the natural world... where attractions are always directed towards bodies'. It is between bodies that the force of attraction acts, not between mathematical points. The third law of motion says that 'the actions of attracting and attracted bodies are always mutual and equal'. In the real world bodies come in different shapes and sizes and densities. Section 11 considers the more complicated problem of two bodies revolving round a common centre of gravity, and their mutual effect on each other. It also determines an alternative model where the force of attraction varies in direct proportion to the distance from the centre, rather than in proportion to the inverse square of the distance. He also considers the three body problem in its relevance to the perturbation of the moon's orbits in relation to the earth and the sun.

In the course of Book 1, he also disposes of a problem

---

[1] John Roche, 'Newton's *Principia*' in *Let Newton Be*, p 56.

Newton describes the Laws of Motion & the System of the World

that had worried him in his early investigation of gravity in 1666 when the apple fell. This was whether, being a small object situated near to the surface of the earth, the apple was being attracted sideways as well as downwards by the surrounding solid matter of the earth. In Section 12, Proposition 70, he demonstrates that there is a cancellation of forces between particles inside a spherical body, which mutually attract each other by an inverse square force, such that a particle outside will be attracted by an inverse square force as if it were situated at a point in the centre of the body whether it be a solid sphere or a shell. (Proposition 71). This holds only for the inverse square law.

Book 1 ends with Sections considering the attraction between non-spherical bodies (Section 13) and very small bodies (Section 14), including the hypothetical corpuscles which Newton thought might be the origin of light rays. He considers the possibility of forces of the same kind explaining the colour fringes which he had seen in reflections or refractions of light and in chromatic aberration, as he explains in the Scholium to Section 14.

Book 2

Book 1 had dealt with bodies moving unhindered in empty space. Book 2 turns to frictional forces and wave motion, and considers a large variety of examples of the motion of bodies in resisting media. This was of particular relevance in Newton's day because of Descartes' widely accepted view that the whole world was filled with rotating vortices, and that the planets were carried around the sun in their currents. In the final Section of Book 2, Newton investigates the property of vortices 'in order to test whether the celestial phenomena could be explained by vortices'. He finds that the periodic times (i.e. the lengths of the 'planetary years') of the parts of a circulating vortex turn out to be proportional to the square of the distances from the centre of motion [i.e. $T \propto r^2$]. This cannot be reconciled with the astronomical observations and Kepler's third Law [which predicts $T^2 \propto \bar{r}^3$]. Later in the Book Newton returns to enlarge on the difficulties of accepting the doctrine of vortices in the opening paragraph of his final General Scholium. Huygens, a keen supporter of the Cartesian mechanical philosophy, commented after reading the *Principia:* 'Vortices [have been] destroyed by Newton.'

Unlike the first book the second reports the results of many of Newton's practical experiments. The first four of the nine Sections deal with the motions of objects in fluid mediums under several different conditions of resistance. He explores the mathematical consequences where the resistance is proportional to the velocity (Section 1), or the square of the velocity (Section 2) or a mixture of the two (Section 3), identifying the factors of tenacity, friction and density as important. His method of fluxions makes its first appearance in print in the course of Section 2. Section 4 investigates the revolving motion of bodies in resisting mediums; Section 5, the density and compression of fluids; Section 6, the motion of simple pendulums, and the effect of the resistance of air or fluids. This book also contains the results of many of the experiments that Newton did with pendulums, following the lead of Galileo and Huygens.

Section 7 deals with the resistance encountered by projectiles; Section 8, the propagation of waves through fluid, containing the first determination of the speed of sound; Section 9, the circular motion of fluids. Newton was the first person to point out that the motion of a solid object through some medium could be studied just as well by having the fluid move past the static object as *vice versa*, and he had some useful observations on the shape which will meet the least resistance which (he points out) could be of use in designing ships. In Sections 6 and 7 he develops a physical theory dealing with the resistance of fluids.

Book 3

After giving a summary of what he has done in the first two books, he announces that he will now demonstrate how the same principles apply throughout the world, something which he proceeds to do with such thoroughness that his results are still valid and useful to astronomers, space scientists, physicists and engineers to this day. His introduction to this third and final book is written in magisterial style:

> It remains that, from the same principles, I now demonstrate the frame of the System of the World. Upon this subject I had indeed composed a third book in a popular method, that it might be read by many; but afterwards, considering that such as had not sufficiently entered into the principles could not easily discern the strength of the consequences, nor lay aside the prejudices to which they have been many years accustomed, therefore, to prevent the disputes which might be raised upon such accounts, I

chose to reduce the substance of the book into the form of propositions in a mathematical way, which should be read by those only who have first made themselves masters of the principles established in the preceding books: not that I would advise anyone to the previous study of every proposition of those books; for they abound with such as might cost too much time even to readers of good mathematical learning...

Newton starts by stating four rules or principles which should be followed by those studying natural philosophy, emphasizing that, as 'Nature is simple and does not indulge in the luxury of superfluous causes', no more causes should be admitted than are both true and sufficient to explain the phenomena [i.e., the experimental findings], and that the evidence so collected should be regarded as true until proved otherwise, and should not be abandoned simply because it conflicts with some theory.

Book 3 is divided roughly into six parts, although it is not formally separated into sections like the two earlier books. The first part contains these four rules. Then comes a second part in which Newton summarizes *the phenomena* [data] which he is concerned to explain: in particular, the motions of the satellites of Jupiter and Saturn and the moon in relation to the earth, and of the planets round the sun. This has been the main topic of mathematical treatment in Book 1 and from it has emerged the universal law of gravity, affecting all the solid bodies in the universe, and manifest as a mutual attraction between any two of them. The laws governing this force are dealt with as 'propositions' [to be tested by further observations in the third section]. They are found to be the same everywhere and for all bodies. This section contains new experimental data on such things as the variability of weight of bodies in different parts of the earth due to small changes in the strength of the force of gravity (what we now term 'g') with height, etc., and consideration of the small variabilities observed in the motions of the moon and the satellites of Jupiter and Saturn.

The fourth section deals with *gravity as a cause of the tides*; and leads naturally into the fifth which describes the results of *Newton's study of the motion of the moon*. He himself felt this study to be incomplete. He said later that trying to sort out the irregularities in the moon's motion was the only thing that had given him a headache! The sixth and last part of the Book was devoted to *the analysis of the great body of data which he had collected on the motion of comets* and the working out of the type of path which they followed, which turned out to be a heliocentric elliptic orbit of the same kind as that followed by the planets of the solar system, but very much more elongated.

The Book abounds in new findings and revolutionary new insights. He demonstrates how to find the masses of the sun and the planets from the mass of the earth, and shows how the earth is flattened at the poles, as are other planets. He shows that the familiar fact that the axis of the earth is tilted so as to make an angle of about 66.5 degrees to the plane in which its orbit lies—something which accounts for the summer and winter seasons in its yearly journey round the sun—means that the equatorial bulge of the earth and the resultant pull of the sun on the part of the bulge which is nearer to it, leads to a slight twisting force which results in what is known as *the precession of the equinoxes*, a very slow wobble which takes about twenty-six thousand years to complete each time. This phenomenon was discovered by Hipparchus in 200 BC. Newton works all this out, and proves that the gravitational pull on the bulge would produce exactly this very slow movement of the direction of the axis as had been observed through the centuries.

Newton added to all this a characteristic proviso (not actually published until the second edition in 1713), refusing to speculate on the cause of the power of gravity, and saying clearly that he did not know how to explain it! This is strongly expressed in a letter to Richard Bentley which he wrote six years after the publication of the first edition of the *Principia*, in which he says:

> You sometimes speak of gravity as essential and inherent to matter. Pray do not ascribe that notion to me; for the cause of gravity is what I do not pretend to know and therefore would take more time to consider of it...

It was in particular the problem of how there could be action-at-a-distance through empty space (and at such enormous distances) which puzzled him and made him suspect the operation of some agent, material or immaterial, mediating the force, as he explains to Bentley in a further letter.

Newton describes the Laws of Motion & the System of the World

> 'Tis inconceivable that inanimate brute matter should (without the mediation of something else which is not material) operate upon and affect other matter without mutual contact; as it must if gravitation in the sense of Epicurus be essential and inherent in it. And this is one reason why I desired you would not ascribe innate gravity to me. That gravity should be innate, inherent and essential to matter so that one body may act upon another at a distance through a vacuum without the mediation of anything else by and through which their action and force may be conveyed from one to another is to me so great an absurdity that I believe no man who has in philosophical matters any competent faculty of thinking can ever fall into it. Gravity must be caused by an agent acting constantly according to certain laws, but whether this agent be material or immaterial is a question I have left to the consideration of my readers.

He was to write in the course of the General Scholium, which he added to the second edition of the *Principia*, published in 1713:

> Thus far I have explained the phenomena of the heavens and of our sea by the force of gravity, but I have not yet assigned a cause to gravity... I have not as yet been able to deduce from the phenomena the reason for these properties of gravity, and I do not feign[1] hypotheses.... It is enough that gravity really exists and acts according to the laws which we have explained, and abundantly serves to account for all the motions of the celestial bodies and of our sea.

[1] The Latin word here is *'fingo'*, which may also be translated as 'frame'.

The Spiritual Awakening of Science

It was to be another two hundred years before Einstein offered an adequate but totally unexpected solution to the problem.

12

THE PUBLICATION OF NEWTON'S *PRINCIPIA* AND ITS AFTERMATH

EDMUND HALLEY — who was born on 6th November 1656 and was therefore fourteen years younger than Newton — was the only son of a prosperous soap manufacturer in the City of London, who came from a family in Derbyshire. His father sent him to St Paul's School where he distinguished himself in both classics and mathematics, and he rose to become captain of the school at the age of fifteen.

While still at school, he developed an interest in, and knowledge of, astronomy which remained with him for the rest of his life. He went up to Queen's College, Oxford, as a commoner in 1673 at the age of seventeen, already equipped with a good grasp of Greek, Latin and Hebrew, and with his own collection of astronomical instruments, which he was soon putting to good use. With a twenty-four foot telescope he observed a lunar eclipse on 27th June 1675, while he was at his London home, and in Oxford in July and August of the following year he recorded the occurrence of a remarkable sun spot, and later the occultation of Mars by the moon. All these observations he recorded and reported to the Royal Society where they appeared in the *Transactions*. Before he was twenty the Society had also published his paper on a *Direct and geometrical method of finding the aphelia and the eccentricity of the planets*. The *aphelia* is the point of the orbit furthest from the sun.

From all he had learnt, Halley realized that there were many errors in the data recording the position of the fixed stars. He thought that it was indispensable that these should be corrected, and recognized that to do so there was a need for data to be collected from the Southern Hemisphere to complement what Flamsteed and Helvelius were currently providing from the Northern one. Copernicus had been satisfied to aspire to an accuracy within ten minutes of arc, but with the technical improvements now available, following Huygens' invention of the pendulum clock and the use of a thread from a spider's web as a measuring graticule mounted in the eyepiece of a telescope, combined with a micrometer to adjust the telescope's direction, it was becoming possible to measure a star's position much more precisely, to within a limit of two seconds of arc.

Meanwhile, Halley, during the month of his twentieth birthday, left the University without taking his degree, and travelled to Saint Helena in a ship belonging to the East India Company, which had been asked by Charles II to provide Halley with transport. His father provided him with an annual allowance of £300. He had no elaborate equipment with him and relied on a large five-and-a-half foot sextant to determine the position of the stars relative to the data provided by Tycho Brahe. While he was away, he made a number of important observations but, unfortunately, the climate in Saint Helena was not favourable for astronomical observation. Nonetheless he succeeded during his eighteen months' stay in accurately determining the position of 341 stars and laying the foundation of austral astronomy, as well as making the first complete observation of the transit of Mercury. On his return Flamsteed called him 'the Southern Tycho'. He presented his *Catalogue of the Austral Stars* to the Royal Society on 7th November 1678 and was elected a Fellow three weeks later at the age of twenty-two. 'Austral' means literally 'belonging to the South'. A few days later he was awarded an honorary M.A. at Oxford at the command of the King. His high standing in the Royal Society at this time is shown by the fact that they shortly afterwards sent him to Danzig for six months as arbiter between Hooke and Helvelius in a dispute on the relative merits of telescopic and direct measurements in determining the position of the fixed stars or planets. He shared the observations of Helvelius for over two and a half months and testified to their accuracy.

Towards the end of 1680 he started on a tour of the Continent with a school friend, Robert Nelson, and, while in Calais, caught sight of the great comet which appeared that year and afterwards made observations on it with Cassini in Paris. These were to prove of great value to Newton later in fixing its orbit. He spent most of 1681 in Italy, returning to England in 1682 and getting married to Mary Tooke, the daughter of the Auditor of the Exchequer, who has been described as 'an amiable and attractive woman'.

The Spiritual Awakening of Science

Halley himself was described as thin and of medium height and as someone who always spoke with an unusual sprightliness and vivacity. His disposition was characterized as 'ardent, generous and candid; he was disinterested and upright, genial to his friends, an affectionate husband and father, and was wholly free from rancour or jealousy. He passed a life of almost unprecedented literary and scientific activity without becoming involved in a single controversy; and was rendered socially attractive by his unfailing gaiety... [which was combined] with a mind of extraordinary penetration, compass, and power.' Among his admirers was Peter the Great of Russia, who in 1697, not only consulted him about ship-building and other projects, but admitted him as a friend to dine with him.

Sadly, Halley's father died suddenly and unexpectedly in 1684, leaving Edmund, with a young wife and family to support, in somewhat reduced circumstances. Yet this was at precisely the period when he became deeply involved with Newton's work on gravity. More than anyone (*not* excepting Newton!) he was responsible for the publication of the *Principia*. Dr Glaisher spoke with justice in an address given much later in Cambridge on 19th April 1688 when he said: '...but for Halley, the *Principia* would not have existed'. It was his visit to Newton in August 1684, and the enthusiasm which he showed at the announcement by Newton that he had successfully proved the association of the inverse square law with an elliptical orbit, that directly led to Newton deciding to devote his series of autumn lectures in Cambridge that year to the topic of the

The Publication of Newton's *Principia* and its Aftermath

movement of orbiting bodies. Shown the nine-page text of these lectures on his further visit to Cambridge in December 1684, Halley was the first to recognize the importance of what Newton had now done and to urge him to allow it to be registered with the Royal Society with a view to publication. This new development was reported by Halley on his return to London, and the manuscript of the Cambridge lectures, *De Motu*, was entered in the Society's records early in 1685 by Aston, an old friend of Newton's youth, who was now the Secretary. After this Halley took on the task of liaising with Newton on behalf of the Society for the period of seventeen months, during which he expanded the original text out of all recognition.

Thirteen months later, on 28th April 1686, the completed manuscript of Book 1 was sent to London, with a dedication to the Royal Society. A week before, Halley had prepared the members for it by giving a *Discourse Concerning Gravity* in which he announced (with reckless optimism!) that Newton's work was almost ready for the press. According to Newton's later letter to Halley, written in the summer of 1686, he had enlarged the original lectures into what became Book 1 in the winter of 1685-6. At this time it also contained twenty-two propositions dealing with the motion of bodies in a resisting medium, which he later separated into what became Book 2.

The Society received the manuscript warmly and ordered that a letter of thanks be written to Newton, and that the book was to be put in the hands of Mr Halley to make a report to the Council. As no Council meeting was held for the next three weeks, Halley raised the matter at the Society's meeting on 19th May, where it was voted that the book should be printed forthwith. But the Society had no funds available, and so Halley, already strapped for cash, had to agree to undertake to publish it entirely at his own expense. This was at a time when his reduced circumstances had already compelled him to accept the humble post of clerk to the Royal Society at a salary of £50 per annum.

He wrote to Newton after the meeting:

> Your Incomparable treatise was by Dr Vincent presented to the R. Society on the 28th past, and they were so very sensible of the Great Honour you do them by your Dedication, that they immediately ordered you their most hearty thanks, and that a Councell should be summon'd to consider about the printing thereof; but by reason of the President's attendance upon the King, and the absence of our Vice-President, whom the good weather had drawn out of Town, there has not been any Authentick Councell to resolve what to do in the matter: so that on Wednesday last the Society in their meeting, judging that so excellent a work ought not to have its publication any longer delayd, resolved to print it at their own charge, in a large Quarto, of a fair letter; and that this their resolution should be signified to you and your opinion therin be desired, that so it might be gone about with all speed.

The letter then goes on less happily to deal with another matter that had arisen:

The Publication of Newton's *Principia* and its Aftermath

There is one thing more that I ought to informe you of, viz., that Mr Hook has some pretensions upon the invention of the rule of the decrease of Gravity, being reciprocally as the square of the distances from the Center. He sais you had the notion from him, though he owns the demonstration of the curves generated thereby to be wholly your own; how much of this is so, you know best, as likewise what you have to do in this matter, only Mr Hook seems to expect you should make some mention of him, in the preface, which, it is possible, you may see reason to prefix. I must beg your pardon it is I, that sent you this account, but I thought it my duty to let you know it, that so you may act accordingly; being in myself fully satisfied, that nothing but the greatest Candour imaginable, is to be expected from the person, who of all men has the least need to borrow reputation.

Newton replied to Halley almost immediately with a long letter, describing in detail the history of his discovery and the clear evidence that Hooke was later than both Sir Christopher Wren and himself in knowing about the inverse square law. He had not only demonstrated it in comparing the force of gravity at the earth's surface and the moon, but also calculated it from Kepler's third Law while he was still a student in 1666. Hooke's claim to be the discoverer was therefore negligible and inaccurate, and he was greatly disturbed by it. He ends by informing Halley that he had originally designed the whole work to consist of three books, of which the second is almost ready, having been finished during the last summer, and only requiring copying. But he continues:

The Spiritual Awakening of Science

The third [book] I now design to suppress. Philosophy is such an impertinently litigious lady, that a man had as good be engaged in law suits, as to have to do with her. I found it so formerly, and I am now no sooner come near to her again, but she gives me warning.

The first two books, without the third, will not so well bear the title of *Philosophiae naturalis Principia Mathematica;* and therefore I have altered it to this, *De Motu Corporum libri duo*, but on second thoughts, I retain the former title. It will help the sale of the book, which I ought not to diminish now it is yours...

Before Newton had posted the letter he received a further report (almost certainly from Edward Paget in London) that Hooke was making a stir and demanding that justice be done. This thoroughly exasperated him and he exploded in a postscript, which is longer than the letter, in which he complains bitterly that all Hooke had done was to publish Borelli's hypothesis under his own name, and to now claim that he had done everything but the drudgery of calculation.

> He has done nothing, and yet written in such a way, as if he knew and had sufficiently hinted all but what remained to be determined by the drudgery of calculations and observations, excusing himself from that labour by reason of his other business, whereas he should rather have excused himself by reason of his inability. For it is plain, by his words, he knew not how to go about it. Now is not this very fine? Mathematicians, that find out, settle, and do all the business, must content themselves with being nothing but dry calculators and drudges; and another, that

The Publication of Newton's *Principia* and its Aftermath

does nothing but pretend and grasp at all things, must carry away all the invention, as well of those that were to follow him, and of those that went before. Much after the same manner were his letters writ to me, telling me that gravity, in descent from hence to the centre of the earth, was reciprocally in a duplicate ratio of the altitude, that the figure described by projectiles in this region would be an ellipsis, and that all the motions of the heavens were thus to be accounted for; and this he did in such a way, as if he had found out all, and knew it most certainly. And, upon this information, I must now acknowledge, in print, I had it all from him and so did nothing myself but to drudge in calculating, demonstrating, and writing, upon the inventions of this great man. And yet, after all, the first of those three things he told me is false, and very unphilosophical; the second is as false; and the third was more than he knew, or could affirm me ignorant of by anything that passed between us in our letters...

Halley showed great tact and understanding in the way in which he replied to Newton's letter. Clearly he himself was anxious about Newton's threat to withhold the third book of his *Principia*. He recounts how Hooke had claimed, during the discussions with Wren and himself, that he had demonstrated the inverse square force for the orbits of the planets but that he would keep his demonstration to himself, that others, by trying and failing, should see how difficult the problem was. And even now, says Halley, Hooke does not produce his demonstration, although he knows very well that Newton has presented his to the Royal Society.

The Spiritual Awakening of Science

But now he says, this is but one small part of an excellent system of nature, which he has conceived, but has not yet completely made out, so that he thinks not fit to publish one part without the other. But I have plainly told him, that unless he produce another differing demonstration and let the world judge of it, neither I nor anyone else can believe it.

Nevertheless, Halley goes on, Hooke has been re-presented to Newton in too unfavourable a light. He did not make his claim at the meeting of the Royal Society, but afterwards, when they had adjourned to a coffee house. And Halley concludes by again begging Newton not to withhold his Third Book.

On learning from Halley that Hooke's coffee house claims had been disallowed by the Royal Society, Newton largely recovered his equanimity.

> '... I am very sensible', he replies, 'of the great kindness of the gentlemen of your Society to me, far beyond what I could ever expect or deserve, and I know how to distinguish between their favour and another's humour. Now I understand he was in some respect misrepresented to me, I wish I had spared the postscript to my last...'

He goes on to say that it was indeed Hooke's letter [of 1679] that prompted him to undertake certain calculations which he then threw by, being upon other studies. And he acknowledges that he did learn from Hooke that falling bodies fall to the south-east in our latitude.

'And now having sincerely told the case between Mr

The Publication of Newton's *Principia* and its Aftermath

Hooke and me, I hope I shall be free for the future from the prejudice of his letters. I have considered how best to compose the present dispute, and I think it may be done by the enclosed Scholium to the fourth proposition...'

The Scholium reads: 'The inverse square law of gravity holds in all the celestial motions, as was discovered also independently by my countrymen, Wren, Hooke, and Halley.' This Scholium was obviously written merely for the purpose of putting an end to the controversy. It was not true, and Newton never supposed that it was. A fortnight later he wrote to Halley telling him that he had just discovered a copy of a letter he had written to Huygens years before and which showed that even then he understood the law of gravitation. And to convince Halley of this fact he copies out part of this old letter. He deals again with Hooke's claims, and points out that the year after the date of the letter, Hooke, in a paper on the motion of the earth, declared that he had not determined the degrees by which gravity decreased, and recommends the subject to the prosecution of others. 'So then in this theory I am plainly before Mr Hooke.'

Sullivan sums all this up well:

Newton was not concerned to prove that he was the first man who had hit on the law of the inverse squares, nor even to assert that he was the only man who had shown that such a law would account for the elliptical orbits of planets. As he states in one of his letters, he was inclined to believe that Sir Christopher Wren had obtained this result independently. He made no exclusive claims, although he would probably have been justified in doing so. It was not Hooke's claim to be an independent discoverer [of the inverse square law] that aroused Newton's resentment, but his assertion that Newton was *not* an independent discoverer. The difference between the motives of the two men in this controversy are perfectly obvious. Hooke resents Newton's intellectual superiority. Newton resents the attack on his moral integrity. To Hooke, Newton was a rival; to Newton, Hooke was a nuisance.

From Newton's point of view, Hooke was one of the 'little smatterers in mathematics' whose criticisms arose from their exaggerated sense of their own importance and who desired to assert their self-superiority rather than to understand and appreciate the truth. Hooke's unscrupulousness in pursuing his ambition for fame in his claim for priority in discovering the inverse square law, is well illustrated by the letter dated September 15th 1689, which he subsequently got John Aubrey to send to the Oxford antiquary and historian John à Wood, who was the author of *History and Antiquities of Oxford* and was about to publish a further volume *Athenae Oxonienses*. The letter appears to have been written at Hooke's dictation and has emendations and passages in Hooke's own handwriting. It states that Hooke had communicated to Newton:

> the whole of his Hypothesis, that the gravitation was reciprocal to the square of the distance, which would make the motion in an ellipse, in one of whose foci the sun being placed, the aphelion and perihelion of the planet would be opposite to each other in the same line, which is

The Publication of Newton's *Principia* and its Aftermath

the whole celestial theory, concerning which Mr Newton only made a demonstration, not at all owning, he received the first Intimation of it from Mr Hooke. Likewise Mr Newton has in the same booke printed some other theories and experiments of Mr Hooke's...without acknowledging from whom he had them.

The letter ends:

Mr Wood! This was the greatest discovery in nature, that ever was since the world's creation: it was never so much as hinted by any man before. I know you will doe him right. I hope you may read his hand: I wish he had writ plainer, and afforded a little more paper.

Tuus, J Aubrey

P.S. Before I leave this town I will get of him [i.e. from Hooke] a catalogue of what he hath wrote, and as much of his inventions as I can; but they are many hundreds; he believes not fewer than a thousand. 'Tis such hard matter to get people to do themselves right.

As Sullivan writes: 'This is the letter of a man whose disappointment and envy have made him distinctly unscrupulous, for even Hooke could not have believed what he wrote here. And that he should adopt so surreptitious a method of trying to discredit Newton shows how little confidence he really had in his case.' He remained bitterly resentful of Newton for the rest of his life, as we know from the entries in his private diary.

* * *

The Spiritual Awakening of Science

In retrospect it is now much easier to get a clear idea of the truth about the claims of both Hooke and Newton. The main facts are these. In 1666 Giovanni Alfonso Borelli, Professor of Mathematics at Pisa, published a book, *Theoricae Mediceorum Planetarum,* in which he analysed the movement of the planets round the sun and the smaller planets circling Jupiter and Saturn in terms of impetus and Plutarch's model of the moon as like a stone whirled round in a sling, representing a force attracting the orbiting planet to the central body. We know that John Collins actually sent Newton a copy of Borelli's book five years later in 1671, but Newton had already worked out the inverse square law at Woolsthorpe in 1666 from Kepler's third Law and the formula for the centrifugal endeavour, v^2/r, independently discovered by himself and Huygens.[1]

Hooke's first paper appeared in the same year as Borelli's book was published and is dated 23rd May 1666. It deals (as Borelli does) with how the path of a celestial body, such as the solar planets or the satellites of Jupiter and Saturn, can be bent into a circle or an ellipse by a force attracting it to a centre, but makes no mention of the falling off of the force with distance. Newton was later to write of this and Hooke's further paper that all he had done was to publish Borelli's hypothesis under his own name. In his second paper eight years later in 1674, Hooke proposes what he calls 'a system of the world, differing in many particulars from any yet known' (a doubtful proposition

---

[1] See Chapter 10, page 206, Note 1.

The Publication of Newton's *Principia* and its Aftermath

in view of Borelli's book, let alone Plutarch!). This is 'based on three suppositions: viz., (1) universal gravitation (2) that all bodies move forward in a straight line until they are deflected by some effectual power and sent into a circle, ellipse, or other more complicated curve; and (3) that these forces are strongest at short distances and fall off in strength as the distance is increased.' But he does not say in this paper how much the force must vary with distance to account for the planetary orbits. Even when he republished this same paper five years later in his collected volume of *Lectiones Cutlerianae* (1679) he writes of the third supposition 'That these attractive powers are so much the more powerful in operating, by how much nearer the body wrought upon is to their own Centers... [but] what these several degrees are I have not yet experimentally verified...'

Newton himself gives credit to Hooke's letters of 1679 as having stimulated him to look again at the problem, which led him to actually calculate the dependence of the *elliptical* planetary orbits on an inverse square centripetal force. But even in 1684, Hooke was still only making unsubstantiated boasts that he had done the same but would keep it secret, so that when he revealed it, people would know how to value it! The value of what Hooke had written was accurately assessed by the French scientist, Clairaut, in the eighteenth century, when he said that it 'served to show what a distance there is between a truth that is glimpsed and a truth that is demonstrated'!

Derek Whiteside, the modern authority on Newton's mathematical papers, appraises Hooke's achievement in these words:

The Spiritual Awakening of Science

In England, supremely, Hooke had over twenty years developed his researches into a loose gathering of all the constituents (elliptical planetary orbits round the sun at a focus, deflection of the planet into its orbit from a linear inertial by a gravitational pull to the sun varying instantaneously as the inverse square of the solar distance) with the exception of Kepler's true areal law — and knowledge, if not acceptance, of that too was becoming increasingly widespread. Unfortunately, too, for Hooke, the ultimate fusion needed a mathematical insight surpassing his moderate talents in that field — a point judiciously if heavily made by Newton when he later recalled his own triumph for Halley.

* * *

Hooke's rancour seems to have had unpleasant repercussions for the unfortunate Halley within the Royal Society, at a difficult time while he was trying to get the *Principia* published. Newton finished the manuscript of Book 2 sometime in the winter of 1686-7, but meanwhile the process of publication in London had come to a halt. On 29th November 1686, the Council suddenly resolved that Halley's continuance in office should be put to a vote and that a new election should be held for a clerk to replace him. This was the day before the Annual General Meeting where elections were being held, and Hooke was elected onto the Council at that meeting. On 5th January 1687, the Council appointed a committee to investigate Halley's performance of his duties. At the same meeting they invited Hooke to submit a proposal to supply meetings with experiments and discourses, for which, of course, he would be paid. The investigating committee reported in Halley's favour on 9th February, saying that the society's books and papers were 'in a very good condition'. Writing to Newton that month, Halley told him that '6 of 38, last generall Election day, did their endeavour to have me put by'.

Halley, now relatively secure in his post again, immediately wrote to Newton for a copy of a sheet of the manuscript lost by the printer, saying that he was going to push forward with the publication towards completion. He received Book 2 from Newton early in March. To his surprise it turned out to be as long as the first book! At this stage he did not know if there was to be a Book 3, but wrote hopefully to Newton:

> You mention in this second [book] your third Book *de Systemate mundi*, which from such firm principles, as in the preceding you have laid down, cannot chuse but give universall satisfaction; if this be likewise ready, and not too long to be got printed at the same time, and you think fit to send it; I will endeavour by a third hand to get it all done togather, being resolved to engage on no other business till such time as all is done: desiring herby to clear myself of all imputations of negligence, in a business, wherin I am much rejoyced to be in any wais concerned in handing to the world that that all future ages will admire.

Halley had already employed a second printer to work on Book 2. In the event, the first printer had nearly finished setting up the first Book in print by the time the third Book arrived a month later, so that it was given to him to do.

The Spiritual Awakening of Science

Halley wrote to tell Newton that he had received the third part of his 'divine Treatise' in April 1687.

Halley's life was still being made difficult by influences emanating from within the Royal Society's Council, which on 15th June 1687, passed a vote to pay Halley the £50 due to him for 1686, but on the same day voted further to pay Hooke before it paid anyone else. The Society was out of funds, many of the members having become lax in paying their subscriptions and worse was to come. In July they offered to pay them both with fifty copies of the Book on the *History of Fishes*, the publication of which had recently landed the Society in financial difficulties.[1] In the end it turned out that Halley remained unpaid until October 1690, when he was paid only for the salary earned in 1687 and subsequent years.

The year Halley spent in setting the *Principia* up in print 'costs me a great deal of time and paines' (as he wrote when excusing himself for other jobs postponed or not done). As well as correcting the proofs of the text, all the diagrams had to be set up from woodcuts. Section 9 in Book 1 on the motion of apsides gave him 'extraordinary difficulty' and he feared it might have to be reset. But on 5th July 1687 Halley was able to write and tell Newton that the book was finished. With this letter he sent him twenty copies 'to bestow on your friends in the University'.

---

[1] See A. Tinniswood, *His Invention So Fertile: A Life of Christopher Wren*, London: Cape, 2001, pp 256-259. Wren became President of the Society in January 1681 and set about trying to reform the finances, but it proved a very slow process.

The Publication of Newton's *Principia* and its Aftermath

Thus the *Principia* was published in midsummer 1687, twenty-one years after the two-year period at Woolsthorpe when the apple fell, and then, only thanks to the benevolent urging and tactful persuasion of Halley, who himself paid for its publication and saw it through the press. The price unbound was six shillings or five shillings for ready money. Halley sent Newton forty copies for sale by the Cambridge booksellers. The first edition was sold out very quickly.

It brought Newton great fame, but many people, including expert mathematicians, found his book difficult to understand. Dr Babington, Newton's colleague at Trinity College, said that some parts of it readers 'might study seven years, before they understood anything of it', and a Cambridge student who passed Newton on the street was heard to remark: 'there goes the man that hath writt a book that neither he nor anyone else understands'! A very competent French mathematician, De Moivre, 'found much of it beyond his comprehension at first reading, and therefore bought a copy which he tore into sheets and carried a few of them in his pocket at a time, so that he could study them whenever he had leisure'. Another good mathematician from France, the Marquis de l'Hôpital, is said to have cried out in admiration on examining *Principia*: 'Good God! What a fund of knowledge there is in that book!' He then asked for every particular that was known concerning Sir Isaac, even down to the colour of his hair, and asked: 'Does he eat and sleep and is he like other men?' He was surprised when Dr Arbuthnot, who had introduced him to the book, told him that Newton conversed cheerfully with his friends, assumed nothing and put himself upon a level with all mankind. Many years later, in old age, he wanted to meet Newton, but died before he could do so.

Two further editions of the *Principia* appeared with corrections and revisions agreed or suggested by Newton himself. Newton entrusted the job of editing it for the press to his brilliant young protégé, Roger Cotes, who, in October 1707, had been elected at the age of twenty-five to be the first Plumian Professor of Astronomy and Experimental Philosophy in Cambridge. The second edition in 1713 has a number of important additions, including the long final General Scholium. Sadly, Cotes died at the early age of thirty-four, shortly after the book's appearance. Newton said of him: 'If Mr Cotes had lived we might have known something.' The printing of a third edition, seen through the press by another friend of Newton's, the much younger physician, Henry Pemberton, began in 1723. It was eventually published in March 1726, less than a year before Newton's death.

It took about fifty years before people began to understand him and the point of view that he took; in particular, his insistence on clearly distinguishing between experimental data gleaned from careful observation (*'phenomena'* as he called them) and *hypotheses* formulated to explain them. Thus a reviewer writing in an eminent French journal commented: 'The work of Mr Newton is the most perfect treatise on mechanics that can be imagined, it

The Publication of Newton's *Principia* and its Aftermath

not being possible to provide more precise or more exact demonstrations than those which he gives... but these demonstrations are mechanical only' and he quotes in evidence Newton's cautious remark that 'Here I design only to give mathematical notions of those forces, without considering their physical causes and seats.' The same critic goes on to say that in the third Book he has shown how the tides could be caused by the pull of the sun and the moon, but that he had not actually proved that the attraction existed!

As time went on, he was more fully understood. Voltaire, who was among the first from abroad to fully recognize Newton's genius, remarked: 'Before Kepler, all men were blind. Kepler had one eye, Newton had two.' By the time D'Alembert contributed his *Histoire des sciences* to the *Encyclopédie* in 1751, he was dismissing Cartesian vortices as ridiculous and speaking of Newton's work as having 'given philosophy a form which it is apparently to keep'. Laplace (1749-1827), the celebrated French mathematician and astronomer, wrote some years later that 'The *Principia* is pre-eminent above any other production of human genius.'

Writing from a contemporary twentieth century standpoint Sir Hermann Bondi praises Newton's achievement in the *Principia* in particular for the brilliant way he selected a problem which was soluble.[1] He points out that:

---

[1] Sir Hermann Bondi, 'Newton and the twentieth century – a personal view' in *Let Newton Be!* pp 241-248.

if you talk about the problems which you meet when you walk about the street, 80 per cent of them are insoluble while 19½ per cent of them are trivial. It is the task of the scientist to select the tiny layer between the insoluble and the trivial, where skill, insight, originality, creativity and application can make a difference. The difficulty of finding this layer is often overlooked...

Newton solved the problem of the movement of bodies in the solar system so totally that not much was left for others to do. In general, the rails of thinking in physics and astronomy tend to be still very much those that Newton laid down...[but]...It took a long time before one began to understand — and the understanding is not yet universal — that his genius *selected* an area where such perfection of solution was possible.

This is misleading (says Bondi) because most of science is not concerned with things like the Newtonian solar system, but with things more like weather forecasting!

Bondi points out that the influence and importance of most scientific papers can be gauged by how often they are cited in other people's publications. Some discoveries are so important that the names of those responsible are perpetuated in scientific language by being associated with units or processes, as in the case of Newton himself — a *newton*, N, is now the unit of force in the international system, equal to the amount of force needed to accelerate a mass of one kilogram by one metre per second. There are many other examples, such as *Ampere, Farad(ay), Galvani(sm), Joule, Ohm* and *Volt(a)*.

The Publication of Newton's *Principia* and its Aftermath

But with the greatest scientific advances there comes a final stage when it is so difficult to imagine what the world was like before it was made that one can hardly get the contribution into perspective... The landscape has been so totally changed, and the ways of thinking have been so deeply affected by Newton that it is very hard for us to realize how total a change he produced[1].

It should be added here that Newton himself would have been among the first to recognize the limitation regarding his achievements in the *Principia* which Bondi speaks of. Indeed his final summing up of his own achievements as like those of a boy picking up a few shells on the sea-shore 'while the great ocean of truth lay undiscovered before him' makes that abundantly clear. It is also worth remembering that much more of his time and interest were given, not to his fruitful studies in physics, but to his much less productive studies in chemistry, his wide-ranging observations into the mechanism whereby nature brought about 'transformations' in living things, to world-history and theological studies. Among one of the last things he interested himself in was electricity. None of these areas was yet ready for a great advance. But he was interested in every aspect of a world, which he saw as the creation of an omnipresent and all-powerful God. As he wrote to Dr Bentley:

When I wrote my treatise about our Systeme I had an eye

---

[1] See Bondi in *Let Newton Be!, op. cit.,* p 242.

The Spiritual Awakening of Science

upon such Principles as might work with considering men for the beleife of a Deity and nothing can rejoyce me more then to find it usefull for that purpose. But if I have done the publick any service that way 'tis due to nothing but industry and a patient thought.

A Foreword contributed by Albert Einstein to a modern reprint of Newton's *Optics*, published in 1931 by G. Bell and Son: London.

FORTUNATE Newton, happy childhood of science! He who has time and tranquillity can by reading this book live again the wonderful events which the great Newton experienced in his young days. Nature to him was an open book, whose letters he could read without effort. The conceptions which he used to reduce the material of experience to order seemed to flow spontaneously from experience itself, from the beautiful experiments which he ranged in order like playthings and describes with an affectionate wealth of detail. In one person he combined the experimenter, the theorist, the mechanic and, not least, the artist in exposition. He stands before us strong, certain, and alone: his joy in creation and his minute precision are evident in every word and in every figure.

Reflexion, refraction, the formation of images by lenses, the mode of operation of the eye, the spectral decomposition and the recomposition of the different kinds of light, the invention of the reflecting telescope, the first foundations of colour theory, the elementary theory of the rainbow pass by us in procession, and finally come his observations of the colours of thin films as the origin of the next great theoretical advance, which had to await, over a hundred years, the coming of Thomas Young.

Newton's age has long since been passed through the sieve of oblivion, the doubtful striving and suffering of his generation has vanished from our ken; the works of some

The Spiritual Awakening of Science

few great thinkers and artists have remained, to delight and ennoble us and those who come after us. Newton's discoveries have passed into the stock of accepted knowledge: this new edition of his work on optics is nevertheless to be welcomed with warmest thanks, because it alone can afford us the enjoyment of a look at the personal activity of this unique man.

ALBERT EINSTEIN

13

THE VITAL SPARK

WE TAKE so much of our modern knowledge of the world and nature for granted that it is difficult for us to put ourselves in the position of those who lived in earlier ages. But even today, what is now common knowledge among experts is scarcely understood by more than relatively few of us, and then only in fields in which we have taken a particular interest.

Consider then, for a moment, how little there was in the experience of our ancestors to acquaint them with the existence of electricity, let alone to provide them with any understanding of its nature. It would surely be true to say that, until relatively recently in history, it manifested itself in only a few rare and incomprehensible phenomena, which were not even connected with each other in any obvious way.

There were, for instance, the occasional sparks experienced by some individuals, often in hot, dry weather, when they touched certain things or combed their hair. They were probably largely ignored or discounted as too unimportant to be worth noticing, or else regarded with awe as psychic phenomena.

Then there was the mysterious and puzzling behaviour of amber, known even to the ancient Greeks, which, when

The Spiritual Awakening of Science

rubbed, could attract light objects, causing feathers, hairs, or small fragments of paper or other objects to dance about and stick to it as if they had suddenly become alive and imbued with the power of movement. This certainly intrigued people who came across it or had it demonstrated to them, and was regarded as mysterious.

Another even stranger, less widely known, and apparently totally unrelated, fact was the strange power of the torpedo fish to stun its prey, a fact known to the Romans and used by them medicinally as a way of relieving headache or the pain of childbirth. Outside the apothecary's shop in Pompeii were found (preserved by the eruption of Vesuvius, which largely destroyed the city) a series of beautifully painted tiles advertising the wares sold within the shop, and one of these shows the Mediterranean torpedo fish, strongly suggesting that it was one of the regular therapeutic agents sold inside. And there are also actual accounts of its use by Scribonius Largus and Pliny in the first century AD, describing how, in the treatment, the two ends of the fish are to be placed across the brows of the patient 'until their senses are benumbed'. The fish was used in this way either to ease labour pains during childbirth or to treat bad headaches. Since, when applied in this way, we now know that the fish is capable of delivering a very effective high-voltage shock of as much as 100-150 volts at high amperage (a talent it uses in its natural life to stun its prey!) it must, as Professor John Fulton has pointed out[1], have been quite capable of making the patient

[1] John Fulton *The Frontal Lobes and Human Behaviour*, Sherrington Lectures 1952, Liverpool: University Press.

The Vital Spark

totally oblivious of his headache This was effectively a Roman version of what we now call electro-shock therapy (or ECT), used about two thousand years before it was re-introduced in 1936, by an Italian doctor from Rome called Cerletti, as a supposedly entirely new method of treatment for relieving certain psychiatric symptoms. Of course, the medical profession now uses modern technology to generate the shock, but the principle is exactly the same. It is not surprising that these relatively few scattered examples of electrical events should not have given anyone the idea of how intimately our whole life and world is bound up with things electrical.

Then, in about the eleventh century, the Chinese discovered the usefulness of a small pivoted magnet or lodestone for navigation. The lodestone (a magnetic stone containing iron oxide) pointed towards the lodestar — the pole-star as we call it — and enabled ships to determine where the North was. This Chinese discovery was introduced into Europe by Muslim sailors a century later.

The first stirrings of scientific thought began in the twelfth and thirteenth centuries, largely as a result of the translation of works from Greek and Arab thinkers like al-Hazen and others.[1] One of the writers of the thirteenth century, Peter de Maricourt, wrote an *Epistola de magnete*, and much influenced his contemporary, Roger Bacon (c.1220-1292), who is often regarded as among the first scientists. Roger Bacon and Robert Grosseteste (c.1175-1253) were also very interested in optics and wrote on the subject.

[1] See Copleston, *op. cit.*, Vol. 2, pp 228-232 and Vol. 3, pp 156-157.

The Spiritual Awakening of Science

Writing in the thirteenth century, the great mystic poet Rumi speaks of amber and the magnet as analogues of the intense relationship between the lover and the beloved object. As he writes:

> Visit once a week is not the ration for lovers; the soul of the sincere lovers has an intense craving to drink .... To the lover one moment of separation is as a year.[1]
>
> The gist is that whenever any one seeks, the soul of the object sought by him is desiring him.
>
> Whether it be man, animal, plant, or mineral, every object of desire is in love with everything that is without (has not attained to) the object of desire.
>
> Those who are without their object of desire attach themselves to an object of desire, and those desired ones draw them (on).
>
> But the desire of the lovers make them lean (while) the desire of the loved ones makes them fair and beauteous.
>
> The love of the loved ones illumines the cheeks; the love of the lover consumes his soul.
>
> The amber loves (the straw) with the appearance of wanting naught, while the straw is making efforts (to advance) on that long road.[2]
>
> Everything in the world draws something (to itself): infidelity draws the infidel and righteousness him who is guided aright. There is both the amber and the magnet (lodestone); whether thou art iron or straw thou wilt come to the hook (thou wilt be attracted);

---

[1] *Masnavi*, VI 2071, 2074.   [2] *Masnavi*, III 4442-4447.

The Vital Spark

The magnet carries thee off if thou art iron; and if thou art straw, thou wilt be in contact with the amber.[1]

About 400 years after this, William Gilbert, a personal physician to Queen Elizabeth, wrote a book in Latin called *De magnete*, published in 1600, collecting the little that was then known about magnetism, including Peter de Maricourt's *Epistola de magnete*. It was he who first introduced the word 'electricity', derived from the Greek word 'elektrou', meaning amber. But if you had tried to suggest to anyone at this time that the whole universe was composed of electromagnetic radiation, they would not have had the vaguest idea of what you were talking about, and could only have dismissed what you were saying as the incoherent ravings of a madman.

Gilbert recognized that the earth itself was a great magnet and that the lodestone compass pointing north was due to this property. He studied electricity and thought it a fluid. He recognized the difference between conductors and insulators, but misunderstood them. One class of objects (such as glass, sulphur and resin) were attracted to the amber after it was rubbed; these he called 'electrics'. The other class of objects (such as copper or silver articles) acquired no such power after rubbing and were called 'non-electrics' by him.

Apart from all these rare and apparently unconnected phenomena, there was, however, one thing that everyone knew and feared from time immemorial, and that was

[1] *Masnavi*, IV 1633-1635.

lightning. But this was certainly not something which was connected with any of the other examples which have been mentioned. Nor was there any reason at all to connect it and them to a common cause.

The awe-inspiring occurrence of thunder and lightning could occur suddenly and unexpectedly in a thunderstorm and strike no one could predict where. It often killed instantly those whom it struck down and set fire to trees or houses without warning, and it was viewed almost universally by mankind with fear and terror. For many hundreds, if not thousands, of years, it was generally felt that these phenomena could only be a manifestation of the intervention of higher powers. It was regarded in the ancient world, for instance, as a manifestation of Jove wielding his 'oak-cleaving thunder-bolts', or the Nordic God, Donner, smiting with his mighty supernatural hammer.

Even in Shakespeare's time, a mere 400 years ago, there was still this feeling that thunderstorms were, in some way, Acts of God, outside the ordinary course of Nature. This was certainly the popular view of such things, even if it was not shared by the more sophisticated. And, on these grounds, they were often felt to be portents of mighty and exceptional events — indicative, in some way, of divine intervention in the ordinary course of Nature.

In this scientific age we have some difficulty in recognizing the superstitious awe with which such phenomena were then viewed, but Shakespeare reminds us of it continually in his plays, written only four centuries ago. It was expected that exceptional events would be mirrored in exceptional events to be seen in the heavens above us, as we learn, for instance when Caesar's wife Calpurnia says:

> When beggars die there are no comets seen,
> The heavens themselves blaze forth the death of princes!

Lightning was therefore connected in the popular imagination with the supernatural and particularly the powers of darkness. The three witches in *Macbeth*, ask each other as they part:

> When shall we three meet again
> In thunder, lightning or in rain?

And the third verse of the dirge in *Cymbeline* recognizes them as a source of universal fear and anxiety:

> Fear no more the lightning flash,
> Nor the all-dreaded thunder-stone,
> Fear not slander, censure rash;
> Thou hast finished joy and moan;
> All lovers young, all lovers must
> Consign to thee, and come to dust.

Prospero asks his servant Ariel at the beginning of the last play:

>   Hast thou, spirit,
> Performed to point the tempest that I bade thee?

To which Ariel answers:

> To every article....
>   Jove's lightnings, the precursors

The Spiritual Awakening of Science

> O' th' dreadful thunder-claps, more momentary
> And sight-outrunning were not; the fire and cracks
> Of sulphurous roaring the most mighty Neptune
> Seem to besiege, and make his bold waves tremble,
> Yea, his dread trident shake.

Ariel goes on to describe to Prospero those on the ship, including Ferdinand, jumping into the foaming water, crying: 'Hell is empty, And all the devils here.'

King Lear, wandering out into the storm, sees it first as an instrument to bring retribution for the ingratitude of man, and in particular to his daughters!

> You sulph'rous and thought-executing fires,
> Vaunt couriers of oak-cleaving thunderbolts,
> Singe my white head! And thou, all-shaking thunder,
> Strike flat the thick rotundity o' the world,
> Crack Nature's moulds, all germens spill at once
> That make ingrateful man.

And later he makes it clear that lightning is to be seen as an instrument of the wrath and justice of heaven, a punishment for wrong-doing:

> Let the great gods,
> That keep this dreadful pudder o'er our heads,
> Find out their enemies now. Tremble, thou wretch
> That hast within thee undivulgèd crimes
> Unwhipped of justice....

All this is not simply a flight of fancy or a poetic

The Vital Spark

exaggeration on Shakespeare's part. It was a matter of widespread belief in his day and later. The writer remembers reading the inscription on the old market cross in Devizes, put up by the local council for the edification of the God-fearing inhabitants of that market town in Wiltshire. It tells the story of a woman who stole some money from someone else while working in the market. She came under suspicion and was challenged, upon which she vehemently denied the charge and said 'she wished that she might be struck down by lightning if she had done it', whereupon she was then and there struck down by a flash of lightning, to serve as an example to all of the swift retribution to be expected for wrong-doing. In this hard-boiled age we are not inclined to see lightning as an effective instrument of divine justice any more. The Americans, anyway, prefer to rely on the more dependable Electric Chair!

But even if lightning was a familiar experience throughout the history of mankind, the central role of electricity in the universe has been something totally unrecognized and unconceived of, let alone understood, for the great majority of the time. These few phenomena that we now recognize to be electrical, may not have been totally unknown to man, but they were not understood or connected. On the contrary, no one had the faintest idea of what they were dealing with.

It was Benjamin Franklin in the eighteenth century who finally deprived the lightning of its mystery by studying the matter scientifically, and showing, by flying his kite during a storm, that it was an electrical discharge which could be earthed. He believed that electricity was an invisible fluid which probably existed everywhere and could accumulate and be discharged through a suitable conductor. He also helped to tame its menace by inventing the lightning conductor.

Apart from thunder and lightning there were also other rare meteorological phenomena which people encountered with a mixture of fear and wonder. One such was the *aurora borealis* or 'Northern (or Southern) Lights'. This extraordinary and spectacular show of flickering lights in the Northern night sky was called 'streamers' or 'merry dancers' by the common people and regarded by many with awe. They were no doubt regarded as an omen of good or ill luck by many, and like the appearance of comets, were often thought of as a manifestation of the supernatural powers at play. To the poet they meant something beautiful but fleeting and insubstantial. Robert Burns compared the transience of all worldly pleasures to these momentarily appearing and disappearing coloured lights, when he wrote that they were 'like the borealis race, That flit ere you can point their place'. The Northern Lights were first studied scientifically by John Dalton in 1787, and clearly recognized by him to be electrical phenomena appearing between 100 and 150 miles above the earth's surface. They are now known to be due to the arrival of showers of cosmic particles within the strong magnetic field at the North and South Poles.

Most of the examples mentioned have concerned what

The Vital Spark

we should now call electrostatic charges. It was only in the late eighteenth and early nineteenth century that the notions of electric currents flowing from one point to another began to be investigated. It was not really until the time of Michael Faraday in the early nineteenth century that it began to be apparent that electricity was a powerful and substantial force which could drive motors and which entered intimately into the chemical reactions in which substances were formed and transformed. Now, just 100 years later and 400 years after Gilbert's book was published, we recognize, as a result of such scientific giants as Clerk Maxwell, Hertz, Rutherford and many others, that our whole universe is actually composed of nothing else but electromagnetic radiation, of which light, as we know it, is one small part. Even on a more practical everyday level, electricity and its properties now dominate our life as a result of our deeper understanding of it, and modern society could not function without telephones, radio and television, lasers, electric clocks and watches, not to mention computers.

The yogis tell us that much the same all-encompassing role is equally true, at a more fundamental level, of life and consciousness. As Marjorie Waterhouse puts it in a brief, but pregnant, remark in *Training the Mind through Yoga*:

> The attitude of the man-in-the-street towards his real Self is rather like our attitude towards the force of electricity. Electricity has presumably been a fact since the world began, and it is now held to be at the root of the Universe, yet no one knows its true nature, and a [few] hundred years ago no one even knew of its existence. To the

majority it still only spells light, warmth and motion, but it is none of these things. They are only manifestations of a fragment of its power. In the same way, man loves, he creates, he acts, he grieves, but these activities are not his real Self, they are not a full manifestation of Spirit, they are only indications of its presence. Man himself, as Spirit, encloses *maya*—time, space and the cosmos—but he is other than these....

Compare the occurrence of life

To the materialist, life is an unimportant chance development in a tiny and unimportant corner of the universe, found (as far as we know) only on one insignificant planet on the outer edge of our galaxy. And mind is a still more fragmentary development of the evolutionary series in man. Under these circumstances, we shall probably be told, the idea that consciousness is immanent in all creation is laughable and must be dismissed as a ridiculous myth, just as the idea of the whole objective universe being made of electromagnetic energy would have been by the Elizabethans.

The typical view of one scientifically enlightened philosopher of the twentieth century can be illustrated by a passage from Bertrand Russell:

> As geological time is reckoned, man has so far existed only for a very short period—1,000,000 years at the most. What he has achieved, especially during the last 6,000 years, is something utterly new in the history of the Cosmos so far, at least as we are acquainted with it. For countless ages the sun rose and set, the moon waxed and waned, the stars

The Vital Spark

shone in the night, but it is only with the coming of Man that these things were understood. In the great world of astronomy and in the little world of the atom, Man has unveiled secrets which might have been thought undiscoverable. In art and literature and religion, some men have shown a sublimity of feeling which makes the species worth preserving...[1]

The underlying assumption of this view is that consciousness is a new and isolated phenomenon, appearing by chance in a vast physical universe totally devoid of consciousness, and characteristic only of an isolated local evolutionary development, apparently random and by chance, first of life, and then of man, in a small, unimportant planet at the periphery of one particular galaxy out of literally millions of others. It seems a bit like the attitude of people towards the fleeting appearance of the *aurora borealis,* before Dalton started investigating it scientifically. The development of life and consciousness and our ability to understand the world, we are told, was just a strange, inexplicable event, which had happened by chance in an out-of-the-way corner of a totally inanimate and unconscious universe—as 'something utterly new in the history of the Cosmos'. One must admit that Russell at least has the grace to add here the proviso 'so far at least as we are acquainted with it'.

And this seems just as well, for, among the many things that we know about the Cosmos is that there are literally many millions of other galaxies, and that we don't even

[1] *Portraits from Memory*, London: George Allen & Unwin, 1958, pp. 232-233.

The Spiritual Awakening of Science

have the faintest idea whether life exists elsewhere in our own galaxy, let alone in any other of those further away. We also know that our sun is only an insignificant star on the outer periphery of the Catherine wheel which is our Milky Way with its myriads of stars. Even statistically, it seems to be pushing things a bit far to suggest seriously that life on earth is likely to be unique!

When we consider the size of the known cosmos in relation to our own empirical existence, the physical conditions for life as we know it to exist *do* seem to be relatively unusual. Even in our own solar system, there is only one planet with conditions at present optimal enough to support life as we know it, and we ourselves have difficulty in surviving in the Antarctic or the desert on our own planet, so that hundreds of thousands of our fellow human beings on this tiny earth are subject to life-threatening famines and droughts. But there are literally thousands of millions of stars like the sun even in our own local galaxy, as well as thousands of millions of other galaxies which we can see spread out as far as the most powerful telescopes can reach, and there is anyway no reason to think that life as we know it is the only form in which life and consciousness can manifest itself.

But, apart from all this, there is an even more striking possibility that we meet if we turn to the teachings of the yogis and the mystics of the West. And it is their insistence on the fact that consciousness is the very stuff from which the entire universe is created, that the absolute reality, the Being from which our world of multiplicity, change and

The Vital Spark

becoming is empirically created, is in its very nature Existence, Consciousness and Bliss *(sat, chit, ananda)*.

The manifestations of life seem at first sight to be rather like the extremely rare manifestations of electricity which were known to our ancestors—the occasional display of lightning, the magnetic phenomena associated with rubbed amber, the strange power of the torpedo fish to stun its prey and (more recently) the mariner's compass. But we now know that electricity is not only all around us, but that the whole of the physical universe is a product of electromagnetic force and nothing else.

So the advent of life and consciousness appears on superficial examination as a rare and random event in the world, only encountered late in the evolution of higher forms of life on our particular planet. But, as in the case of electricity, it is, say the yogis, the stuff of which all experience is woven and it is as immanent in the world of so-called inanimate nature as in ourselves. What we are pleased to call the non-living and inanimate world of nature is as much a phenomenal evolute of the creative power of consciousness as is the world of living things. To use a simile given by Swami Rama Tirtha, the consciousness hidden in the physical world is like the light of the sun shining on the vast, silent fields of ice and snow on the Himalayan peaks. It is immanent or hidden in the whole of so-called inanimate creation, but not evident because there is no clear reflection of the sun in the frozen snow-fields. The individualized consciousness only becomes fully manifest in the self-conscious individual through the progressive awakening process in nature when the ice melts under the heat of the sun and becomes clear water. Self-consciousness appears in the course of evolutionary development with the appearance of the antahkarana or inner organ of experience in the brains of the higher animals and man. The sun is clearly reflected in the melted water contained in the pot.

If this is so, then, just as the lower knowledge of the world of nature, the sphere of relativity within time, space and causation, has been revolutionized by our understanding of the fundamental role of electromagnetic energy in its make-up, so the higher knowledge of the role of the transcendent Consciousness in the stream of experience can revolutionize our understanding of our own experience. But this is not simply a matter of theory. Yoga promises us a means by which we can realize this true Self of ours through experimentally verifying it in our own experience.

Even the man-in-the-street has a few experiences which point towards this truth, although he does not credit them with much importance. They are like the occasional sparks which, when understood, bear testimony to the ubiquitous presence and importance of electricity.

One of George Washington's Rules of Civility and Decent Behaviour was: 'Labour to keep alive in your breast that little spark of celestial fire, called conscience.' And the great figures in early Christianity used to talk of the divine spark hidden within the personality of each and every man. They called it the *scintilla conscientiae* or *synderesis/synteresis* [which literally means, that which carefully keeps guard

The Vital Spark

and watches over the individual and guides his conduct. It was a faculty which passed judgement both on the acts which one was thinking of doing and also those which one had already committed *(synethesis)*]. This divine spark was spoken of originally by St Jerome, St Thomas and St Albert the Great as the power of conscience existing in all men which admonishes them of the good and opposes evil.[1]

The word scintilla comes from the same root from which we get the word scintillating. And this 'inner light' was seen as something which continually gives out flashes or sparks of light in the surrounding darkness. One might say it was rather like the guiding light from his home glimpsed from afar through the trees by some late traveller returning through the dark forest—seen, now more clearly, now less so, so that our view of it is intermittent and uncertain and yet clearly indicative of the right direction in which we must go and beckoning us onwards.

Such is the Inner Light, 'that of Christ in every man' of which the Christian mystics speak, 'the Buddha nature' within the heart, 'the face that you had before you were born', as the Zen tradition puts it.

From the point of view of the ordinary man, we can legitimately say that all this talk about the divine spark of conscience in his own experience may seem pretty insignificant, like the occasional sparks experienced by our ancestors when they were still ignorant of any real

[1] F.C. Copleston, *A History of Philosophy*, Burns Oates & Washbourne, 1953, Vol. 3, pp 201-202.

knowledge of electricity, let alone the important and all-embracing role it played in the constitution of the physical world and their own bodies and brains.

But the mystics insist that exactly the same is true of our life and conscious experience. On the spiritual plane this is the clue to the reality which creates and sustains the whole world. This is not only a doctrine of the Vedanta. Meister Eckhart, one of the greatest of the Catholic mystics, who lived in Germany in the thirteenth century, says that:

> God created all things, not to stand outside Himself, like other craftsmen, but he called them from nothingness, that is from non-existence, to existence, which they found and received and had in Him for He himself is existence.[1]

This is exactly what Vedanta says in describing the nature of the absolute as Existence (*sat*). As Eckhart puts it, 'outside God there is nothing, inasmuch as it would be outside existence'. He also says that 'creation is a work of God who is outside time' and that speaking of it as occurring 'in the beginning' simply means 'in Himself', for He creates Time too and for Him there is no past or future. It is for this reason that He is called 'the first and the last'. Creation takes place in the indivisible 'now' of eternity, says Eckhart. It is worth remembering these words of Eckhart, written so many hundreds of years ago before we knew anything of modern physics, when one reads the accounts of the Big Bang in Stephen Hawking's *Brief History of Time*.

---

[1] Copleston, *op. cit.*, pp 187-188.

The Vital Spark

But Eckhart has an even more striking echo of the Vedantic truth that the supreme reality is of the nature of both existence and consciousness when he says that God's nature is One and Unnumbered in that He understands or comprehends in one perfect unity of experience the whole of the multiplicity of the created things. This characteristic is, Eckhart maintains, more fundamental even than existence. Consciousness (*chit*) is more fundamental than mere existence (*sat*). And he points out that St John says that 'In the beginning was the Word and the Word was God' and not 'In the beginning was being and the being was God.'[1]

Just as the clues to electricity were there, even before their significance was realized, so the verse from the *Upanishad* says: 'The Self is the clue to this all for by it one knows this all.' In other words, just as the spark is a tiny clue to the existence of electricity, which turns out not only to be intimately involved in everything in the universe, but to be the very thing out of which the whole universe is made, so 'the [conscious] Self in the individual is the clue to the spiritual reality underlying the whole universe, for by investigating it one comes to know the nature of this reality'. This is the message of the Yoga, and its practice provides the means for achieving it.

Shri Shankara speaks of this process in his commentary on the *Bhagavad Gita* when he says that at the outset the self appears as the relatively insignificant individual identified

---

[1] Copleston, *op. cit.*, p 184.

with a particular body and mind, but that it turns out, when its nature has been fully realized, to be none other than the Supreme Reality, lying behind the whole universe.

Christ hints at this discovery when he speaks towards the end of his empirical life of returning 'to the glory that I had with Thee, O Father, before this world began'. And Jesus also speaks of the point of creation in terms which remind one of Eckhart's contention that God creates the world and time in the 'now' of eternity, when he says: 'Before Abraham was, I am.' He does not say: 'Before Abraham was, I was' because, as Eckhart points out, for God there is neither past nor future. There is something *uncreated* in the core of the personality of each and every man, says Eckhart, and this is the element, called Atman by the yogis, which enables man to achieve God-realization.

14

AN EXAMPLE OF GREATNESS

IN THE third chapter of the *Bhagavad Gita* there is a verse which proclaims:

> Whatsoever a great man does, the same is done by others as well. Whatsoever standard he sets, the world follows.

Something of the same sentiment is echoed in the lines of Longfellow:

> Lives of great men all remind us
> We can make our lives sublime,
> And, departing, leave behind us
> Footprints on the sands of time.
>
> Footprints, that perhaps another,
> Sailing o'er life's solemn main,
> A forlorn and shipwrecked brother,
> Seeing, shall take heart again.

These lines come from Longfellow's *A Psalm of Life*, and some other lines from this poet equally remind us that there is truth also in Shri Shankara's saying that the achievement of Truth does not come without effort like a ripe fruit falling into the palm of the outstretched hand.

> The heights by great men reached and kept

The Spiritual Awakening of Science

Were not attained by sudden flight,
But they, while their companions slept,
Were toiling upward in the night.

Yoga tells us that the potentiality for greatness is hidden in each and every man. But in practice we don't really believe it. We have to remember that Yoga is important, not because it is some very unusual and exotic teaching introduced from the Far East, but because it deals with the human personality and the nature and significance of the human experience which is common to all of us. Swami Rama Tirtha says clearly that where individuals are successful and inspired, they are putting into practice the principles enunciated by the Vedanta, whether they know it or not.

Let us take a specific example, a man who has been described as 'the greatest of all experimental investigators of physical nature' and 'a member of the small class of supreme scientists, which includes Archimedes, Galileo, Newton, and Darwin'. Perhaps you can guess who it was. If not, let me tell you some more about him. He was the son of a blacksmith who came from a small village in Yorkshire and his mother was the daughter of a local farmer. The family moved to London before he was born and he went to school only between the ages of five and twelve. He himself later said: 'My education was of the most ordinary description, consisting of little more than the rudiments of reading, writing and arithmetic at a common day school. My hours out of school were passed at home and in the

An Example of Greatness

streets', (where he used, incidentally, to play marbles). When he was nine years old, the family was so poor that it was on public relief and the boy was receiving an allowance of one loaf of bread to last him a week.

At the age of twelve he left school to become an errand boy to a bookseller and newsagent called Riebau, who had a shop in Blandford Street, close to Manchester Square. His duties included the early morning paper round. He also had to dust the room and black the boots of a lodger to whom the bookseller rented a room above his shop. The lodger was a French refugee who was a good professional artist (he had earlier painted Napoleon's portrait) and he took a liking to the boy and gave him lessons in drawing. After a year's probation, the boy was apprenticed to the bookseller and, as well as working in the shop, was set to learn the art of book-binding. He used to read as much as he could of the books given to him to work on. He first became interested in science at this time by reading an article on electricity in an encyclopaedia that he had to bind. He also particularly liked a book called *Conversations in Chemistry* by a Mrs Marcet.

After some years the bookseller allowed him to go occasionally in the evening to hear some lectures on Natural Philosophy delivered in a house near Fleet Street. The fee for each lecture was one shilling, which was a lot of money then, but the boy's elder brother, who was now himself a blacksmith, paid the entrance fee for him. The lectures were in fact the beginnings of what later became Birkbeck

The Spiritual Awakening of Science

College. The boy's father had died seven years after he started in the shop, when he was nineteen, and his mother at that time kept herself by taking in lodgers until her sons could support themselves and her. The boy went on working as a book-binder for eight years in all (that is, until he was twenty-one). One could hardly have a more unpromising start to a career of greatness.

The man's name was Michael Faraday. At the age of twenty-one he had done virtually nothing of any importance, but—if more evidence of what he was to go on to achieve were needed—one can quote the remark by Einstein that the history of physical science contains two couples of equal magnitude: Galileo and Newton, and Faraday and Clerk Maxwell. The first two transformed our idea of the nature of the physical world in the sixteenth and seventeenth centuries by recognizing the laws of motion governing gravity and the movement of the stars, as well as the movement of all physical objects. Faraday and Clerk Maxwell were the two people who successively brought about an equally momentous scientific revolution by recognizing and clarifying the nature of electromagnetic forces and their fundamental role in the constitution of the physical world. As such they were the true fathers of the Theory of Relativity and of a large part of modern technology.

How did this ill-educated errand boy and book-binder of twenty-one come to bring this about? His first, not very important, scientific research was not published until he was twenty-five and he made no important discovery until

An Example of Greatness

he was over thirty. His major contributions to changing the conceptual basis of science did not begin until he was about forty-five.

One major factor in the formation of Michael Faraday's character and the shaping of his life lay in his spiritual life. His father was a member of a very small sect called the Sandemanians, which had been founded by a Scottish Presbyterian minister, who left the Church because he believed that it should not be subject to any worldly covenant, but should be governed only by the doctrines of Christ and his Apostles. He held that Christ had come to teach the existence of eternal life and not to establish any worldly power, and that no church could become the established religion of any nation without being perverted. The Sandemanians did not try to convert anyone and the congregations were small. They simply tried to follow the teachings of Christ. They used to try and follow the practice of the Apostles, breaking bread together on the Sabbath and eating a common meal in the room next to the chapel after the Sunday service. They had no priests; they were led by a number of elders, who were elected unanimously by the congregation and who presided in turn at the services. They considered the saving of money sinful and Faraday was scrupulous about this throughout his life. He never discussed religion without invitation and considered that it was concerned with an order of truth different and higher than natural truth. He continued to attend these services all his life. He was elected an elder at the age of forty-nine, by which time he was world-famous as a scientist. It was said of his readings from the Bible:

The Spiritual Awakening of Science

The perfection of the reading, with its clearness of pronunciation, its judicious emphasis, the rich musical voice, and the perfect charm of the reader, with his natural reverence, made it a delight to listen.

Elders were expected to attend every Sunday without fail and on one occasion Faraday absented himself in order to obey the command from Queen Victoria to dine with her at Windsor. The congregation would not accept that this excuse was reasonable and his eldership and membership were temporarily suspended, although he continued to attend the services regularly.[1] Faraday was soon re-admitted to his Church, but was not re-elected as an elder for many years.

While still employed by the bookseller and attending the evening lectures on Natural Philosophy, Michael Faraday became acquainted with a well-educated Quaker youth, called Benjamin Abbott, who was younger than he was, and started a correspondence with him. In it he explains that he is lacking in a knowledge of grammar and in the art of composition, but would like to improve his knowledge by correspondence with Abbott. He tells Abbott that he has made already a few simple experiments into the principles of electricity, himself making a voltaic battery and studying the electrolytic decomposition of magnesia. In another letter he replies to Abbott who has complained

---

[1] One is reminded of the reprimand suffered by the former Lord Chancellor, Lord Mackay, another devout member of a small Scottish Church which had seceded from the Presbyterian Church, for attending the Memorial Services of two Roman Catholic colleagues.

An Example of Greatness

of his own shortage of philosophical ideas, that a philosopher cannot fail to abound in subjects for investigation, and that his main problem is that he is short of time.

> O, that I could purchase at a cheap rate some of our modern gents' spare hours, nay, days; I think it would be a good bargain both for them and me.

One of the great principles enunciated by the spiritual teachers is 'Seek and ye shall find'. As the Lord says in the *Bhagavad Gita*: 'By whatever path men approach Me, so do I reward them'. So it was with Faraday.

It happened that a Mr Dance, who was a member of the Royal Institution, was a customer of the shop where Faraday worked, and the young bookbinder impressed him so favourably that he gave him tickets for the last four lectures to be delivered by Humphry Davy in the Royal Institution between February and April 1812. Faraday went and took notes at these lectures, and copied them out fully afterwards in a quarto volume, adding some beautiful illustrations, and sent them to Davy, asking to be enabled to quit trade, which he found vicious and selfish, and to devote himself to science. The notes covered 386 pages of manuscript and this famous book still exists in the library of the Royal Institution. In his letter Faraday said that he wished to serve science, which he imagined made its pursuers amiable and liberal. He therefore asked for any laboratory appointment that might be available. Davy wrote back as follows:

The Spiritual Awakening of Science

December 24th 1812

Sir

I am far from displeased with the proof you have given me of your confidence, and which displays great zeal, power of memory and attention. I am obliged to go out of town, and shall not be settled in town till the end of January. I will then see you at any time you wish. It would gratify me to be of any service to you. I wish it may be in my power. I am, Sir, your obedient humble servant

H. Davy

Early in the following year Davy sent for Faraday and talked to him about the job of an assistant in the laboratory. However, he advised him not to give up his prospects as a bookseller's apprentice, telling him that science was a harsh mistress. He smiled at Faraday's notion about the superior moral feelings of the followers of science, saying that he would leave it to the experience of a few years to set him right on that matter. Having recommended him to stick to book-binding, he promised to send all the Royal Institution's book-binding orders to him, and to recommend him as a book-binder to his friends. But he engaged Faraday for some days as an amanuensis, to take down dictation from him, after he had injured his eye during experiments with nitrogen chloride. So Faraday soon went back to the shop.

In his lectures Swami Rama Tirtha makes the point that as soon as you have truly renounced a strong desire, it is almost automatically achieved. The principle 'Seek and ye

An Example of Greatness

shall find' (he says) is only half the truth; we also have to remember that other great spiritual principle enunciated by Christ: 'Seek ye first the kingdom of heaven and all these other things shall be added unto you'.[1]

One evening some weeks later, while Faraday was undressing upstairs, he was startled to hear a loud knock at the front door. A carriage had drawn up outside the house, and Davy's footman left a note requesting him to call next day at the Royal Institution. Davy asked him whether he still desired to be engaged in scientific work. It turned out that Davy had had to sack his laboratory assistant, and thought of offering the position to Faraday. He would get two rooms at the top of the Royal Institution to live in, and 25 shillings a week. Faraday was twenty-one years old.

Shortly after moving into the Royal Institution, Faraday wrote a long letter to his friend, Abbott, about what makes a good lecture, preceding his remarks with a passage which gives a delightful flavour of his personality at this time:

> As when on some secluded branch in forest far and wide sits perched an owl, who, full of self-conceit and self-created wisdom, explains, comments, condemns, ordains and orders things not understood, yet full of his importance still holds forth to stocks and stones around — so sits and scribbles Mike.

At twenty-one Michael Faraday's *curriculum vitae* was not impressive. He had had no proper education and his

---

[1] See, for instance, *In Woods of God-Realization*, Volume 2, pp 277-278.

work experience was of nine years, first as a newspaper boy and general factotum in a bookseller's and later as a bookbinder. His only knowledge of science was what he had picked up from reading one or two popular books and what he learned by occasionally going to hear the evening lectures on natural philosophy delivered by a Mr Tatum. It was a fairly unpromising start to his career. But an opening to science, which he was already beginning to love, had been offered to him in the shape of the tickets to Humphry Davy's four lectures at the Royal Institution and he had grasped it with both hands, as evidenced by his producing the notes and illustrations to send to Davy.

Being appointed Davy's lab boy was the turning point in Faraday's career, but events still took a totally unforeseen, and not necessarily favourable, turn. Davy, who had been a great chemist with a lot of discoveries to his credit, was beginning to settle down to enjoying the fruits of fame and success and spent more and more of his time hob-nobbing with the aristocracy. He had recently been knighted and, shortly after appointing Faraday, he decided to resign from the Royal Institution and to marry, unwisely choosing someone who was rather a snob herself. He then decided that he would travel abroad in Europe and the Near East, visiting notable scientists, and he invited Faraday to accompany him and to assist him. He took with him a small case of chemicals with which he proposed to do experiments *en route* and he wanted Faraday to assist him in these and in taking down his writings to dictation.

An Example of Greatness

Sir Humphry and Lady Davy set out, with Faraday accompanying them, in October 1813, travelling to France, Italy, Switzerland and the Tyrol, keeping a journal of all the eminent men of science whom they visited. Faraday had never before been more than twelve miles from London and he was first impressed by the scenery in Devonshire which they passed through on their way to Plymouth, where they were taking ship for France. France was at war with England at the time—it was only two years before the battle of Waterloo—but such was Davy's reputation as one of the foremost chemists of the time that he had special permission for his party to enter France. While they were there, they met many of the most eminent men of science, including Ampère and Gay-Lussac. Faraday saw Napoleon in his carriage on the way to a state visit to the Senate. While in France, Davy also carried out experiments on the newly discovered element, iodine.

Then they travelled on to Italy, where, during a stay in Florence, they burned diamonds in oxygen, using the Grand Duke of Tuscany's great lens. They also met the elderly Volta, who had invented the battery in 1800, some 15 years before, and saw Vesuvius in eruption, picnicking on its slopes, before going on to Switzerland and Germany.

On this journey Faraday had the great good fortune to meet many of the foremost scientific minds of the day, which widened and deepened his love and knowledge of science; but the experience was by no means an unmitigated joy for him. Davy had been unable to engage a valet and gradually called on Faraday more and more to act as his valet as well as carrying out all his other duties. Davy treated Faraday quite well, but Lady Davy treated him as a menial and continually scolded him. Faraday wrote home to his friend Abbott that he had seriously considered ending his appointment, but that he had decided to complete it. The opportunity of working with Davy was not to be missed. He comments wryly in the letter: 'I should have but little to complain of were I travelling with Sir Humphry Davy alone, or were Lady Davy like him...' He adds that he will probably return to book-binding when he gets home.

In Switzerland, they stayed in Geneva with Davy's friend, the scientist De La Rive. At first Faraday was sent to have his meals with the servants, but when De La Rive got to know him, and found out that he was not a valet, but Davy's lab assistant, he was shocked, and proposed that Faraday should dine with the family. Lady Davy would not agree, however, and De La Rive reacted by arranging for Faraday to have his meals served in his own room. Faraday used to speak appreciatively in later life of the way that De La Rive treated him at this time. In one of his letters to Abbott he speaks of the ills and trials of life, comparing them to 'clouds which intervened between me and the sun of prosperity, but which I found were refreshing, reserving to me that tone and vigour of mind which prosperity alone could enervate and ultimately destroy'. His letters to his mother are full of affection.

When the party got back to London in 1815 Faraday was re-engaged by the Royal Institution as a laboratory assistant

An Example of Greatness

at an increased salary of 30 shillings a week. Outwardly he could be said to have had very few assets at this juncture, other than his association with Sir Humphry Davy as lab boy and general factotum. But he already had a deep love of science, dating from before he knew Davy, and he had a strength of character and a faith, founded on his spiritual convictions, which proved a far more powerful asset than superior education or worldly advantages could have done. From then onwards he devoted himself to his experiments and to the pursuit of scientific truth.

He was soon working with Davy on the invention of the miner's safety lamp. A year later he gave his first lecture and his first small research paper, written jointly with Davy, was published. We cannot go into all his scientific achievements in this account, but they are dazzling in their variety and importance, although it was not until the age of twenty-five that he ever expected to do anything in research and he was twenty-nine before his first important discovery was published.

To begin with, he produced some very simple papers in collaboration with, or annotated by, Davy, but gradually he became more independent and in 1823, eight years after he had got back to London, he was proposed as a candidate for Fellowship of the Royal Society by one of the other members, called Wollaston. Davy, who by this time was President, far from supporting the proposal, vigorously opposed it. One can call this small-mindedness or jealousy or just a typical example of a prophet not being recognized in his own country. Presumably, Davy still regarded

Faraday merely as a particularly bright lab boy whom he had benevolently patronized, although Faraday had already by this time made many important independent contributions to science. Davy even asked Faraday himself to withdraw his name, but Faraday said that, as he had not proposed himself, he could not have it withdrawn. Davy then said that, as President, he would remove the name from the list himself. Faraday did not react to Davy's hidden jealousy and vanity; he simply replied that he was sure Davy would do what was best for the Royal Society.

Parenthetically, it may be said that one could hardly ask for a clearer example of someone practising the teachings of Yoga on not being concerned with the fruits of action, as expressed in the *Bhagavad Gita* (2.48):

> Do thy work, abandoning attachment, with an even mind in success and failure, for evenness of mind is called Yoga.

In spite of Davy's opposition, Faraday was elected a Fellow in the following year. There was only one vote against him at the election. It was apparent that no one else but Davy had any doubts about his worthiness for the honour! In the following year (1825) Faraday's position at the Royal Institution was much improved when he was appointed Director of the laboratory under the Professor of Chemistry, Brande. Faraday started evening meetings, at which members could see experiments and discuss researches which were being carried out at the Institution and elsewhere. He also started a Christmas series of children's lectures. Contemporaries spoke of the grace,

An Example of Greatness

earnestness and refinement of his whole demeanour when lecturing, his lucidity being at its best when lecturing to children.

The Royal Institution had been founded in March 1799 following a proposal by Count Rumford

> ...for forming in London by private subscription an establishment for feeding the poor, and giving them useful employment, and also for furnishing food at a cheap rate to others who may stand in need of such assistance, connected with an institution for introducing and bringing forward into general use new inventions and improvements, particularly such as relate to the management of heat and the saving of fuel, and to various other mechanical contrivances by which domestic comfort and economy may be promoted.

Rumford particularly wanted to make it fashionable to care for the poor and indigent. In the end the Society for Bettering the Condition of the Poor was separated from the Research Institution and the latter was set up in a house in Albemarle Street, where it still is. By the time that Faraday was appointed to the staff, some sixteen years later, the Institution was still in considerable financial difficulties and this state of things continued for some time, so that when at the age of thirty-four he was appointed Director, as well as lecturing and carrying on his scientific researches, he had to devote a great deal of time to trying to keep it financially afloat. Two years later, in 1827, he was offered the relatively well-paid Chair of Chemistry in the newly founded London University, but he refused it because (as he said):

The Spiritual Awakening of Science

I think it is a matter of duty and gratitude on my part to do what I can for the good of the Royal Institution in the present attempt to establish it firmly. The Institution has been a source of knowledge and pleasure to me for the last full fourteen years; and though it does not pay me in salary what I now strive to do for it, yet I possess the kind feelings and goodwill of its authorities and members, and all the privileges it can grant or I require; and, moreover, I remember the protection it has afforded me during the past years of my scientific life.

Things did not get better, however, and he had to tell the Board of Management that 'we are living at the parings of our skin' (or, as we might now say, by the skin of our teeth!). The Committee considered that they could not make any reduction in Mr Faraday's salary which was at that time £100 per annum plus a house, and a supply of coals and candles for heat and light. Thus Faraday as Director of the Institution was getting less than twice as much as when he was first employed by Davy as a lab boy. The Committee expressed their regret that the circumstances of the Institution did not justify them increasing his salary to what he undoubtedly merited. Faraday was then forty-one, having made his most famous discovery the year before and having received by that time the highest honours bestowed by international learning. He never complained about his salary.

Faraday throughout this period remained true to his religious conviction. John Tyndall, his successor, said that he came nearer than anybody else that he knew to the

An Example of Greatness

fulfilment of the Christian precept: 'Take no thought for the morrow'. He had absolute confidence that, in case of need, the Lord would provide. With such feeling and such faith he was naturally heedless of laying anything by for the future. He used to have his dinner each day at two o'clock and would begin his meal by lifting both hands over the dish before him, and in the tones of a son addressing a father, of whose love he was sure, asked the blessing on the food. In his earlier years at the Royal Institution, he used to make a little extra money by what he called 'commercial work', advising people on scientific and chemical problems. Between 1823 and 1837 he made between £240 and £310 per annum from this source, but he then gave this up altogether in favour of concentrating on his scientific research on electromagnetism. He wanted to concentrate all his time and effort on what he considered to be worthwhile in the search for truth. It was the period of his greatest discoveries in science.

Faraday can truly be said to have demonstrated his faith in the spiritual principle enunciated by the Lord in the *Gita*: 'O Arjuna, in the case of my devotees, I provide what they need and protect what they have.' We can find essentially the same teaching in the Christian Gospels in the passage on the lilies of the field.[1]

At the age of thirty, in 1821, Faraday married a twenty-

---

[1] Matthew 6.25-34; Luke 12.22-34.

one year old girl called Sarah Barnhard, who was also a member of the Sandemanian Church. He had the formal ceremony in which he seriously committed himself to enter the life of the community a month later. Although he had been brought up in the group and had long been an attender, this was a definite step undertaken by serious members to commit their future life to following the way of Christ in accordance with its tenets. At the same time he was, in his scientific work, determinedly tackling the problem of electromagnetism; and on Christmas Day, 1821, he took his young wife into the laboratory to show her the rotation of a magnetic needle near an electric current passing through a wire, the first demonstration of this particular effect, which was to be the origin of the electric motor.

He was also researching very actively in chemistry, working on the vaporisation of mercury and preparing liquid chlorine for the first time. He went on to liquefy a number of other gases and demonstrated clearly the principle that all gases were simply substances in a gaseous state which could be liquefied by lowering the temperature or increasing the pressure. He experimented with alloys of steel and made the first stainless steel. In 1825 he discovered the new compound of carbon and hydrogen ('bicarburet of hydrogen'), which later came to be called benzene and led in time to the development of aniline dyes. He also turned his attention to the production of different kinds of glass with varying optical properties, presenting the results in three lectures in 1829.

An Example of Greatness

But his main theme—and his most important contribution to future knowledge—lay in his studies of electricity and magnetism and the induction of one by the other. He steadily worked on these problems for over ten years, trying (but without success) to see if magnetism could be converted into electricity in the same way that magnets could be deflected by currents flowing in wires in their vicinity. He also tried to see if a current flowing in one wire could induce a current in a second nearby wire connected to a sensitive galvanometer. No matter how large the steady currents he used he was unable to do this. It was not until 1831 that he discovered that it was only at the moment when a steady current was turned on or off that a current could be induced in a nearby 'secondary' coil of wire and that this effect could be increased by the introduction of an iron core (e.g., in the form of an iron ring round which the two coils were wound). The iron became magnetized with the steady current, and produced a surrounding magnetic field, which was built up or collapsed at the moment when the current was turned on or off, inducing the current in the secondary wire. Similarly, when a magnet was *moved* in the neighbourhood of a coil of wire, a current was induced in the wire at the time of the movement. This was when (what Faraday called) the 'lines of force' of the magnetic field surrounding the magnet were moving relative to the nearby wire. It was therefore the relative movement or change of the electromagnetic fields surrounding a current or magnet which caused the interaction and induced the effects. Electromagnetic forces interacted when there was a *change of strength, direction or movement*, either of the current or the magnet, correlating with the movement of the lines of force making up the surrounding electromagnetic field.

This discovery, made by Faraday in 1831, showed how electricity could be generated from mechanical movement and led to the dynamo. It was the most important of all his many discoveries, the result of long and intense enquiry and experiment, which had gradually revealed the fundamental nature of electricity and magnetism as forces characteristic of a single all-pervading field underlying the physical world.

In 1833, at the age of forty-two, he read a paper to the Royal Society on the fundamental identity of the electricity which manifested itself in many different phenomena. His work on electrochemistry had suggested that electricity was in some way made up of definite 'packets' as if it were composed of particles, atoms or corpuscles, an observation which foreshadowed the discovery of the electron. He had worked out the quantity of electricity needed to bring about chemical changes such as the release of iodine from potassium iodide through electrolysis. He studied the production of gases during electrolysis and showed that it depended solely on the amount of electric current passed irrespective of the size of the battery or the composition of the plates, and that the same law applied to the decomposition of all chemical substances by electrolysis, when one also took into account their chemical equivalents (i.e. the proportions in which they were combined in different substances). He thus showed that 'the decompositions of

An Example of Greatness

the voltaic battery are as definite in their character as those chemical combinations which gave birth to the atomic theory'. He commented in a paper in 1834:

> Although we know nothing of what an atom is, yet we cannot resist forming some idea of a small particle which represents it to the mind; and though we are in equal, if not greater, ignorance of electricity, so as to be unable to say whether it is a particular[1] matter or matters, or mere motion of ordinary matter, or some other kind of power or agent, yet there is an immensity of facts which justify us in believing that the atoms of matter are in some way endowed or associated with electrical powers, to which they owe their most striking qualities, and amongst them their mutual chemical affinity. As soon as we perceive, through the teaching of Dalton, that chemical powers are, however varied the circumstances in which they are exerted, definite for each body, we learn to estimate the relative degree of force which resides in such bodies; and when upon that knowledge comes the fact that the electricity we appear to be capable of loosening from its habitation for a while and conveying from place to place, whilst it retains its chemical force, can be measured out, and being so measured is found to be as definite in its action as any of those portions which, remaining associated with the particles of matter, give them their chemical relations, we seem to have found the link which connects the proportion of that we have evolved to the

---

[1] By the word 'particular' here, Faraday, of course, means 'made up of particles'.

proportion of that belonging to the particles in their natural state.[1]

Faraday continued his investigations of electricity throughout the 1830s, turning to the problem of the nature of static as distinct from current electricity. He studied the charges induced in two concentric spheres separated either by air or by other substances and demonstrated the properties of what we would now call capacitative charge and the dielectric of capacitors.

In 1841, at the age of fifty, his health broke down under the strain of overwork and he did no science for three years. During this time he went to Switzerland with his wife and brother-in-law and, since he was still physically robust, went on long excursions. On 12th August 1841 he visited the falls at Giessbach and noted in his journal:

> The sun shone brightly, and the rainbows seen from various points were very beautiful. One, at the bottom of a fine but furious fall, was very pleasant—there it remained motionless while the gusts of cloud and spray swept furiously across its place, and were dashed against the rock. It looked like a spirit strong in faith and steadfast in the midst of a storm of passions sweeping across it; and, though it might fade and revive, still it held on to the rock, as in hope, and giving hope.

As soon as his health permitted he returned and resumed his work and soon became equally productive. He

---

[1] Cited in J G Crowther, *British Scientists of the Nineteenth Century*, London: Kegan Paul, 1935, pp 110-111.

An Example of Greatness

demonstrated that the plane of polarized light passing through glass could be rotated by a magnetic field. And he then proceeded to the discovery of what is called diamagnetism. He studied the effects of a magnetic field on a flame and on the flow of gases, establishing that oxygen was strongly magnetic but that nitrogen was neutral 'like space'. This led on to an investigation of the effect of the atmosphere on the earth's magnetism. He applied the findings to the effect of magnetic storms and to the annual and diurnal variations in the earth's magnetism and also to the effect of temperature on the earth's magnetic field. In 1850 he sent papers to the Royal Society on these topics.

It has been said that 'a strong vein of metaphysics runs through the speculations of Faraday, but his experiments are always handled with regal power'. In fact Faraday saw beyond the atomic theory of his contemporaries, realizing that the atom was not the hard solid object which they imagined, but a centre of force. He held that in the conception of molecules or atoms separated by inter-molecular space 'space must be taken as the only continuous part of a body so constituted'. If space is a conductor (he argues) it cannot exist in insulating bodies, and if it is an insulator it cannot exist in conducting bodies. So it cannot be either. He recognized chemical combinations as being due to electric forces of attraction and repulsion between atoms, quantified in definite and characteristic amounts, anticipating in this (as Helmholtz was later to point out) the existence of the electron as the unit of charge in ion exchanges during electrolysis. He also conceived of particles as concentrations in fields of force and amounting to that alone. In 1846 he suggested the electromagnetic theory of light and expressed doubt about the existence of the ether, asking:

> whether it was not possible that the vibrations which…are assumed to account for radiation and radiant phenomena may not occur in the lines of force which connect particles and consequently masses of matter together; a notion which, as far as it is admitted, will dispense with the ether which, in another view, is supposed to be the medium in which these vibrations take place.

He points out that the velocity of light and electricity are known to be approximately the same. In these prophetic words he presages the findings of the experiment of Michelson and Morley in 1877 and the Theory of Relativity. The existence of electromagnetic waves was not experimentally established and generally accepted until Hertz discovered radio waves, also in 1877.

Perhaps these few short indications can give an idea of how it could be said that 'Faraday was the greatest physicist of the nineteenth century and the greatest of all experimental investigators of physical nature'.

His friend and successor John Tyndall says that Faraday was a man of strong emotions, generous, charitable, sympathizing with human suffering.

His five pound note was ever ready for the meritorious man who had been overtaken by calamity. The tenderness of his nature rendered it difficult for him to refuse the

An Example of Greatness

appeal of distress. Still, he knew the evil of indiscriminate alms-giving, and had many times detected imposture; so that he usually distributed his gifts through some charity organisation which insured him that they would be well bestowed. He used to give a large part of his meagre income to charity.

His faith never wavered, but remained to the end as fresh as in 1821 when he made his profession of faith on formally joining his Church; and in later life, when questioned about his religious belief by Lady Lovelace, he described himself as belonging to 'a very small and despised sort of Christians, known—if known at all—as Sandemanians; and our hope is founded on the faith as it is in Christ'. He made a strict distinction between his religion and his science, believing that man could not know God by means of his reason, but that the soul could have direct communion with God.

He could not bear indecision and said that even a bad decision was better than no decision. Later in his life he was given a pension of £300 by Sir Robert Peel and was also, through the initiative of Prince Albert, given a grace and favour house at Hampton Court. He resigned from the Royal Institution at the age of seventy in 1861 and died aged 75 in 1867.

John Tyndall, who was appointed Professor of Natural Philosophy at the Royal Institution under Faraday in May 1853 and had a long and harmonious collaboration with him, wrote of Faraday's character:

The Spiritual Awakening of Science

Faraday's intellectual power cannot be traced to definite antecedents; and it is still more difficult to account by inheritance for the extraordinary delicacy of his character. On a memorable occasion, a friend who knew him well, described him thus: 'Nature, not education, made Faraday strong and refined. A favourite experiment of his own was representative of himself. He loved to show that water, in crystallising, excluded all foreign ingredients however intimately they might be mixed with it. Out of acids, alkalis, or saline solutions, the crystals came sweet and pure. By some such natural process in the formation of this man, beauty and nobleness coalesced, to the exclusion of everything vulgar and low.

The experiment could stand as representative of that transformation of the human personality of which the yogis speak, in which the pure Self of man emerges, as if crystallized from the personality with all its impurities, by the process of meditation and spiritual enquiry (*vichara*), culminating in self-realization.

15

Herald of the Future

ASKED WHO was the greatest scientist of the nineteenth century, most people would probably answer Charles Darwin, but they would be wrong. Charles Darwin's major achievement in discovering and propounding the theory of evolution has changed the world, but he is not alone among those who have done this. A much less recognized scientist, who went about investigating and revolutionizing our understanding of the world, is James Clerk Maxwell. Recently he has, at last, been celebrated for his many achievements in the world of physics, physiology and statistics. He demonstrated that the world consisted, not so much of so-called matter, but of electricity, the laws of which he determined and promulgated. All this is now presented clearly and simply in a short book by Basil Mahon, *The Man Who Changed Everything*[1], published by Wiley. Furthermore, the man himself provides a perfect answer and rebuttal to those who think that science and religion are in any way antipathetic to each other or irreconcilable. Like Newton, Maxwell was a deeply religious man. He loved poetry, George Herbert most of all. When dying, he repeated Herbert's poem, 'Aaron'. His knowledge of the Bible was remarkable.

[1] See page 323.

The Spiritual Awakening of Science

It is to Clerk Maxwell, taking up the investigation started by Faraday, that we owe the recognition that electricity and magnetism are the basic material from which the world is made. The reason why we can have radio, television and astronomy is because the whole of creation is a product of electromagnetism. Light itself, which encompasses the world and brings us information about the most distant heavenly bodies, consists of several wavelengths which are visible to us, because the eye is sensitive to them and them alone. Electromagnetic waves bring us all this information of the cosmos and they constitute the basic material from which the stars and other heavenly bodies are created.

Clerk Maxwell worked out the relationship between electricity and magnetism, recognizing that light, as we appreciate it, was one band of wavelengths in the ocean of electromagnetic waves. Having discovered this, he set to work on the mathematics of the behaviour of the media in these terms and wrote *A Treatise on Electricity and Magnetism* in two volumes, which immediately became a classic.

The story of his life is remarkable, if at times rather sad. He was born into the family of a Scots lawyer. John Clerk Maxwell worked in Edinburgh but he had also inherited a small estate in Kirkcudbright in the southernmost part of Scotland, which was called Glenlair. He was a kind and friendly man but a little unconventional. He had a passion for finding out about the burgeoning new technology being invented at this time in the factories of the industrial revolution. He seems to have passed on this major interest to his son, even at the time when he was still an infant, because James became well known by those who met him as a boy, by the way he would point at something and ask, 'What's the go o' that? What does it do?' Nor was he content with a vague answer. Unless a satisfactory answer was forthcoming, James would insist, 'But what's the particular go of it?' Thus James enjoyed a youth spent at Glenlair, the country estate of his parents. Both were devout Christians, but of two different traditions, the father Presbyterian and the mother Episcopalian, but living together in complete amity.

James Clerk Maxwell was destined to transform our understanding of the world by elucidating the nature of electricity and magnetism, and showing them to be the fundamental nature of matter. In doing so he swept away the dominant view of the world as a product of matter existing in a real time and space, replacing these Newtonian concepts with a relatively immaterial product of electromagnetic force.

When the full implications of these changes began to be felt and realized, the hard materialistic picture of nineteenth century science could have been said to have changed into the elusive spectacle spoken of by Prospero at the end of Shakespeare's *Tempest*:

> Our revels now are ended. These our actors,
> As I foretold you, were all spirits and
> Are melted into air, into thin air:
> And, like the baseless fabric of this vision,
> The cloud-capp'd towers, the gorgeous palaces,

The Spiritual Awakening of Science

> The solemn temples, the great globe itself,
> Yea, all which it inherit, shall dissolve
> And, like this insubstantial pageant faded,
> Leave not a rack behind. We are such stuff
> As dreams are made on, and our little life
> Is rounded with a sleep.

Maxwell's idea was so revolutionary and so difficult to understand for those who did not have the knowledge of physics and mathematics needed to appreciate it, that it was accepted with admiration only by a very few of the greatest scientists of his time. In 1879 Hermann Helmholtz, the professor of physics at Berlin University, persuaded the Berlin Academy of Sciences to offer a prize for conclusive experimental verification of Maxwell's theory. One of Helmholtz's brightest pupils, Heinrich Hertz, succeeded in providing this proof eight years later in 1887.

The Spiritual Awakening of Science traces the origin of science in the ancient Greek world, through the times of the Arab Caliphate at Cordoba, and later the advent of the mediæval church with the emergence of such great figures as Leonardo, Galileo, Kepler and Newton in the Renaissance. The publication of Newton's two greatest works, the *Principia Mathematica* and *Optics*, seemed to settle the methods and conclusions of science about the world at large, but the one phenomenon which was still little understood was the nature of electricity. Benjamin Franklin was able to show, by flying his kite at the end of a wire during thunderstorms, that the dangerous effect of lightning coming to earth could be mitigated by the provision of lightning conductors. We see that, with the invention of storage devices like the Leyden jar and batteries, rapid progress was made in handling relatively small currents and voltages in the laboratory.

But it was not until the early nineteenth century that major systematic advances in the understanding of electricity were initiated by great figures such as Faraday and Clerk Maxwell. Faraday's contribution is the subject of the chapter preceding this one. It is reproduced from an earlier book, *Yoga for the Modern World*, as part of the present narrative. It also seemed worthwhile inserting before this the article on 'The Vital Spark', which gives a very cursory account of the attitude to so called 'electric phenomena' from ancient times until now. In 2003 *The Man Who Changed Everything* was published on the life of James Clerk Maxwell, by the contemporary author, Basil Mahon, giving a splendid account of Maxwell's importance in the history of electricity and magnetism. The paperback version was published by Wiley in the following year. Mahon's book on Maxwell deserves to be welcomed and widely read as the most important contribution to modern knowledge for the general reader published since the death of James Clerk Maxwell. It is very readable and approachable, even for the relatively uninformed reader, and will render him at home with the scientific facts which Maxwell discovered and promulgated during his tragically short life.

There is only one other major book describing Maxwell's life, published in 1882, three years after his death in 1879, by a dear friend of his, Lewis Campbell, who had

The Spiritual Awakening of Science

known him since schooldays in Edinburgh, while the scientific details of his work were contributed by William Garnett, who had collaborated with him for most of his career, both at King's College in London and later in the last five years of his life, when he was the Director of the New Cavendish Laboratory in Cambridge, where Garnett was his demonstrator. This 662-page volume by Campbell and Garnett, entitled *The Life of James Clerk Maxwell*, is a rich source of information about his childhood, youth and education. It sets out his main subsequent achievements from different university posts in the course of his career, accompanied by an amazingly large collection of letters to and from Maxwell and his friends. This is followed by a 110-page section on his contributions to science and a 74-page section containing his verses and translations, both juvenile and adult. (Four pages from this source have been reproduced on pages 329 to 332.)

The subsequent neglect of the details of Clerk Maxwell's life is extraordinary, when compared with other major figures in eighteenth and nineteenth century science, like Charles Darwin, William Thomson (Lord Kelvin), Hermann Helmholtz and others. But his importance is very adequately recognized and proclaimed by such figures as Albert Einstein who said: 'One scientific epoch ended and another began with James Clerk Maxwell,' or the even more emphatic view of one of the leading American figures in physics, Richard Feynman, who has written: 'From a long view of the history of mankind—seen from, say, 10,000 years from now—there can be little doubt that the most significant event of the nineteenth century will be judged as Maxwell's discovery of the laws of electro-dynamics.' Basil Mahon, in the introduction to his book, gives an admirable account of Maxwell's achievements, which is well worth quoting verbatim:

> In 1861, James Clerk Maxwell had a scientific idea that was as profound as any work of philosophy, as beautiful as any painting, and more powerful than any act of politics or war. Nothing would be the same again.
>
> In the middle of the nineteenth century the world's best physicists had been searching long and hard for a key to the great mystery of electricity and magnetism. The two phenomena seemed to be inextricably linked but the ultimate nature of the linkage was subtle and obscure, defying all attempts to winkle it out. Then Maxwell found the answer with as pure a shaft of genius as has ever been seen.
>
> He made the astounding prediction that fleeting electric currents could exist not only in conductors but in all materials and even in empty space. Here was the missing part of the linkage; now everything fitted into a complete and beautiful theory of electromagnetism.
>
> This was not all. The theory predicted that every time a magnet jiggled, or an electric current changed, a wave of energy would spread out into space like a ripple on a pond. Maxwell calculated the speed of the waves and it turned out to be the very speed at which light had been measured. At a stroke, he had united electricity, magnetism and light. Moreover, visible light was only a small band in a vast range of possible waves, which all

travelled at the same speed but vibrated at different frequencies.

Maxwell's ideas were so different from anything that had gone before that most of his contemporaries were bemused; even some admirers thought he was indulging in a wild phantasy. No proof came until a quarter of a century later, when Heinrich Hertz produced waves from a spark-gap source and detected them.

Over the past one hundred years we have learnt to use Maxwell's waves to send information over great and small distances in tiny fractions of a second. Today we can scarcely imagine a world without radio, television and radar. His brainchild has changed our lives profoundly and irrevocably.

Maxwell's theory is now an established law of nature, one of the central pillars of our understanding of the universe. It opened the way to the two great triumphs of twentieth century physics, relativity and quantum theory, and survived both of those violent revolutions completely intact. As another great physicist, Max Planck, put it, the theory must be numbered among the greatest of all intellectual achievements. But its results are now so closely woven into the fabric of our daily lives that most of us take it wholly for granted, its author unacknowledged.

What makes the situation still more poignant is that Maxwell would be among the world's greatest scientists even if he had never set to work on electricity and magnetism. His influence is everywhere. He introduced statistical methods into physics; now they are used as a matter of course. He demonstrated the principle by which we see colours and took the world's first colour photograph. His whimsical creation, Maxwell's *demon*—a molecule-sized creature who could make heat flow from a cold gas to a hot one—was the first effective scientific thought experiment, a technique Einstein later made his own. It posed questions that perplexed scientists for sixty years and stimulated the creation of information theory, which underpins our communications and computing. He wrote a paper on automatic control systems many years before anyone else gave thought to the subject; it became the foundation of modern control theory and cybernetics. He designed the Cavendish Laboratory and as its founding Director, started a brilliant revival of Cambridge's scientific tradition, which led on to the discoveries of the electron and the structure of DNA.

Some of his work gave direct practical help to engineers. He showed how to use polarized light to reveal strain patterns in a structure and invented a neat and powerful graphical method for calculating the forces in any framework; both techniques became standard engineering practice. He was also the first to suggest using a centrifuge to separate gases.

An interesting report on Maxwell's 'demon' appeared recently in the *New Scientist*. The issue of the 21st June 2008 explained that it was an imagined creature, created in 1871, which was capable of seeing individual atoms in a container of gas that had a central barrier with a tiny trapdoor. It could sort the atoms according to their energy by opening or closing the trapdoor to incoming atoms, depending on their speed. It appears to bring order to chaos without expending energy. The report carried news of research at the University of Oregon which recreated the demon using a pair of parallel lasers that act as the trapdoor. 'They are making a sorting system, which is exactly like Maxwell said, and it's a beautiful demonstration,' commented David Leigh of the University of Edinburgh. Last year his own group used a nanoscale technique to make a demon that could sort and move ring-shaped molecules. Besides offering a way of trapping and cooling atoms so that their properties can be studied precisely, Maxwell's demon may also be useful in quantum computing and gravity-mapping to determine the location of deposits of oil, water or minerals.

Maxwell was born in 1831 and lived for only 48 years. He was not only a great scientist but a man of extraordinary personal charm and generous spirit. His friends found him inspiring, entertaining and entirely without vanity. They loved and admired him in equal measure and felt better for knowing him. From his earliest days he was fascinated by the world and determined to find out how it worked. His parents, like all parents, were assailed with his questions. A casual comment about a blue stone brought the response: 'But how do you know it's blue?' Maxwell's childhood curiosity stayed with him and he spent most of his adult life trying to work out the 'particular go' of things. At the task of unravelling nature's deep secrets he was supreme.

There follow four facsimile pages from the first biography of James Clerk Maxwell by his friends, Lewis Campbell and William Garnett, published in 1879, beginning with an engraving of Mrs Clerk Maxwell and James.

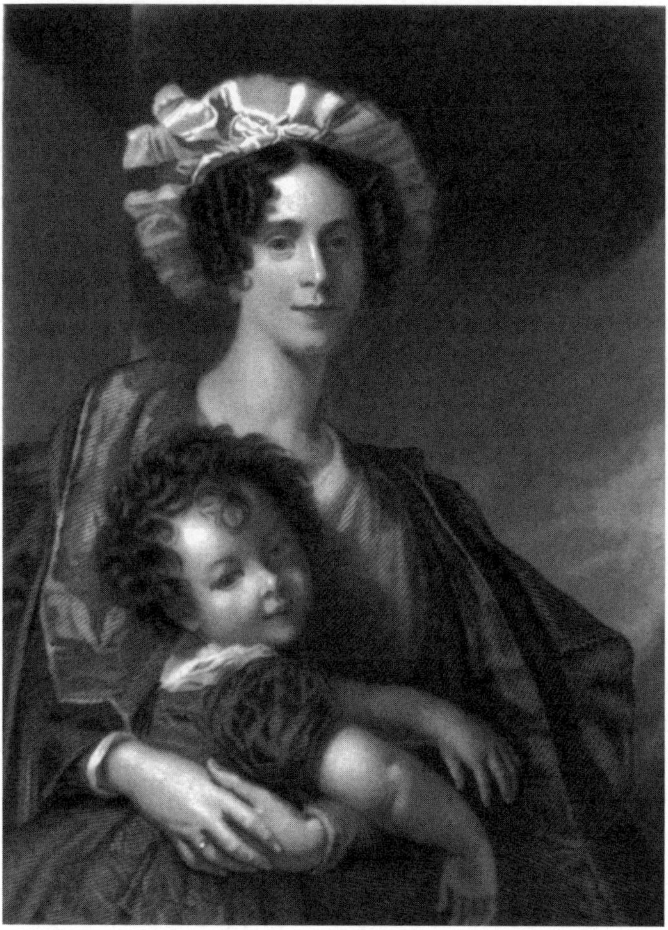

members his interest in colours—" that (sand) stone is red; this (whin) stone is blue." " But how d'ye know it's blue?" he would insist. He would catch insects and watch their movements, but would never hurt them. His aunt, Miss Cay, used to confess that it was humiliating to be asked so many questions one could not answer " by a child like that."

But the child was not always observing, or asking questions. Ever and anon he was engaged in *doing*, or in *making*, which he liked better still. And here his inventiveness soon showed itself. He was not long contented with " tossing his hat about," or fishing with a stick and a string (as in an early picture of Miss Cay's); but whenever he saw anything that demanded constructive ingenuity in the performance, that forthwith took his fancy, and he must work at it. And in the doing it, it was ten to one but he must give it some new and unexpected turn, and enliven it with some quirk of fancy. At one time he is seated on the kitchen table, busily engaged in basket-making, in which all the domestics, probably at his command, are also employed. At another he is "making seals"[1] with quaint devices, or improving upon his mother's knitting. For he must early have attained the skill, of which an elaborate example still exists, in "Mrs. Wedderburn's Abigail," which will be described in the next chapter, and was worked by him in his twelfth year.

Of his education in the narrower sense during this period little is known, except that his mother had the entire charge of it until her last illness in 1839, and that she encouraged him to "look up through Nature to Nature's God."[2] She seems to have prided herself upon his wonderful memory, and it is said that at eight years old he could repeat the whole of the 119th Psalm. His knowledge of Scripture, from his earliest boyhood, was extraordinarily extensive and minute; and he could give chapter and verse for almost any quotation from the Psalms. His knowledge of Milton also dates from very early times. These things were not known merely by rote. They occupied his imagination, and sank deeper than anybody knew.

But his most obvious interests were naturally out of doors. To follow his father "sorting" things about the farm, or "viewing" recent improvements; by and

---

[1] As mentioned in his letter to Miss Cay of 18th January 1840.

[2] When James, being eight years old, was told that his mother was now in heaven, he said, "Oh, I'm so glad! Now she'll have no more pain." Already his first thought was for another.

ture. Master James is in the duck-pond, in a wash-tub, having ousted the ducks, to the amusement of the young "vassals," Bobby and Johnny, and is paddling himself (with some implement from the dairy, belike), out of reach of the tutor, who has fetched a rake, and is trying forcibly to bring him in. Mr. Clerk Maxwell has just arrived upon the scene, and is looking on complacently, though not without concern. Cousin Jemima has been aiding and abetting, and is holding the leaping-pole, which has probably served as a boat-hook in this case.

Glenlair
1841

The achievement of sailing in the tub was one in which James gloried scarcely less than Wordsworth's Blind Highland boy in his tortoise shell. It is referred to in the following letter, written by the boy of ten years old to his father, who had gone for a short visit to St. Mary's Isle:—

Herald of the Future

In 1860, after recovering from smallpox, James was appointed Professor of Natural Philosophy at King's College, London, and he was awarded the Rumford Medal by the Royal Society of London for his work on colour vision. Living in London, he was able to attend lectures at the Royal Institution. Faraday was now in his seventies and his memory had begun to fail, but he and James took pleasure in each other's company — as Mahon imagines them, 'two modest and genial men from different backgrounds but sharing a passionate interest, whose combined endeavours brought about a metamorphosis in science and technology.'

In 1861 James gave a lecture on colour at the Royal Institution with a visual demonstration that any colour could be made by mixing the three primaries. With the help of Thomas Sutton, a colleague at King's and an expert photographer, using red, green and blue filters, he took three pictures of a tartan ribbon, developed the plates, and projected the world's first colour photograph. In fact, there had been a chain of favourable coincidences, since the plates used by James and Sutton were insensitive to red light. As Mahon explains: 'The red dye in the ribbon happened to reflect some ultra-violet light as well as the red, and the solution used by Sutton as a red filter happened to have a pass-band in the same ultra-violet region. Moreover, although the emulsion used on the plates was not at all sensitive to red, it happened to be sensitive to ultra-violet. So the parts of the picture which appeared red had actually been obtained with ultra-violet light, well beyond the range of the human eye!' This was all finally elucidated about a hundred years later by a team at Kodak Research Laboratories.

Three weeks after his colour show, and one week before his thirtieth birthday, James was elected to the Royal Society, in recognition of his work on Saturn's Rings and colour vision. It must have given him some gratification to be welcomed formally into the top rank of British physicists, but the event seems to have barely registered in the Maxwell household. Perhaps he had the private wistful thought that his father would have enjoyed it.

At the time he joined King's College, James had published only one paper on electricity and magnetism, and that had been five years before. But the subject was never far from his mind and ideas had been steadily brewing. He believed strongly in the power of subconscious thought to generate insights. As a student he had expressed this theory in a poem, 'Recollections of Dreamland', written in 1856 in Cambridge:

> There are powers and thoughts within us, that we know not, till they rise
> Through the stream of conscious action from where Self in secret lies.
> But when Will and Sense are silent, by the thoughts that come and go,
> We may trace the rocks and eddies in the hidden depths below.

He put the same idea in a letter written in 1857 to his friend,

R. B. Litchfield: 'I believe there is a department of the mind conducted independently of consciousness, where things are fermented and decocted, so that when they are run off they come out clear.'

The impression Clerk Maxwell made on his friends and associates

Lewis Campbell, a fellow student in Trinity, gives this picture of James as his friends knew him: 'His presence had by this time fully acquired the unspeakable charm for all who knew him which made him insensibly become the centre of any circle, large or small, consisting of his friends or kindred.' And Campbell quotes the memory of another student who was not a particular friend: 'Of Maxwell's geniality and kindness of heart you will have had many instances. Everyone who knew him at Trinity can recall some kindness or some act of his which left an ineffaceable impression of his goodness on the memory — for 'good' Maxwell was in the best sense of the word.' As Campbell writes in the closing chapter of his biography 'the leading note of Maxwell's character is a grand simplicity'.

William Garnett was Maxwell's demonstrator at the Cavendish. He collaborated with Campbell in writing the standard biography of James Clerk Maxwell, published in 1882. He contributed a 110-page section on Maxwell's contribution to science, but this is inadequate from our perspective (as Mahon says) because nobody at the time had a proper grasp of the immense significance of Maxwell's work. But Garnett's admiration, and indeed love, for the great man shines through and the account has charm as well as historical interest.

Dr J W Lorraine, who attended Maxwell at Glenlair, wrote in a letter dated 5th October 1879, a month before James died in Cambridge: 'I must say he is one of the best men I have ever met, and a greater merit than his scientific attainments is his being, so far as human judgment can discern, a most perfect example of a Christian gentleman.' The recipient of this letter, Dr Paget in Cambridge, wrote to William Garnett: 'There is a deep interest in the fact of how such a man as Maxwell met the trials of sickness and the approach of death. They are severe tests of amiability and unselfishness, and of the genuineness of religious convictions. It is something to say of a man that his unselfishness and composure remained undisturbed, and it is interesting physiologically and psychologically, that in the very extremity of bodily weakness, when the nourishment of the brain must have become so reduced, the mind remained perfectly clear.'

A few months before Maxwell died he wrote a letter to David Peck Todd at the Nautical Almanac Office in Washington. This letter dealt with the extreme accuracy entailed in any measurement of the 'ether drift' — the motion of the earth through the ether which was believed to permeate space and to be the medium by which light waves were transmitted. Todd had this letter published and Albert Abraham Michelson read it. Taking it as a challenge, he developed his interferometer, an instrument which used the tiny wavelengths of light itself as units of measurement.

Herald of the Future

With Edward Morley, his colleague, he then embarked on the experiment to determine the difference in speed of the two parts of a light beam split at right angles. This difference would give them the ether drift. Michelson and Morley carried out their famous experiment in Cleveland, Ohio, in 1887. To their amazement, however, there was no difference – the speed of light in each direction was identical. Michelson was disappointed and never recognized the fundamental significance of their experiment. Albert Einstein finally solved the puzzle. Despite what our senses tell us, there are no absolute measures of space or time: all are relative. The only absolute quantity is the speed of light, which is the same for all observers in unaccelerated motion, no matter how fast or in what direction they are moving. And the speed of light is completely determined by Maxwell's theory. His equations are the very core of special relativity, providing the link between space and time. This is the explanation of the results of Michelson's and Morley's subsequent experiment, which is now recognised as one of the most important in the history of physics. Maxwell's philosophy was never to dissuade a man from trying an experiment, no matter how slim the prospect of success, because he might find something entirely unexpected.

A leading article in *The Times* of Monday, 8th September 2008 about the opening on the following Wednesday of the Large Hadron Collider (LHC) at the CERN physics laboratory, reads as follows: 'Discoveries that change the world more often take a different route. They happen when clever men and women are free to follow their intellectual

The Spiritual Awakening of Science

interests as they choose. Their insights can then be exploited by others. When James Clerk Maxwell developed the equations that describe electro-magnetism in the nineteenth century, he was not seeking to invent electronics and computers... We do not yet know what applications the LHC's discoveries may bring. But even in the unlikely event that they find none, no protons will have been smashed in vain. For the pursuit of pure knowledge for its own sake is in itself worthwhile. In pushing back the barriers of ignorance, it adds to our freedom of spirit. It inspires and delights, no less than Beethoven's symphonies or Titian's paintings. It is a celebration of what it means to be human.'

Main Index

See separate index for people, page 346.

f-n = footnote

absolute, 211-212, 232, 286, 290, 337.
action-at-a-distance, 211, 214-215, 228, 230, 244.
alchemy, 28-29, 35, 196 f-n.
Almagest, 26-27, 204.
Alexandria, 9-12, 22, 24-25, 28, 42.
Arabic, 23, 25-28, 39 f-n.
astronomy, 2, 4, 8, 12. 15, 26-29, 35, 51, 95, 141, 143, 152, 154, 202-203, 218, 247, 249, 266, 268, 285, 320.
atman, 82, 292.
atomic theory, 7, 313, 315.
aurora borealis, 282, 285.
Bhagavad Gita, 65, 67-70, 78, 80, 104-105, 236, 291, 293, 299, 306, 309.
bondage, 66.
calculus, 143, 145-146, 172-173. *See also* **fluxions**.
calendar, 2.
Catholicism, 199.
Cavendish Laboratory, 324, 327.
chemistry, 28-29, 184, 197, 269, 306-307, 310, 312.
Christian Gospels, 309.
Christianity, 24-25, 37, 49, 288.
Church, 22, 33, 36-37, 43-44, 46-50, 91, 93, 96, 212, 297-298, 310, 317, 322.
circular motion, 150, 206 f-n, 210, 215, 217, 226-229, 241.
colour vision, 333-334.

colours, 115, 117-118, 145-146, 157-164, 166-167, 170-171, 177, 223-224, 271, 327.

comet, 143, 218-219, 225-226, 232, 243, 249, 279, 282.

Communism, 42, 87, 91.

compassion, 65, 100-101.

conscience, 49, 288-289.

consciousness, 19, 80, 104, 283-288, 291, 334.

Creation, 20, 34, 38, 269, 284, 290, 292, 320.

Dark Ages, 9, 12, 30, 92, 106.

delusion, 66, 85.

discipline, 68, 103.

DNA, 87 f-n, 327.

electricity, 216, 269, 273, 277, 281-283, 287-288, 290-291, 295, 298, 311-314, 316, 319-323, 325-326, 334.

electron, 312, 315, 327.

elliptical motion, 94, 183-186, 204-205, 210, 213-214, 217-220, 229-230, 237, 243, 250, 255, 257-258, 260, 262.

energy, 221, 227, 235, 284, 288, 325, 327-328.

evil, 68, 73, 82-83, 129, 289.

evolution, 46, 284-285, 287-288, 319.

experience, 17-18, 45, 53-56, 64, 66, 80, 98, 102, 106-110, 118-121, 210, 271, 273, 287-288, 294; spiritual, 38, 43, 288-291.

experiment, 8, 12, 21, 29, 34-35, 42, 49-50, 53-55, 71, 95, 106, 113, 127, 131, 136, 143, 154, 158-159, 161, 164-173, 177, 183-184, 202, 212, 216, 223, 225, 228-229, 240, 243, 259, 262, 266, 271, 294, 298, 300, 303, 305-306, 310, 312, 315-318, 322, 327, 336-337.

experiment, in Yoga, 104, 288.

faith, 34, 305, 309, 314, 317.

fluxions, 143, 146, 155, 172, 240.

Main Index

freedom, 32, 42, 45, 46, 48, 62, 64-66, 338.

God, 18-19, 30, 34, 38, 47-48, 54, 56, 82, 89-91, 93, 109, 128, 200, 211-212, 215, 269, 278, 290-292, 317.

gravity, 130-135, 145-150, 153, 186, 200-201, 210-211, 216, 218, 223, 225-231, 238-245, 250-257, 296, 328.

Greek City States, 1.

gunas, 235-236.

hypnotism, 45.

ignorance, 35, 66-67, 80, 102, 313.

illumination, 95, 115.

illusion, 81.

inductive logic, 71.

inertia, 210, 214-218, 231-235, 262.

information, 109-110, 219, 320, 326-327.

intellect, 35, 46, 67, 98, 101, 104, 187, 258, 317, 326.

Islam, 22, 25, 31.

judgement, 55, 67, 116, 120-121, 208, 289, 336.

Koran, 12, 23.

Last Supper, 60, 124, 126.

Laws of Motion, 145, 186, 196-198, 221, 223, 232ff, 296.

laws of nature, 12, 57, 130, 145, 326.

light, 27, 29, 57, 95, 106, 111-122, 145, 147, 156-172, 177, 223, 224, 226, 239, 271, 282-283, 315-316, 320, 325, 327, 333, 336-337; **light, spiritual**, 289.

love, 54, 61-62, 65, 84, 86, 101, 109, 124, 130, 138, 276, 284, 302, 305, 319, 328, 335.

magnetism, 71, 216, 219, 221, 231, 275, 277, 282-284, 287-288, 296, 309-312, 315-316, 320-321, 323, 325-326, 334, 338.

material world, 18, 211.

mathematics, 2-4, 8, 12, 15-16, 26, 28, 34-41, 44, 52, 95, 110, 127, 132, 142-146, 156, 172, 185, 193, 198, 200, 207-209, 212-214, 247, 258, 260, 320, 322.

matter, 7, 148, 158, 199, 200, 201, 211-212, 221, 223, 227, 230-234, 239, 244-245, 313, 316, 319-321.

maya, 284.

meditation, 130, 138-139, 144, 156, 176, 181, 192-193, 197, 318.

memory, 67, 104, 120-121, 300, 333, 335.

Middle Ages, 26-27, 33, 35, 37-38, 46.

mind, 17-18, 20, 40, 44-46, 49, 52, 55, 64-69, 78, 80-82, 100, 102-104, 109-110, 113, 118, 120-121, 123, 127, 130, 135, 138-140, 143, 147-148, 164, 169, 191, 193, 196, 198-199, 211-212, 221, 250, 284, 292, 304, 306, 334, 336.

Monte Cassino, 30.

morality, 3-4, 70, 81, 100, 101, 164.

natural philosophy, 16, 36, 84, 146, 168, 173, 177, 181-182, 199, 215, 221, 225, 242, 254, 295, 298, 302, 317, 333.

nature, 12, 16-17, 34-38, 41, 44, 53-72, 80-82, 93, 97, 103, 110, 119, 122, 164, 194, 215, 221, 225-226, 235, 237, 242, 256, 259, 269, 271, 273, 278, 287, 288, 294, 316, 328.

Neo-Platonism, 25, 31.

New Scientist, 327.

objectivity, 13, 16-17, 21, 62, 100, 103.

observation, 12, 16, 33, 35, 37-38, 41, 50, 53, 56, 71, 92, 94-95, 106, 111, 133, 200, 203-204, 206, 218-219, 225, 236, 240-243, 247-249, 254, 266, 269, 271, 312.

optics, 26-29, 35, 51, 57, 116 f-n, 141, 145, 155-156, 224 f-n, 275.

Optics (Newton's), 216, 271-272, 322.

Optics (Ptolemy's), 27.

Main Index

Panchadashi, 118.
parabolic model, 229.
pendulum, 134, 228, 230, 240, 248.
perception, 54, 119, 120-122, 232; **spiritual**, 110.
perspective, 62, 117-118.
philosophy, 3, 25 f-n. 31-32, 36-37, 66, 70, 78, 84, 86-87, 106, 110, 141, 146, 167-168, 173, 221, 235-236, 240, 267, 325, 337; *see also* **natural philosophy**.
physics, 8, 9, 12, 16, 26, 51, 71, 84, 95, 145-146, 153, 184-185, 213, 268-269, 290, 319, 322, 326-327; *see also* **natural philosophy**.
plague, 129, 144, 146, 154, 165, 206.
prakriti shakti, 221, 235.
precession of the equinoxes, 26, 244.
Principia Mathematica, 172, 187-199, 207 f-n, 212, 214, 217, 220, 221-240, 244-245, 247-269, 322.
purity, 3, 65-66.
Quantum Theory, 41, 326.
Quantum Wave Mechanics, 20.
real, 18, 85, 238, 283-284, 321.
reality, 17, 85-87, 212, 286, 290-291.
reflection (light), 35, 115, 162, 227, 239, 287; **(figurative)** 37, 128.
Reformation, 47, 49.
relativity, 41, 288, 296, 316, 326, 337.
religion, 31, 45-46, 88-89, 104, 147, 285, 297, 317, 319.
Renaissance, 26, 39, 42ff, 64, 80, 85, 91, 106, 322.
Restoration, 154.
Roman Empire, 31, **(Holy)**, 43.
Royal Institution, 299-309, 317, 333.

Royal Society, 154, 156, 159, 162-169, 172, 175-180, 183-186, 192, 212, 223, 247, 249, 251-252, 255-256, 262, 264, 305-306, 312, 315, 333-334.

scientific method, 53.

self, 21, 66, 68-70, 78, 82, 105, 194, 283-284, 287-288, 291, 318, 334.

self-knowledge, 21, 81, 103-104.

self-control, 3, 68.

sensation, 29, 113, 118, 120-121, 158, 224.

senses, 30 f-n, 54, 67, 99, 104, 120-122, 274, 337.

sensus communis, 116, 120-121.

silence, 110, 176.

sin, 47, 68, 104.

soul, 4, 5, 8, 20, 52, 62, 66, 107, 110, 119-122, 128, 212, 276, 317.

space, 113-114, 118, 136, 158, 201, 206, 210-211, 215, 225, 232, 234, 239, 241, 244, 284, 288, 315, 321, 325, 336-337.

spectrum, 145, 159, 223-224.

spirit (including **spiritual**), 20, 36, 37, 38, 43, 46-48, 65-66, 68, 80-83, 100, 122, 127, 284, 290-291, 297, 299-300, 305, 309, 314, 318; **of free enquiry**, 2, 35, 44, 46.

telescope, 35, 95, 162-165, 171, 178, 200, 212, 218, 247, 248, 271, 286.

The Man Who Changed Everything, 319ff.

Theory of Relativity, *see* relativity.

thought, 1, 8, 9, 12, 31, 36-37, 40, 42, 64, 78, 86, 91, 98, 99, 106, 124, 138-140, 169, 188, 222, 270, 275, 309, 327, 334.

Timaeus, 38.

time, 2-3, 61-62, 119, 132-135, 146-147, 181-182, 190, 196, 204-205, 211, 214, 217, 228, 232, 237, 240, 244, 284, 288, 290, 292, 321, 337.

Main Index

tolerance, 3, 36, 46, 65-66.

transmigration, 4.

trigonometry, 27-28, 142.

truth, 2, 13, 14, 16, 31, 34-35, 37-38, 40, 42, 45-46, 54-56, 64-66, 73, 80-81, 83-89, 91, 95-98, 102-103, 106, 110, 168, 173, 176, 194-195, 200, 220, 222, 258, 260-261, 269, 288, 291, 293, 297, 305, 309.

universal, 12, 97, 130, 145, 211, 219, 223, 230, 238, 242, 261.

Upanishads, 21, 106, 236, 291.

Vedanta, 21, 106, 236, 291.

vision, optical, 116-118, 121-122, 333-334; **psychological**, 100; **idealistic**, 232; **spiritual**, 38.

vortices, 201-202, 206 f-n, 239-240, 267.

wave-theory of light, 111, 145, 224, 320, 325-326, 336.

will, 16, 19, 67-68, 102-104, 334.

wisdom, 3, 35, 52, 56, 64, 70, 75, 80-85, 97-1-4, 221-223, 301.

Yoga of Self-knowledge, 21, 106.

Yoga for the Modern World, 323.

yogis, 85, 99, 104, 136, 283, 286-287, 292, 318.

Zen, 289.

Index of People

Abbott, Benjamin, 298, 301, 304.
Al-Ghazali, 110.
Al-Hazen, 29, 35, 115, 275.
Albert the Great, St, 33, 44 f-n, 289.
Albert, Prince, 317.
Alexander the Great, 9.
Ampère, André Marie, 303.
Andrade, E N da C, 146-147, 154, 187, 194.
Apollonius, 213.
Aquinas, Thomas, St, 31, 33-34, 36, 38, 44 f-n.
Archimedes, 9, 10, 23, 25, 28, 108, 190, 294.
Aristarchus, 10, 92-93, 223.
Aristotle, 9, 23, 25, 28, 31, 33-40, 95, 108, 130-132, 135, 141, 158, 161, 199, 200, 232.
Arya-Batha, 28.
Aubrey, John, 258-259.
Augustine, St, 37.
Averroes, 31, 33.
Avicenna, 31, 33.
Babington, Dr, 265.
Babylonians, 1-3, 26, 42.
Bacon, Roger , 34, 35, 39, 43, 44 f-n, 64, 102, 275.
Bacon, Francis, 70-78, 81-82, 103, 165 f-n.
Barrow, Isaac, 142, 144, 155-156, 171, 178, 208, 213.
Bellarmine, Cardinal, 95.
Benedict (Saint) of Nursia, 30.
Bentley, Richard, 244, 269.

Index of People

Bhaskara, 28.
Blake, William, 78.
Bondi, Hermann, 267-269.
Borelli, G A, 200, 254, 260-261.
Bowen, C D, 75-76.
Boyle, Robert, 175.
Brahe, Tycho, 94, 200, 203, 248.
Brahmagupta, 28.
Briggs, Henry, 29.
Bruno, Giordano, 36, 43, 46.
Burns, Robert, 282.
Campbell, Lewis, 323-324, 328, 335.
Cassini, Giovanni Domenico, 119 f-n, 249.
Caxton, William, 49.
Cecil, William, 73.
Cerletti, Ugo, 275.
Charlemagne, 31.
Charles II, King, 154, 178, 199.
Chaucer, Geoffrey, 49.
Christ, 34, 47-48, 58, 69, 124-125, 127, 129, 289, 292, 297, 301, 309-310, 317.
Clement III, Pope, 34.
Clerk Maxwell, James, 138, 283, 296, 319-338.
Collins, John, 178, 260.
Columbus, Christopher, 32.
Copernicus, Nicholas, 10, 27, 152, 200, 202-203, 248.
Cotes, Roger, 266.
Cromwell, Oliver, 175.

da Vinci, Leonardo, 8, 30, 41, 50-72, 80-82, 85, 88-92, 97-98, 102-127, 130-133, 152, 157-159, 165, 231, 322.

D'Alembert, Jean le Rond, 267.

Dalton, John, 282, 285, 313.

Dampier, William, 223 f-n.

Darwin, Charles, 36, 55, 81, 104, 294, 319, 324.

Davy, Humphry, 164, 299-308.

de Chardin, Teilhard, 37.

de Fontenelle, Bernard, 169, 177.

de l'Hôpital, Marquis, 265.

de la Rive, Auguste-Arthur, 304.

de Maricourt, Peter, 275, 277.

de Moivre, Abraham, 265.

Democritus, 7.

Descartes, René, 17, 118, 141-142, 158, 161, 201-202, 206-207, 209-215, 227, 239.

Deussen, Paul, 236.

Diophantus, 28.

Dürer, Albrecht, 117.

Eckhart, Meister, 33, 36, 43-44, 290-292.

Egyptians, 1, 2, 39.

Einstein, Albert, 55, 63, 81, 104, 137, 26, 271-272, 296, 324, 327, 337.

Elizabeth I, Queen, 70, 73, 75, 277.

Empedocles, 4.

Epicurus, 245.

Euclid, 9, 23, 25-26, 142, 144, 191, 193, 213.

Index of People

Faraday, Michael, 8, 55, 81, 104, 164, 283, 293-318, 320, 323, 333.

Ferdinand II of Aragon, King of Spain, 22, 32, 43.

Fermat, Pierre de, 213.

Feynman, Richard, 324.

Flamsteed, John, 218-219, 248-249.

Francis I, King of France, 58, 90.

Franklin, Benjamin, 281, 322.

Frederick II, Emperor, 31, 39 f-n, 44.

Frederick II, King of Denmark, 203.

Galen, 25.

Galileo Galilei, 8, 27, 36, 41, 43, 94-96, 132-137, 141, 152-153, 162, 200-202, 209, 228-229, 232, 240, 294, 296, 322.

Garnett, William, 324, 328, 335, 336.

Gassendi, Pierre, 141.

Gay-Lussac, Joseph Louis, 303.

Gilbert, William, 277, 283.

Greek philosophers, 1, 23.

Gregory, David, 145, 222.

Griffiths, Bede, 37.

Grosseteste, Robert, 34, 44 f-n, 275.

Grotius, Hugo, 132.

Gutenberg, Johann, 49.

Halley, Edmund, 181, 185-187, 198, 219-220, 247-257, 262-265.

Haroun-al-Raschid, 25.

Hawking, Stephen, 290.

Hegel, 99, 101.

Helmholtz, Hermann, 81, 315, 322, 324.

Helvelius, 248-249.

Herbert, George, 319.
Hertz, Heinrich, 283, 316, 322, 326.
Hipparchus of Nicaea, 26-27, 244.
Hippocrates, 25.
Hobbes, Thomas, 141, 153.
Hooke, Robert, 165, 168-170, 173, 176-177, 180-185, 200, 213-216, 219-220, 224, 229, 249, 253-264.
Hunter, William, 61.
Hus, Jan, 47.
Huygens, Christian, 111, 162, 165, 206, 214, 240, 248, 257, 260.
Hypatia, 24.
Isabella of Castille, 22, 32-33, 43.
James II, King, 199.
Jeans, James, (quoted), 3, 8, 11, 26, 96, 118-119, 132-133, 136, 146, 202, 223-224.
Jerome, St, 289.
Jews, 32, 39, 43.
John Paul II, Pope, 96.
Justinian, Emperor, 25.
Kepler, Johannes, 94, 141, 146, 150, 162, 185, 200-207, 211, 214, 217, 220, 230, 236-237, 240, 253, 260, 262, 267, 322.
Keynes, John Maynard, 139.
Laplace, Pierre-Simon, 267.
Largus, Scribonius, 274.
Lavoisier, Antoine-Laurent de, 46.
Leo III, Pope, 31.
Leo X, Pope, 57.
Leonardo of Pisa, 39.

Index of People

Leucippus, 7.
Linus, Francis, 166-168.
Lollards, 48.
Lomazzo, Gian Pauol, 123-124.
Longfellow, Henry Wadsworth, 293.
Lorraine, J W, 336.
Luther, Martin, 47.
Machiavelli, Niccolò, 56, 69-71, 73, 75, 78, 80-83, 85, 87.
Mahon, Basil, 319, 323, 325, 333, 335.
Marx, Karl, 86.
Melzi, Francesco, 52-53, 59, 89-90, 152.
Mencius, 69.
Michelson, Albert Abraham, 316, 336-337.
Milton, John, 69, 153.
More, Henry, 141.
Morley, Edward, 316, 336-337.
Muhammed, 22, 42.
Newton, Humphrey, 188, 190-191.
Newton, Isaac, 8, 41, 55, 81, 104, 129-272 (Chapters 7-12), 294, 296, 319, 322.
Oldenburg, Henry, 159, 163, 168, 175-177.
Pacioli, Luca, 52.
Pascal, Blaise, 138.
Paul, St, 37.
Peel, Robert, 317.
Peter the Great, 250.
Pilate, Pontius, 84.
Planck, Max, 326.

Plato, 23, 25, 34, 37-41, 141.
Pliny, 26, 28, 49, 274.
Plotinus, 20.
Plutarch, 3, 200, 223, 260-261.
Proclus, 25.
Ptolemy, Claudius, 23, 26-28, 94-95, 152.
Pythagoras, 3-7, 13-14, 94, 202, 204, 224.
Rama Tirtha, Swami, 44-45, 101-102, 104, 287, 294, 300.
Smith, Barnabas, 137, 180.
Rumford, Count, (Sir Benjamin Thompson), 307, 333.
Rumi, Jalalu'ddin, 276.
Russell, Bertrand, 83, 85-87, 97-102, 284-285.
Rutherford, Ernest, 283.
'Salai', Giacomo, 127.
Sandemanians, 297, 310, 317.
Schrödinger, Erwin, 12, 17-20, 81, 103.
Servetus, Michael, 46.
Sforza, Lodovico, 51, 54, 58, 127.
Shakespeare, William, 4, 5, 75, 77-78, 278, 281, 321.
Shankara, 291, 293.
Shastri, Hari Prasad, 65-66, 82.
Sherrington, Charles Scott, 19.
Snow, C P, 98.
Socrates, 84.
Spinoza, Baruch, 175.
Stevinus, Simon, 132, 134.
Stukeley, William, 148, 191.
Sullivan, J W N, 139, 168-169, 185, 185, 187, 192-193, 257, 259.

Index of People

Sureshvara, 118.
Sutton, Thomas, 333.
Sylvester II, Pope (Gerbert of Aurillac), 39.
Thales, 3, 14, 15.
Thomson, William (Lord Kelvin), 324.
Trevelyan, G M, 46.
Trotsky, Leon, 87.
Tyndall, John, 308, 316-317.
Umar, 12.
Valturius, Robertus, 52.
Vasari, Giorgio, 59, 65, 88, 90, 124.
Verrocchio, Andreas del, 51.
Victoria, Queen, 298.
Viète, François, 207.
Volta, Alessandro, 303.
Voltaire, 267.
Wallis, John, 142, 172, 207.
Washington, George, 288.
Waterhouse, Marjorie, 283.
Whitehead, A N, 38, 40-41.
Whiteside, Derek, 143, 196, 261.
Wood, John à, 258.
Wren, Christopher, 185, 220, 253, 255, 257, 264.
Wycliffe, John, 47-49.
Xenophon, 8.
Young, Thomas, 271.

Two books by A M Halliday that present the teachings of Advaita Vedanta in a contemporary setting

YOGA FOR THE MODERN WORLD

Man's life is more than ever dominated and shaped by the influence of science and technology. Yet only the deeper values, upheld by the great spiritual traditions, can ensure that the outer progress rests on a corresponding inner progress in peace, goodwill and enlightenment.

The Vedanta tradition has always emphasized personal enquiry and experiment, and, like science, seeks to realise the deeper truth behind phenomena. Its inner discoveries in the field of self-knowledge should be of no small interest to those currently investigating the nature of consciousness.

These nineteen lectures consider various aspects of contemporary life, and show how the ancient wisdom of the Upanishads and the Bhagavad Gita, pregnant with valid and practical insights, has the power to infuse modern life with meaning and purpose.

402pp paperback   978-0-85424-047-0

FREEDOM THROUGH SELF-REALISATION

These eighteen lectures place the teachings of the Bhagavad Gita and the Upanishads in a modern context, and show the way to an inner development open to everyone.

'All the talks deal with timeless, enduring themes, still very relevant to contemporary life. The author, a pupil of the late Hari Prasad Shastri, enlivens his text with well-chosen passages from the writings of philosophers, poets and mystics....The book offers clear, practical advice from a Vedantic viewpoint, on techniques of meditation and good living.' *Yoga and Health*

225pp Paper   978-0-85424-040-1

SCIENTIST AND MAHATMA
The life and teachings of Swami Rama Tirtha

Swami Rama Tirtha (1873-1906) was an outstanding spiritual personality who had achieved the goal of life: realisation of the Absolute. In the language of the ancient Upanishads, he saw his own Self in all beings and all beings in the Self.

Through intellectual acumen and an unwavering will, he was set for a brilliant scientific career, becoming a Professor of Mathematics in Lahore. But the call of the Infinite overpowered all empirical considerations. He renounced the world in order to pursue the supreme science of God-realisation.

The book includes a moving account of Swami Rama Tirtha's life, his quest and achievement, told by Hari Prasad Shastri, who knew and revered the Mahatma.

Swami Rama Tirtha visited America in 1902-1904 and gave many lectures, fusing his lively appreciation of Western culture and society with the ancient Vedic wisdom. This new edition has been greatly enhanced by presenting substantial extracts from these talks, as well as other writings.

Also included are several of the Mahatma's poems and one of his last writings, the essay called 'Upasana' (Worship).

'He was one of the greatest souls, not only of India, but of the whole world. I adore his ideals.' *Mahatma Gandhi*

320pp paperback   978-0-85424-018-7

*Original works on Adhyatma Yoga
and its application in daily life*

◆

by Hari Prasad Shastri

THE HEART OF THE EASTERN MYSTICAL TEACHING

MEDITATION - ITS THEORY AND PRACTICE

SEARCH FOR A GURU

WISDOM FROM THE EAST

YOGA HANDBOOK

◆

by Marjorie Waterhouse

TRAINING THE MIND THROUGH YOGA

POWER BEHIND THE MIND

WHAT YOGA HAS TO OFFER

◆

also from Shanti Sadan

SHORT COURSE OF MEDITATION

THE CREST JEWEL OF WISDOM
Viveka Chudamani
A classic of Advaita Vedanta

The commentary by Hari Prasad Shastri demonstrates the practical validity of the teachings of Adhyatma Yoga, while the translation by A J Alston puts the verses into approachable English, faithful to the Sanskrit original, which is included in romanised script. The text covers some sixty key Vedanta topics ranging from the qualifications of the enquirer to his final enlightenment.

336pp paperback   978-0-85424-047-0

Classical texts translated by Hari Prasad Shastri

ASHTAVAKRA GITA

AVADHUT GITA

DIRECT EXPERIENCE OF REALITY
Aparokshanubhuti
with commentary

PANCHADASHI
A 14th Century Vedanta Classic

TEACHINGS FROM THE BHAGAVAD GITA

TRIUMPH OF A HERO
Vira Vijaya of Swami Mangalnath

VERSES FROM THE UPANISHADS
with commentary

WORLD WITHIN THE MIND
Teachings from the Yoga Vasishtha

The Śaṅkara Source Book
in six volumes

Dr A J Alston's pioneering study presents an authoritative account of Śaṅkara's position, which many regard as the summit of Eastern philosophical thought and spiritual wisdom.

ŚAṄKARA ON THE ABSOLUTE
Sources of Śaṅkara's doctrine: His Life and Work
The Doctrine of Nescience Knowledge of the Absolute
The Absolute as Being, Consciousness and Bliss

ŚAṄKARA ON THE CREATION
The Absolute as Creator and Controller
The World and its Presiding Deities
The Acosmic View

ŚAṄKARA ON THE SOUL
The Soul and its Organs and Bodies
The States of the Soul and their Transcendence

ŚAṄKARA ON RIVAL VIEWS
Refutation of Inadequate Brahminical Doctrines
Refutation of Non-Vedic World Views

ŚAṄKARA ON DISCIPLESHIP
Adopting the Path The Veda and the Teacher

ŚAṄKARA ON ENLIGHTENMENT
The Indirect Path The Direct Path
The Enlightened Man

Set of six volumes:978-0-85424-061-6
Single volumes are also available

*Descriptive booklet and order form
available from Shanti Sadan.*

*Extracts from each volume may be found on our website
www.shantisadan.org*

SELF-KNOWLEDGE YOGA QUARTERLY

devoted to spiritual thought and practice

Do you appreciate clear instructions on the inner phase of the Yoga teachings? Do you see Yoga as essentially a universal teaching, in harmony with the key insights of the great religions? Do you believe that the human mind is constructive and potentially a way to peace, a source of illumination?

Then you'll enjoy *Self-Knowledge,* Shanti Sadan's long-established journal of practical Yoga and Vedanta.

Annual subscriptions (as at 2010) £10.00 worldwide.

Free sample issue available on request.

We commend this journal to all who have an interest in Eastern philosophy and prefer their instruction free from glamour and sensation. Of a high standard, it is most readable, and not only widens our horizons but elevates the mind.

Science of Thought Review

Lectures and Courses arranged by Shanti Sadan

Lectures on the Yoga of Self-Knowledge are given on Wednesdays and Fridays at 8.00pm during term time at Shanti Sadan, 29 Chepstow Villas, London W11 3DR.

Special courses, including instruction in spiritual meditation, are also held at other venues in Central London.

For details of all these activities, please contact Shanti Sadan or consult our website: www.shantisadan.org

The Illustrated Book Catalogue
of all Shanti Sadan publications is available from
Shanti Sadan, 29 Chepstow Villas, London W11 3DR, UK

The Shanti Sadan website includes extracts from many of the books.